OF DISHES AND DISCOURSE

Classical Arabic Literary Representations of Food

CURZON STUDIES
IN ARABIC AND MIDDLE-EASTERN LITERATURES

Editors

Curzon Studies in Arabic and Middle-Eastern Literatures is a monograph series devoted to one or more aspects of the literatures of the Near and Middle East and North Africa both modern and pre-modern. It is hoped that the provision of such a forum will lead to a greater emphasis on the comparative study of the literatures of this area, although studies devoted to one literary or linguistic region are warmly encouraged. It is the editors' objective to foster the comparative and multi-disciplinary investigation of the written and oral literary products of this area.

OF DISHES AND DISCOURSE

Classical Arabic Literary Representations of Food

Geert Jan van Gelder

CURZON

First Published in 2000
by Curzon Press
Richmond, Surrey

Typeset in Garamond by LaserScript Ltd, Mitcham, Surrey
Printed and bound in Great Britain by
TJ International, Padstow, Cornwall

British Library Cataloguing in Publication Data
A catalogue record of this book is available from the British Library

Library of Congress Cataloguing in Publication Data
A catalogue record for this book has been requested

ISBN 0-7007-1174-0

Contents

Preface

Several friends and colleagues, having been exposed to parts of this book mostly in the form of talks and papers, have helped me with their comments. My thanks are due to Dr James E. Montgomery in particular, for his useful comments and corrections after having read the whole text, and for recommending its publication in his Series. As usual, Sheila van Gelder-Ottway improved my English for no remuneration other than being assured of the gratitude of her loving husband.

I thank my (now former) colleagues of the Department of Languages and Cultures of the Middle East for their support and friendship during the twenty-three years of my employment at the University of Groningen.

Geert Jan van Gelder, Oxford

CHAPTER I

Introduction

Pleasures may be divided into six classes, to wit, food, drink, clothes, sex, scent and sound. Of these, the noblest and most consequential is food.

Thus wrote a certain Muḥammad Ibn al-Ḥasan al-kātib al-Baghdādī in the introduction to his cookery book.[1] With 'sound' he meant, in all likelihood, above all music and singing, but in view of the pride generally taken by the Arabs in their language and their eloquence, it is obvious that these considerable sources of pleasure must also be included in the category of 'sound'. The saying is a variation on a theme; Hippocrates (Buqrāṭ) is credited with a similar statement: 'The principal pleasures of this world are four: the pleasures of food, drink, sex and sound'. Unlike the professionally biased cook from Baghdad, he prefers 'sound' (*samā*ᶜ), however, since it is the only pleasure that may be had without toil and trouble, and of which there cannot be too much.[2]

That those noble subjects, sound and food, or literature and eating, may interrelate, and even happily cooperate, is known to every literate person. In life and in language the two are closely linked in many ways; suffice it, for the meantime, to mention the word 'entertainment', which may refer to providing food or pleasurable conversation. There are numerous studies on the literary aspects of food and eating in the various literatures.[3] My book would seem to be an emulation of Michel Jeanneret's stimulating study *Des mets et des mots: Banquets et propos de table à la Renaissance*,[4] although I became acquainted with it only when my own text was near its completion. In recent years our knowledge of Arabic literature as well as Arab gastronomical and culinary history has been enriched with important studies. As for food, one may mention for instance the recent editions of medieval

Arabic cookery books like *al-Wuṣla ilā l-ḥabīb* (loosely rendered as 'The Way to the Heart is through the Stomach') by a 13th-century author from Aleppo, Ibn al-ᶜAdīm,[5] the 'Cookery Book' (*Kitāb al-ṭabīkh*) by the 10th-century Ibn Sayyār al-Warrāq from Baghdad[6] and the anonymous late mediaeval cookbook *Kanz al-fawā'id fī tanwīᶜ al-mawā'id* ('The Treasure of Things Propitious: On Preparing Varied Dishes');[7] or the several studies by specialists like Peter Heine, David Waines, Manuela Marín, Lucie Bolens and others.[8]

However, the interaction of eating and literature is still a relatively unexplored territory, compared with other literatures or with related subjects in Arabic studies, such as drinking and literature. There exist, after all, a number of good studies on bacchic poetry. Of course this is because so much wine poetry has been produced in Arabic, far more in fact than poetry about food. But there is, nevertheless, an abundance of literary texts on food. To some extent these have been exploited, it is true, by the culinary authorities mentioned above, but only as interesting and sometimes informative sources for culinary and gastronomic history;[9] as if one studied, for instance, Dutch 17th-century still-lifes as a source for eating customs without regard for their artistic merit. This is perfectly legitimate and valuable; but I should like to approach the material from a different, literary angle. Maxime Rodinson, in a pioneering study on Arabic culinary history, gave a quick survey of the literary sources.[10] Two relevant texts are briefly studied by Manuela Marín in her 'Literatura y gastronomía'. An article by Sabry Hafez,[11] though important, deals almost exclusively with modern literature and discusses the pre-modern period very briefly. He suggests that culinary elements in Classical Arabic literature play a 'one-dimensional role' and appear in a static, less 'immediate and dynamic form' than in modern literature. He is able to do so, it seems, because he unnecessarily restricts his discussion of classical literature to the Qur'ān, proverbs and lexicographical works. Fortunately, there is rather more than this.[12] From the bibliography it will be seen that a fair number of sources have been employed for this study; needless to say, I do not claim that the list is exhaustive, for there are still many other works, printed or still in manuscript, that are bound to offer more material. I have merely used a manageable quantity of readily available texts, keeping in mind that one is enjoined, in Arabic eating etiquette, to help oneself only to what is near at hand.

Although I have called food a 'noble subject', in literature it may seem a very earthy, low subject. Bacchic poetry, for instance, has always enjoyed a much higher status than poems on food, for various reasons – wine as being more 'spiritual' – but surely partly as the result of what J. Christoph Bürgel has called a not well-founded prejudice.[13] The theme lends itself eminently to the lighter genres, such as descriptive epigrams, amusing anecdotes, parodies and satires. It plays an important supporting role in fairytales and children's stories; witness for instance the books for children by Roald Dahl. In Arabic literature too all this may indeed be found; yet, in spite of the earthy aspect there is often a strong link not only between eating and etiquette, which is obvious,[14] but also between eating and ethics. The Arabic word *adab*, today meaning 'literature', and sometimes used in the Classical period for something like 'belles-lettres', means 'erudition' but also 'good manners, etiquette'. The many works that we are wont to call 'typical works of *adab*' regularly possess a moralistic component, not too obtrusively or persistently, but unmistakably present in the background. Just as eating is, ideally, both sustaining and pleasant,[15] so is *adab* instructive and entertaining at the same time. The connection between eating, ethics and literature is visible symbolically in the apparent etymological link between *adab*, 'literature/good behaviour', and *ma'duba*, 'meal or banquet for guests'.[16]

An unknown authority maintained that tasty food, together with a nice drink (*sharāb*, probably wine being intended) and listening to singing, may be helpful in making poetry.[17] While this may be contested by less worldly-minded poets and critics – another unknown connoisseur warns would-be poets against eating or drinking their fill[18] – it is incontestable that food has inspired much literature from the trivial to the great. The literary representations of food naturally provide links between eating and aesthetics. This adds an extra dimension to the links that exist already between aesthetics and real food, which should gratify the stomach and the senses, taste, smell and sight, as is often stressed in cookery books. Food, like *adab* literature, should be pleasant and useful at the same time. Both food and literature combine the intensely personal and individual with the social.[19]

Eating and speaking, or food and literature, are physically linked by the obvious biological fact that both concern the mouth. Put in crude terms, food goes in where words come out. In all ages satirists have linked this superior level of the mouth with the inferior end of the digestive tract. 'Words are to the mouth what excrement is to the anus', as Jeanneret puts it.[20] Montaigne calls his *Essays* 'the droppings of an old mind, sometimes hard, sometimes squittery, but always ill-digested';[21] John Wilmot, Earl of Rochester, while putting his unsavoury words into the mouth of an opponent, speaks of 'the excrement of my dull brain'.[22] His Egyptian contemporary al-Shirbīnī (fl. 1097/1686) likewise describes his diatribe on the peasants as a piece of dung;[23] al-Wahrānī (d. 575/1179) prescribes a diet for an unfortunate poet who is constipated with poems.[24] It will be observed that the oral-anal analogy is incomplete if the lower orifice's output is not matched with an input or intake. In the context of Arabic literature, with its plenitude of homoerotic verse, the missing part is evidently the phallus, and thus, circuitously, sex is brought in. Of course the links between eating and sex are far more directly located in the mouth, which thereby, having a third function, establishes its superiority over the anus, *pace* Abū l-ᶜAnbas al-Ṣaymarī, ninth-century literary buffoon, who wrote a treatise, unfortunately not preserved, on the superiority of the latter to the former.[25] Kissing has its origins in feeding by mouth, mock cannibalism ('I want to eat you') is an amorous commonplace.[26] Metaphorical connections exist between literature and sexual reproduction, when, for instance, poems are called the offspring of the poet. The metaphor of literature as food, where a book may be said to offer various dishes for literary gourmets, and where 'taste' and several other items of critical metalanguage are derived from gustation, is as common as it is ancient. Francis Bacon, in his essay 'Of Studies', used this metaphor in his oft-quoted dictum on books to be tasted, or swallowed, or (rarely) chewed and digested.[27] The trope is, in fact, so trite that I have decided not to yield to the temptation of giving the chapters of this study fancy headings, from 'Starters' to 'Dessert', with the occasional excursus posing as hors-d'oeuvre.

The themes of food, literature, sex and coprology, then, are intimately connected; the purpose of this study is to explore some strands of this in Arabic texts. It is concerned with the place of food in literature from various points of view: how food is depicted and shaped in literary contexts, and how literary texts are shaped by the theme of food. I have followed no strictly predetermined paths and methods; too many writers of literary studies have let themselves be partly or totally submerged in the surges of reigning Theorrhoea. I dare say, however, that even though trying to avoid the footsteps of theory addicts, while browsing on the pastures of literary studies, I too have soiled my soles to some extent in this respect, for no one studying literature can afford to keep wholly aloof from contemporary jargon and ideas - ideas that may actually be fertilizing if applied in the right place, time, and dosage.

Literature, in any case, remains the starting point and the focus of this book. It is hoped that it will be of some use at least to those primarily interested in the culinary history of the Middle East, yet for the purpose of this study culinary history is considered merely as one of the tools for the understanding, interpretation and appreciation of literary texts. It is true that in pre-modern Arabic literature, as in many other pre-modern literatures, the distinction between literary and non-literary is difficult and the borderlines blurred. Nevertheless in most cases the distinction is neither pointless nor impossible.

It would have been possible to combine in this study the theme of food with that of drinking. After all, there are many substances - honey, various broths or soups - where the distinction is uncertain. It has been decided, however, to leave the liquids out, in order not to swell or dilute the already copious material by adding to it the very extensive body of bacchic poetry in Arabic. Although the definitive study of drinking in Arabic literature (including wine, milk, and water) still has to be written, more work has been done on drinking than on eating, as pointed out before. An additional justification for separating eating and drinking may be found in the Arab custom, often observed in literary texts, of not letting banquet and symposium coincide but rather letting the latter follow the former.

In this book I am interested more in dishes than foodstuffs, in concoctions rather than ingredients, leaving the study of the contrast between the cooked and the raw to others. Relatively little attention is given, for instance, to the numerous epigrams on kinds of fruit, in which the visual aspects usually dominate the alimentary and gustatory characteristics: on the whole, they are more akin to poems on flowers (*zahriyyāt, rawḍiyyāt*) than to banquet poems. But obviously some primary foodstuffs, such as dates or honey, cannot be neglected in any discourse on Arab gastrology.

Descriptions of food and eating behaviour in literary texts always function within a system that may be called the culinary semiotic code, knowledge of which helps the interpretation of these texts.[28] Food may act as a marker of a multitude of things such as time, place, class, status, nationality, ethnicity, religion, gender, character and, of course, 'taste' in several senses; it functions in comparisons both as *primum* and as *secundum comparationis*; it may be a metaphor, a symbol, a vehicle of allusion and insinuation, praise and blame. Culinary elements in a text stand in some relationship to other elements in the text, to other texts, and to extra-textual matters: the 'real world' (or at least concepts of it) and, of course, the hearer or reader of the text. A survey and an analysis of the material could be structured on the lines of these various relationships. However, I thought it more convenient to abandon this idea of systematic treatment by categories that are rather abstract and seem to require a kind of critical discourse written in more than the single dimension offered by a linear text. Instead, I shall deal with the several literary genres or modes roughly one after the other, starting with the earliest. This means that pre-Islamic poetry is the first course. The most important watershed in pre-modern Arabic literature is the transition from the heroic and bedouin, which belongs, or pretends to belong, to the nomadic or semi-nomadic world of the bedouins, to the urban literature of the Abbasid period. For the study of gastrology, the latter is much richer ('richer' in terms of the quantity of the material as well as the quality of the dishes). In the presentation of the genres of this long period, the focus will have to oscillate between the centuries and shift from region to region, at the risk of suggesting, unintentionally, that the period is monolithic, devoid of both literary developments and regional distinctions. Since *adab*, in its diverse senses, is a central concept in this study, the middle, fourth, chapter is devoted to it, which does not mean that *adab* plays no part in the other chapters. The closest possible connections between food and text will be discussed in the central section of this central chapter.

Although I have mentioned, and will mention, a few studies on western gastrology, this is intended merely as a hint for future research, or to highlight the occasional striking parallel or striking difference, and lastly because I find it difficult to resist the odd reference and comparison, for this is no systematic comparative study. Many parallels are indeed to be found, but it would be difficult to pinpoint any definite influences, for instance from Greek on Arabic Abbasid literature. For all its riches, Arabic literary history has no Athenaeus with his stunning *Deipnosophists* or Plutarch with his *Symposiaka*, to mention the two most important works on food and conviviality.[29] Not a few Arabic texts could be called, anachronistically, Rabelaisian in their celebration of eating and other bodily functions; yet there is no Arabic Rabelais. Arab readers may find some consolation in the fact that Athenaeus, at least, was born in Egypt.

CHAPTER II

Early Poetry: Feeding as Good Breeding

1. Food and Glory

In pre-Islamic and early Islamic poetry the old Bedouin virtues are central: bravery and generosity, especially the latter. The commonest Arabic words for generosity and open-handedness, *jūd* and *karam*, both have the more general sense of 'nobility, goodness'. It is well known that generosity, together with hospitality which is inseparable from it, is the Bedouin virtue *par excellence*, in the past and the present. Extreme poverty may not keep the Bedouin from regaling his[1] guests with all he has to give. There is usually a good rational explanation for any kind of altruism. Sharing one's livelihood with members of one's clan or tribe, particularly the poorer and weaker ones, strengthens the tribe as a whole, physically and morally. But hospitality extends beyond one's own group, to complete strangers belonging to non-allied and therefore in principle hostile tribes. Extreme and extravagant liberality is neither the expression of unselfish charity, nor a means to get to Heaven, but the appropriate way to gain honour and glory for oneself, one's clan and one's tribe. Thus one acquires a form of immortality, not in the Hereafter but on earth, in stories and poetry.

Here lies the most obvious and the most important connection between food and literature. Generosity consists before anything else in providing food. This is more obvious in Bedouin society than in urban society, where extravagant givers regularly bestow costly robes of honour, pearls and jewels, or large round numbers of dirhams and dinars. Yet the banquet has always remained an important means to show largesse to large numbers. Indeed, the prime role of food is expressed eloquently in a 'mirror for princes', written by al-Thaᶜālibī for Ma'mūn Ibn Ma'mūn Khwārazm-Shāh (*r.* 399-407/1009-1017):

> Some early authority (*baᶜḍ al-salaf*) has said: 'If there is anything that resembles being a deity (*al-rubūbiyya*), it is feeding people. How few are the princes that are characterized by this noble quality, and how numerous are those among them that are generous with large gifts but stingy with the least bit of food!'[2]

Amongst Bedouins, generosity with food involves, naturally, ordinary Bedouin fare such as milk products, cereals and dates; but, if at all possible, the arrival of a guest ought to be celebrated as a feast day with the slaughtering of one or more camels. Liberality with meat may be displayed with a concrete purpose; thus poor ᶜUrwa Ibn Ḥizām, lover of ᶜAfrā', does not stand a chance when a wealthy rival appears who wins over her family by killing many camels and feeding her parents and their whole tribe.[3] The more famous instances of liberality, however, are those of what would seem pointless, even reckless, extravagance. Ḥātim al-Ṭā'ī, the pre-Islamic Bedouin poet who as a young man is said to have killed a whole herd of several hundred camels for a party of strangers, is celebrated, as a paragon not of stupidity but of honour and generosity – even though the camels belonged to his father (or his grandfather, according to some), who was far from pleased. 'Where are the camels?', he asked. 'Father,' answered Ḥātim, 'with them I have given you immortal glory, like the [indelible] ring of the ringdove, and honour that men will forever carry in verses in praise of us, in return for your camels.' The father swears he will no longer live with his son and leaves; but it is Ḥātim's name, not his father's, which has become proverbial.[4] Generosity was the prime concern to anyone who cared for his reputation. The poet al-Namir Ibn Tawlab, who died in the early years of Islam, had been a generous host to many guests during his long life; in his dotage he kept mumbling phrases like 'Give the rider his morning draught! Give the rider his evening draught! Bring the food! Slaughter a camel for the guest!', until he died.[5] By feeding others one lives not merely gloriously and posthumously, but one also lives, as it were, multiple lives through others: 'I divide my body in many bodies', said the famous pre-Islamic poet-hero ᶜUrwa Ibn al-Ward.[6] Feeding has almost become like procreation, another means to live on in bodies other than one's own. Through generosity one lives on both in the flesh and in the spirit, in texts: 'people are texts, (or stories, *aḥādīth*)'.[7] And ultimately, feeding others is a means to procreate:

the reputation and glory that it brings greatly enhance the opportunities to marry (like ᶜAfrā''s suitor, mentioned above) and to have affairs, adulterous or otherwise (like Imra' al-Qays, in his *Muᶜallaqa*, on which see below). Throughout human history, the main purpose of ostentatiously displaying one's generosity has been to acquire power or glory, not for its own sake, but in order to increase one's progeny.[8]

ᶜAmr Ibn ᶜAbd Manāf, the Prophet's great-grandfather, got his nickname Hāshim (Bread-Crumbler) because, according to an often-told story, he provided his tribe Quraysh with crumbled bread brought by caravan from Syria in a year of famine. Thus he was the first to make *tharīd*, which was eaten together with the camels slaughtered upon arrival.[9] Throughout the history of Islam, the much-honoured genealogical indicator Hāshimī has survived as a reminder of the generosity of the Prophet's clan. Hāshim's son ᶜAbd al-Muṭṭalib, the Prophet's grandfather, is also described as an ostentatious feeder of people. After slaughtering many camels for the people of Mecca, he orders more animals to be killed on a near-by hilltop so that the birds could eat of them and he is able to boast, in verse: 'We feed until the birds eat what is left, while the hands of (other) hosts tremble'.[10]

In order to decide whose honour was superior, contestants either boasted of their liberality with food, or tried to outdo each other in actual fact, in a duel of extravagant competitive camel-slaughtering (*muᶜāqara* or *munāḥara*): a form of potlatch. The connections between food and words, or food and literature, are here particularly close, because such a contest is only effective if accompanied by vaunting and invective poems or speeches, and, most importantly, recorded in poetry or prose. As Huizinga, not an Arabist, observed in his *Homo ludens*, Arabic lexicographers explain *muᶜāqara* not only as 'competing in slaughtering camels' but also in a derived sense as 'to contend in reviling'.[11] In the famous public verbal duel (*munāfara*) in prose (partly rhyming prose) of ᶜĀmir Ibn al-Ṭufayl and ᶜAlqama feeding is one of the main themes. It is mentioned by ᶜĀmir several times during the duel ('I slaughter more milch-camels . . . I give away more food in a year of drought . . . I slaughter more young camels and provide more pieces of boneless meat'), but on the day the decision is to be made, it is ᶜAlqama who produces real food in the form of slaughtered camels. Rebuked by his partisans for his negligence, ᶜĀmir quickly orders the same number of cooking-pots and camels to be brought.[12] In a year of drought during the reign of caliph ᶜUthmān (23–35/634–44) a slaughtering match takes place between Ghālib Ibn Ṣaᶜṣaᶜa (the grandfather of the poet al-Farazdaq) and the warrior and poet Suḥaym Ibn Wathīl, both feeding the hungry tribe of Yarbūᶜ. Suḥaym tries to keep up with his rival, first killing one camel, then two more, then ten, and so forth to a total of one hundred (or four hundred, according to others), at which point Suḥaym has to give up. Some years later, during the caliphate of ᶜAlī (35–40/644–61), Suḥaym slaughters two hundred camels at Kufa, while people flock towards him armed with baskets, trays and ropes to carry the meat away. The caliph sees what is going on and attempts, possibly in vain, to dampen the general elation at this act, by now frowned upon as a relic of a heathen age, by pointing out that the meat was not properly killed in the prescribed Islamic ritual manner, with pronouncing God's name over the victim. The narrator adds that this act of generosity on the part of Suḥaym still did not make him the victor.[13]

In a number of *munāfara*s the slaughtering of camels is postponed: a number of camels are set aside by both parties as a stake; when an arbitrator has pronounced which person is nobler, the winner then feeds the people to underline his nobility.[14] Thus it is told how Umayya Ibn ᶜAbd Shams in vain tried to rival Hāshim's generosity, related above. Mocked by the people, he challenges Hāshim to a formal *munāfara*. Hāshim reluctantly agrees, suggesting a stake of fifty camels. A judge, after passing a test of his divinatory power, declares Hāshim to be the winner. Only then are the camels killed and fed to the people.[15] The story has to be read, of course, in the light of political ideology: the Abbasids, descendants of Hāshim, are superior to their predecessors, the Umayyads.

It seems that the old habit was not merely frowned upon but was actually repressed in Islamic times. The Umayyad governor ᶜUbayd Allāh Ibn Ziyād imprisoned Murra Ibn Maḥkān, tribal chief, poet, a noble and generous man, nicknamed Abū l-Aḍyāf ('Father of guests'), because of his competitive slaughtering and feeding (*al-munāḥara wa-l-iṭᶜām*). After another poet has made some scathing verses on the governor, Murra is released and kills one hundred camels, thus topping his rival who had killed one hundred sheep.[16] Bedouin competition reached grotesque proportions in some reports which, if not necessarily true, at least show the importance of the theme in popular lore. In a contest of the Umayyad period, a certain Ḥawshab Ibn Yazīd beats his rival, ᶜIkrima Ibn Ribᶜī. The latter then procures a large quantity (*ṣafā'in*, bargeloads?) of flour. He orders his people to make all of it into dough and to put it into a hole in the earth. They then contrive a ruse to make Ḥawshab's horse fall into the pit, up to its neck. Now they are able to raise a cry that does not fail to impress: 'Come and help, you Muslims, save Ḥawshab's horse, for it has fallen into ᶜIkrima's leaven!' After the horse has been rescued, ᶜIkrima is declared victor.[17] The episode is said to have taken place in an army camp; it sounds like a mere soldiers' prank, but one may imagine that generals and governors were displeased at such acts, not so much for their wastefulness as their potential for incensing internal discord and tribal rivalry between armies and societies that had only recently and with difficulty been welded together.

For the same reason the authorities tried to curb, mostly in vain, the poets of satirical and vituperative poetry (*hijā'*). In this invective verse the virtues of panegyric and vaunting poetry are reversed: bravery becomes cowardice, noble descent becomes bastardy, generosity becomes stinginess. It is striking how many of the lines singled out by the critics as outstanding lines of *hijā'* are about food, or rather its absence. The following are three out of many.[18] Al-Aᶜshā says of his opponent's clan:

> You spend the night, in your winter-quarters, with full bellies, but your female neighbours [under your protection, *jārātu-kum*] are starving and spend the night with empty stomachs.

Al-Akhṭal describes vividly how a clan avoids attracting the attention of passing strangers, in order not to have to feed them:

> People who, when the approaching guests make their dogs bark, say to their mother, 'Piss on the fire!'

Jarīr also depicts someone dodging possible guests:

> The Taghlibite, saying 'Ahem!' when his hospitality is expected, scratches his arse and quotes platitudes.

According to another interpretation of this line the bedouin hems, hoping that he himself will be entertained. This, too, is shameful; it depicts him as a sponger or *ṭufaylī*. The countless anecdotes and poems on parasites, however, belong to Abbasid literature rather than pre- or early Islamic times, and therefore the first interpretation seems more likely to be correct. In Bedouin ethos refusing to provide hospitality is far worse than begging for it.[19]

2. *The* Qaṣīda *or 'Ode'*

The most important Arabic poetic genre is the *qaṣīda*, often translated as 'ode': a polythematic piece of some length, to be distinguished from the more informal and occasional shorter piece called *qiṭᶜa*. The term *qaṣīda* (collective: *qaṣīd*) has been explained as 'poem with a purpose (*qaṣd, maqṣid*)'.[20] However, since many Arabic technical terms referring to verse are related not so much to its content as to its prosodical form, I think it far more likely that *qaṣīda* should be connected with *qaṣada* 'to split in two' and with the fact that a normal line may be divided into two metrical halves. One could compare the term *qarīḍ* ('poetry' excluding the metre *rajaz*, the lines of which are not bipartite) and the verb *qaraḍa* 'to cut'. Incidentally, both *qaṣīd* and *qarīḍ* are related to food, meaning 'marrow-bone' or 'marrow' (acquired through splitting a bone) and 'cud', respectively, while others explain *qaṣīd* as 'dried meat'.[21]

In the old Arabic *qaṣīda*[22] the camel plays a dual part. It is the vehicle transporting the poet-hero (always the 'I' of the poem) from the isolation of the empty desert to the society of the tribe; moreover, slaughtered and prepared in the cooking-pot, it is the instrument for obtaining glory. It is not surprising that, in those rare cases where the camel's own feelings about this treatment are presented, he should resent being first consumed by exhaustion, then consumed by humans or sometimes animals by mouth. The poet and prose writer Abū l-ᶜAlā' al-Maᶜarrī (d. 449/1057), himself a vegetarian, lets a camel vent his anger in his *Risālat al-ṣāhil wa-l-shāḥij* ('The Epistle of Neigher and Brayer'):

> One of the strange acts of humans is that, when they want to travel in a country without water, they deprive the camels of water for eight days, then, when they are all but exhausted from thirst, they let them drink their fill. Then they go into the desert; and if water is scarce, they cut their bellies open and drink the liquid contained in it . . .[23] They drink our blood, which they let in times of drought . . . No animal has to suffer from humans what camels have to suffer: they exhaust them while travelling, and feed them in the desert to beasts and birds of prey . . . Juwayriyya Ibn Asmā', from the tribe of Fazāra, boasts of having slaughtered his mount for a wolf that he met in the desert [the poem in question is quoted] . . . Has not a camel more rights than a wolf? Does not somebody who

> is close deserve more respect than some stranger? Had his guest been a human being, someone of his own kind, he would at least have had an excuse.[24]

Of the two functions of the camel, being both mount and meat, the former is regularly elaborated at length in detailed descriptions of camel and desert. The second theme is less prominent: the killing and preparing of the camel are often mentioned but not often described in detail. Bedouin dishes do not readily lend themselves to lyrical effusions, even though one may imagine how a starved Bedouin, who has lovingly described his she-camel, may not remain unmoved upon seeing a chunk of nourishing meat. Ibn Qutayba's *Kitāb al-maᶜānī l-kabīr* ('The Great Book of Motifs', on early poetry) has a chapter entitled *al-Ṭaᶜām wa-l-ḍiyāfa* ('Food and Hospitality').[25] It opens with verses describing the cooking-pot, black with soot and bubbling; after that, the large dishes. The seething contents of the cauldrons make noises like quarrelling women or groaning camels.[26] 'The pots are milch camels that may be milked as much as has been entrusted to them', a line by Labīd[27] that is explained by Ibn Qutayba: 'Praise, good repute and honour may be 'milked' from them [which is worth] more than the food put into them'.[28] The meat itself is described only rarely. Here is a passage, in Lyall's translation, from a poem by Ibn al-Ahtam, a contemporary of the Prophet Mohammed, which may offend present-day sensibilities, even those of non-vegetarians. He tells us how he has entertained many a guest, arriving after an arduous journey through wind, cold, rain and darkness:

> I have entertained him well, and have uttered no unkind word to him, nor have I said, that I may dismiss him from my hospitality, 'Sooth, there is no room in my tent'.
>
> I said – 'Welcome to thine own people, to a place both easy and broad! See, here is the morning draught set ready for thee, and a friend.'
>
> Then I went to the sleeping line of couching beasts, where the camels great and fat in the hump, like towers, the best of their kind, protected themselves from slaughter
>
> By putting in my way a fine white camel, wont to bring forth her young in the early spring, great as a stallion when she reared herself in front of the other camels ten months gone in calf.

I made for her with a sword-blow on the shank, or with a wide wound, spouting blood, in the stabbing place with its gash in front of the shoulders;

Then two butchers set to work upon her, and mounting atop of her they flay away her hide while yet she is breathing in the last gasps of death;

And there were drawn towards us her udder and her hump, and a white camel-calf that was just trying to stand, of purest breed,

Cut out of its mother's belly: a brother bound to me by the brotherhood of the good, a true comrade, clears away from it with his sword the membrane that enwraps it.

And throughout the night, in the dark hours, there was set before us and the guest a roast of her flesh, rich with fat, and abundance to drink;

And he passed the night with quilts upon him, and smooth soft bedding, as a defence against the east wind – and cold it was!

Yea, every honourable man wards off blame by good cheer to his guest; . . .[29]

According to Ibn Qutayba, who quotes the penultimate verse of this passage, the quilts and the bedding are metaphors: the quilts stand for the food and the 'smooth soft bedding' is the milk. This interpretation is rejected by Lyall as being absurd, but at least it indicates that to the ancient commentators food is the basis of hospitality. No doubt Lyall was right,[30] but the metaphorical interpretation fits in well with the old Arab concepts. According to this explanation the guest protects himself with camel meat against the deadly cold, just as the sleeping camel herd 'protects' itself from slaughter by means of the same camel, which is sacrificed and loses its protection: she is flayed and her calf robbed twice of its covering: its mother's belly and the membrane. In a sense, the tribe protects itself against a bad reputation (also a kind of death) by one of its members, who sacrifices his most precious possession and thus 'wards off blame'. The honour, *ᶜirḍ*, of a man or a tribe is often metaphorically imagined as a piece of clothing, and thus the circle of imagery is completed.

The *Muᶜallaqa* of Imra' al-Qays, surely the most often studied Arabic *qaṣīda* of all time,[31] is remarkable for referring to food twice, representing the raw and the cooked: the slaughtering of the camel for the girls with whom the poet's persona dallies, early in the poem, the girls tossing the bits of flesh (apparently yet uncooked) 'with fat like fringes of twisted silk', and the roasting and boiling of the meat by the cooks after a successful hunt, towards the end of the poem. Suzanne Pinckney Stetkevych makes much of the contrast between the two passages: on the one hand raw meat, unconsumed, in the case of the virgins, just as the love-relationship between the poet and the girls remains immature and unconsummated (I have my doubts here); on the other, cooked meat for a commensal feast, standing for aggregation and fulfilment.[32] However, the contrast, if at all relevant, is only weakly present in the poem. The cooking is described in merely one line; that the meat is eaten is not mentioned in either of the two passages, and the tribe partaking of the food in the latter passage is passed over in silence. And surely it is implied that the virgins will eventually eat the meat after cooking it, as is described explicitly in the anecdote (Imra' al-Qays's adventure at Dārat Juljul) that accompanies the poem. I see no reason why it would be misleading to accept this anecdote as 'a straightforward fleshing-out' (as Stetkevych aptly calls it) of the passage.[33] We can only conclude that, compared with more heroic and amorous themes, such as the hunt and the adventures with women, which take up most of the poem, food does not inspire the poet to expatiate. It seems obvious, however, in view of the heavily eroticized introduction of the poem and even more of the accompanying story, that the poet offers food to the virgins in order to have a sexual affair, or several. 'The female proves more likely to have sex with the males that are more generous with meat':[34] this refers not to humans but to chimpanzees, which means that the story of Imra' al-Qays and the girls has very ancient roots indeed. The food offered to the tribe at the end of the poem ultimately has the same function.

This picture, of food being important but not itself described in detail, does not differ much when other *qaṣīda*s are considered, although the eaters are often mentioned, as in the poem by Ibn al-Ahtam discussed above, or towards the end of Labīd's *Muᶜallaqa*:

> Often when a camel is to be slaughtered and divided by lot (mine the invitation to her death) with gaming sticks evenly-matched of shaft,
>
> I invite (at the sharing out, by them, of a barren or maybe a mother beast, freely offered) the assembled folk to feed on her flesh:

> so the chance guest and the alien sojourner seem to have come down to Tabala, lushness clothing its depths.
>
> Shelter at my tent-ropes is there for any poor wretch of a woman (as starved as the grave-camel) scantily clad in her rags;
>
> and they pile with food, when winds blow rough, trenchers laid out to be eagerly attacked by the orphans.[35]

In several studies Suzanne Stetkevych has described the pre-Islamic *qaṣīda* as basically patterned as a rite of passage. A communal meal often marks the final stage, of reaggregation and integration.[36] The ritual role of many kinds of meals cannot be denied and is underlined by the various Arabic names for meals on special occasions connected with transitions in one's life. The following alphabetical list indiscriminately gives some pre-Islamic and Islamic terms: *^{c}aqīqa* (meat eaten on the occasion of a special ceremony for a newborn child), *^{c}atīra* (a kind of thanksgiving, e.g. when one's flock reached the total of one hundred head; also associated with the beginning of the month of Rajab), *fara^{c}* ('thanksgiving' on the birth of young animals), *ḥidhāq* (also called *khatm*, on completing the memorization of the Qur'ān), *i^{c}dhār* (or *^{c}adhīra, ^{c}idhār*, circumcision meal), *khurs* (after a birth), *milāk* (or *imlāk* or *shundukhī*, on a betrothal), *naqī^{c}a* (either the same as *milāk* or a meal on the return of a traveller, also called *sufra*), *^{c}urs* or *^{c}urus* (wedding banquet, also called *walīma* which is a more general term for a communal meal), *waḍīma* (funeral meal), *wakīra* (on building a house).[37]

These many sacrificial and festive meals, it must be stressed, are not described in the *qaṣīda*: doling out food is not done for very specific reasons, other than relieving the hungry, or wanting to show one's generosity, or in the context of the curious convivial pastime called *maysir*, a kind of game of chance, forbidden by the Koran, involving marked arrow-shafts whereby the stakes of one or more slaughtered camels are apportioned to the players.[38] Although a number of poems seem to fit the pattern of the *rite de passage*, Stetkevych goes too far in extending this idea to the early Arabic *qaṣīda* in general. In any case, reference to eating at the end of a poem is found in merely a small minority of *qaṣīda*s and it does not invariably provide a happy ending, as the poems selected by Stetkevych seem to suggest. Muzarrid produced a parody of the commensal meal in the final lines of a poem describing a poor hunter:

> And he [the hunter, coming home after an unsuccessful hunt] said to her, 'Is there anything to eat? For I can only complain to you, damn you, about people'.
> 'Yes,' she said, 'Here's the well and its water, and a burnt bit of shrivelled skin, a year old'.
> When he had eaten his fill of her food, worn out in the evening, worried by no trivial thing,
> he covered himself, wanting to sleep, with the edge of his coat. But cares prevent slumber from reaching his eyes.[39]

A none too appetizing picture of the meat that is consumed is given by ᶜAbda Ibn al-Ṭabīb, not at the end of the poem but in the middle, during a journey; rather than being a communal feast, it expresses the hardships of desert life:

> When we halted there, we raised above us [on our spears] as a shelter our sheets, and the cauldrons bubbled with meat being cooked for the party –
> [Meat], some dark-red, some red mottled with white which the cook had not thoroughly cooked: as soon as the boiling had changed its colour somewhat, it was taken and devoured.
> Then we turned to our short-haired steeds, branded with our device, and their manes were the napkins with which we wiped our hands.[40]

In a similar context Dhū l-Rumma (d. 117/735) describes in quasi-riddling manner how he and his companions eat bread and meat in the desert:

> One beaten without sin, innocent [i.e. a loaf baked in the sand from which the sand and ashes are beaten], I have broken hastily for my companions;
> A black one like a shield [i.e. a liver] the sides of which I quarrelled over with my friends – we could not endure being without it;
> A white one wearing a transparent shift [i.e. a heart in its membrane] I took and gave to the men, [having slaughtered it] even though it was not sick;
> . . . And one with several prongs [a forked spit] the gaps of which one day I clothed for the raiding party with red bits [of meat] . . .[41]

The pre-Islamic poet ᶜAlqama says boastingly,

> Often I was in the company of people whose food was the green provision-bags (*khuḍr al-mazād*) and meat that had begun to stink.[42]

Ibn Qutayba explains:

> When on a raid, or travelling, they cut meat in pieces and put it into a animal's stomach. After some days it begins to rot . . .; the stomach turns greenish when the meat decays. He compares its colour to that of provision-bags when they turn green from the water. Thus they eat the stomach and what its contains when they have travelled a long distance.[43]

Another commentator[44] has a different explanation: *khuḍr al-mazād*, 'the green of the provision-bag', refers to the liquid in the camel's stomach, which is drunk in emergencies and is called *faẓẓ*. It is, according to a modern specialist, of 'a rather startling green colour and has a strong odour but in emergency could certainly be used as a drinking water supply for humans with no other source'.[45]

Food should not be depicted in too lush and appetizing a manner, it seems, as if the poet, in that case, might be thought to relish it. Here is one of the basic and obvious differences between early bedouin food descriptions and those of later, urban poetry, in which the poet tries to match the appeal of the dish with the attractiveness of the verse that re-presents it. Rather, the bedouin poet-hero should disdain food, neither partaking of it nor depicting it lovingly. The poet's abstention while feeding others is a recurrent topos. Some seem to have lived up to the ideal: Abū Khirāsh, a pre-Islamic poet, it is told, refused a sheep roasted for him by a woman, even though he had not eaten for several days.

> His stomach rumbled, so he struck it with his hand, saying, 'You rumble because of the smell of the food. But, by God, I shall not feed you with any of it!' Then he said, 'Madam, haven't you got anything bitter (*ṣabir aw murr*)?' 'What will you do with it?' asked the woman. 'I want it', he said. She brought him some which he devoured. Then he rushed to his camel and mounted it. The woman implored him, but he refused. 'Did you see anything wrong, or was there something you did not like?' she asked. 'No', he said. Then he went away, while saying:

I bury hunger away until it is bored with me; then I live while neither my clothes nor my body is soiled.
In the morning I drink pure water and I have enough, while weaklings find the food tasty.
I restrain the fierce snake of my belly, you know that; I had rather that others, like your children, would eat.
It is because I am afraid to live basely and contemptibly; death is better than a contemptible life.[46]

If generosity with meat gives prestige, then its opposite, receiving meat, is close to being dishonourable. Perhaps Abū Khirāsh's disdain was strengthened by the fact that the sheep was offered by a woman, whereas doling out the meat has almost always and everywhere been the man's prerogative.

3. *The* Qiṭᶜa *or Short Poem*

Food description is, on the whole, a rarity in the *qaṣīda*, which normally only accommodates some elaboration of the preliminaries to feeding (hunting, slaughtering, playing the *maysir* game) and its paraphernalia (the cooking-pots, the stones supporting it, the bowls). The *qaṣīda* is, moreover, almost exclusively concerned with the heroic diet compatible with lofty diction and themes: meat. The humbler and far more common dishes - bread and other cereals, with milk, butter and dates - are not as a rule mentioned, let alone described, in a *qaṣīda*. Even though the *qaṣīda* is by no means as conventional and rigid as it is often made out to be, it is especially in the *qiṭᶜa* or short poem that the poet is free to deal with anything he likes. But even here, food is not often described in the early period. *Qiṭᶜa* literally means 'piece' or 'fragment', which suggests, wrongly, that it is taken from a larger whole such as a *qaṣīda*. It is often impossible, however, to decide whether a piece originally formed part of a longer poem or was created as an independent composition. There are even single verses that serve as one-line epigrams, such as one by Ḥassān Ibn Thābit, a contemporary of the Prophet:

The butter at the edges of the *tharīd* are like the stars of the Pleiades, or cats' eyes.[47]

This line is usually quoted by itself, only once preceded by another line - perhaps added later - that seems to parody the *qaṣīda*:

> My friends, both of you! Turn aside, dismounting from your hackneys, now that *tharīd* made of curdled milk (?) is brought towards us![48]

What interested the anthologists was the comparison of butter to stars or cats' eyes, which ensured the survival of the line as an epigram, even though a single line, rhyming with nothing else, does not strictly count as a poem.

An early culinary epigram is ascribed to the pre-Islamic Muzarrid, the same who made the original poem on the poor hunter and his scanty fare discussed above. As a boy, it is told, Muzarrid felt slighted by his mother who favoured her other children with the best food. When the mother was away for the day he raided her stores and prepared a meal for himself, while saying the following lines:

> When my mother went out to feed her daughters in the morning, I raided the forbidden tied-up stores.
>
> I mixed a *ṣāʿ*[49] of dates (*ʿajwa*) with two *ṣāʿ*s of wheat flour (*ḥinṭa*), adding one *ṣāʿ* of ghee (*samn*) that floated on top.
>
> I set up the stones under the cooking-pot, equal in size, like the heads of small sheep, cut off on the day that they were gathered.
>
> And I said to my belly, Good cheer today! This is taken from Mother's sanctuary, from what she stores and takes away.
>
> Now if you are empty, this is your medicine; if you are starving, this is the day that you will eat your fill.[50]

This poem may be one of the first versified recipes in Arabic, even though the quantities mentioned are surely a poetic hyperbole. Instead of generosity towards others while himself abstaining, the poet displays a greedy determination to eat the lot himself; nor is the food described of the heroic kind. Rather, it contains a mock-heroic element in the daring raid on forbidden things and the boasting of culinary exploits. Straight from *qaṣīda* conventions is the third line, on the cooking-pot. By not saying 'I am going to eat this' but, instead, addressing his belly as if it were another person, Muzarrid seemingly conforms to the demands of heroic behaviour. In the anthologies this story of young Muzarrid and his poem is told by the philologist al-Aṣmaʿī to the caliph Hārūn al-Rashīd, who is being served with the well-known delicacy called *fālūdhaj* and wants to be told the story again. When al-Aṣmaᶜī has finished the anecdote, the caliph laughs ('until he fell over backwards', in one version, 'so that he had to hold his belly and fell over backwards' in another).[51] Why did the caliph laugh? Possibly on account of the contrast between 'high' *fālūdhaj* and 'low' Bedouin food; but he may have appreciated the mock-heroic elements mentioned before.

Neither Muzarrid nor al-Aṣmaᶜī informs us of the name of the dish concocted by the poet. Judging by the ingredients it could have been *rabīka*, which is made of wheat (*burr*), dates and ghee.[52] The list of Bedouin dishes is long and monotonous (*sakhīna, ḥarīqa, ṣaḥīra, ghadhīra, gharīqa, raghīda, khazīfa, raghīfa, rabīka, bakīla, walīqa, lawīqa, ᶜakīsa*, etc.); as al-Thaᶜālibī says, 'they are all of the pattern *faᶜīla* and similar in quality, being composed of flour, milk, ghee and dates'. It is in fact surprising that so many different dishes could be made from so few ingredients.

Another early epigram looks like a straightforward recipe:

Dates and ghee together, sour cheese next:
There you have your *ḥays*, only not mixed.[53]

According to al-Murtaḍā al-Zabīdī (d. 1205/1791), author of the great dictionary *Tāj al-ᶜarūs*, this anonymous couplet in the simple *rajaz* metre was 'famous, quoted by jurists or Hadith scholars'; he refutes the received opinion that the lines imply that in *ḥays* the ingredients are not mixed. The poet means, he argues, that if the ingredients are present, the dish is present potentially (*bi-l-quwwa*). It is not clear if the couplet ever formed part of a longer poem. As it stands, it is neither boasting verse, as in Muzarrid's lines, nor invective, but pure factual description: perhaps the first versified true recipe. However, one may assume that in the poet's age everyone knew what *ḥays* was and did not need to be told. Therefore one must conclude that the couplet is meant as a little joke. Whenever food is the theme of even the blandest kinds of literature, one must look out for hidden layers of parody and jesting.

CHAPTER III

Eating and the New Ethos

1. From Generously Abstaining to Pious Abstinence

The first literary Islamic text, the Koran, speaks of feeding 'the poor, the orphan and the prisoner' (76:8), or 'feeding on a day of famine' (90:14). But the Bedouin insistence on hospitality is lacking. The word *karīm*, 'noble, generous', often refers to God, to the Koran itself and various other concepts, but not to humans; the word *jūd*, 'liberality, generosity', as well as its synonym *sakhā'* is absent altogether. In the Koran food is associated not with hospitality and honour but with enjoyment and prohibition. The 'good things' in life, *al-ṭayyibāt* (which could also be translated as 'nice things') is an expression often used in connection with eating, as (2:172): 'You that believe, eat of the good things that we have provided for you'; (5:4–5) 'The good things are allowed to you (. . .) and the food of those who have been given the Book is allowed to you'; (5:87–88) 'You that believe, do not forbid such good things as God has allowed to you (. . .) and eat of what God had provided you as lawful and good'. Fish is recommended: 'It is He who has subjected the sea so that you may eat of it fresh flesh' (16:14, cf. 35:12).

Good food is one of the essential pleasures of Paradise. There are some indications that European fantasies about the Land of Cockaigne or Cloud-Cuckoo-Land owe something to the translation into Latin of the Koran.[1] The absence of a corresponding flourishing Arabic tradition of an imaginary yet earthly land of plenty is most likely explained by the fact that its heavenly equivalent in Islam was so much more powerfully present in people's imagination, having more to offer, gastronomically, than its Christian counterpart. In the Hereafter the believers may expect 'of every fruit two kinds' (55:52), 'fruits, palm-trees and pomegranates' (55:68), 'thornless lotus-trees, thickly-growing bananas[2] (. . .) and fruit abounding'

(56:28, 31). Not just vegetarian fare: 'and flesh of fowl, as they desire' (56:21). Especially in sura 56, *al-Wāqiᶜa*, food and drink are important elements in contrasting the ultimate *locus amoenus* of Heaven with the dystopia of Hell, where the food is the fruit of the *zaqqūm* tree that boils in the bowels (56:52, cf. 37:62, 44:43). It does not matter that nobody seems to know exactly what this fruit looks like: its very obscurity strengthens its horrible nature. The food in Hell is ironically called a 'festive reception' (*nuzul*, 56:56, cf. 56:93, 18:102, 37:62). Naturally, the imaginations of later generations were kindled by such passages. In his great compendium of Muslim practice and belief *The Revivification of the Religious Sciences* the theologian al-Ghazālī (d. 505/1111) describes, nearly at the end of the work,[3] the food of the inhabitants of Heaven, citing a few traditions ascribed to the Prophet. 'You will look at the fowl in Paradise; as soon as you desire it, it falls down, roasted, in front of you'. Some of these birds are as big as Bactrian camels; appetites will be commensurate, for people will be able to eat a hundred times more than they used to. Among the things the Paradisial inhabitants will eat is the liver of the great fish (*al-ḥūt*), and the 'ox of Paradise that used to graze at its outskirts' will be slaughtered for them; the fish and ox, or bull, remind one of the cosmological creatures that support the earth in popular creation stories.[4] There is no lack of variety either: according to ᶜAbd Allāh, son of the caliph ᶜUmar, servants will go round with seventy golden plates, each with a different dish. When a Jewish opponent of the Prophet slyly asks whether the eaters will have to excrete, he is told that instead of earthly excrements the bodies will exude a musk-like sweat.[5]

The Koranic passages in favour of enjoying food as one of God's blessings have done useful service in the justification of culinary pleasures in Islam, as can be seen, for instance, from the preambles of cookery books.[6] The mortification of the body, so prominent in many strands of Christianity, finds little encouragement in the Koran, although like any civilization Islam had its share of it.

In Bedouin society abstaining from food for the sake of feeding others is a means to make oneself immortal on earth; in Islam one of the ways to obtain eternal life is by abstaining from forbidden food, such as pork or black-pudding, and by periodic fasting, as in Ramadan. Both are primarily intended to save the individual soul of the believer, yet both have a social dimension. The two Islamic forms of abstinence strengthen the solidarity between the believers, especially since a meal is, preferably, a communal affair: eating by oneself is generally condemned. Ascetics fast in order to reduce the importance of food; to ordinary Muslims fasting serves only to magnify its importance as one of God's blessings. Surely no month is more concerned with thoughts about food than Ramadan. Whereas in Christianity Carnival takes place just before the period of fasting, in Islam a great celebration, one of the Two Feasts, occurs at the end of Ramadan, when the fasting is finally over. Called 'the Minor Feast', it usually surpasses its 'major' counterpart, the sacrificial feast during the Pilgrimage, in conviviality and consumption of food.

Koranic food regulations cannot be called very detailed or burdensome, compared, for instance, with those of Judaism. There are many references to kinds of food in the *Ḥadīth*, the sayings and acts ascribed to the prophet Mohammed. As a whole, these underline the generally positive attitude of the Koranic text towards eating 'the good things'. In a story that is reminiscent of the New Testament story of Jesus' miraculous feeding of the five thousand, Mohammed is given a number of barley loaves and some butter with which he proceeds to feed eighty people in shifts of ten, 'until they had eaten their fill'; on another occasion he feeds 130 people with the liver of one sheep, again until they had satisfied their appetite.[7] A poem attributed to the early grammarian Quṭrub (d.206/821) on Mohammed's miracles has the following lines:

> And there was a dish of *tharīd*, food for one person:
> with it he sated a crowd, while the crowd was witnessing it.
> Three hundred were fed from it and had enough,
> whereas it had not been enough for one ascetic (. . .)
> Twenty-one dates were in a bag, as is related
> in reports transmitted by a chain of authorities:
> Three thousand people had their fill from them,
> and what they left over still filled the bag.[8]

In the course of time the numbers tend to grow and the feats become more and more fantastic. If these stories are told primarily to attribute miracles to the prophet, then this is not rubbed in too emphatically in the earliest stages. The way they are told often seems to stress the prophet's generosity rather than his ability to perform miracles. To the ninth-century compiler, al-Bukhārī, the point of the stories is, first of all, to show that eating one's fill was not blameworthy, judging by the chapter-heading 'Those who ate their fill'. Not surprisingly, another *ḥadīth* affirms that Mohammed was himself a moderate eater: 'God's Apostle left this world never having eaten his fill of barley bread'.[9] According to one of his sayings, a true believer eats with one stomach, an unbeliever with seven stomachs.[10] Nevertheless, 'he loved sweets and honey', according to ᶜĀ'isha,[11] his favourite wife whom he jokingly called 'superior among women just as *tharīd* (a bread and meat broth) is superior among dishes'.[12] It is said that he never condemned a dish but merely abstained from things he disliked,[13] which in another story is illustrated by his behaviour when offered a dish of that bedouin speciality, lizard. Unaware of its nature, the prophet is about to eat it when a woman who is present feels that he ought to be told. He retracts his outstretched hand. When Khālid Ibn al-Walīd, the future conqueror, asks, 'Is it forbidden?', Mohammed replies, 'No, but it was not found in the land of my tribe, so I find that I dislike it.'[14]

Lizards and locusts (the latter eaten by the prophet on several occasions[15]) were not unknown to the town-dwelling contemporaries of the prophet, whose diet cannot have differed very much from that of the nomadic or semi-nomadic bedouins. Yet a distinction began to be felt between urban and bedouin food habits. Eating lizards was used as a topos in invective poetry to stigmatize uncouth tribes and became one of the stock themes of the anti-Arab Shuᶜūbiyya movement, as will be discussed in more detail below, while some measure of urban luxury had reached Mecca already towards the end of the sixth century, before Mohammed's activity as a prophet. ᶜAbd Allāh Ibn Judᶜān[16] was famous for his rich banquets, where *fālūdh* (often called *fālūdhaj* or *fālūdhaq*) was served, a dish made of wheat and honey with which he had become acquainted at the court of the Sāsānian emperor.[17] In a eulogy on Ibn Judᶜān, Umayya Ibn Abī l-Ṣalt says that he issued a general invitation to many people to partake of 'large bowls of ebony, filled with wheat flour mixed with honey'.[18] The reference to the bowls is traditional in poetry; what is novel here is that the ingredients of the dish are given. In spite of its apparently simple nature, *fālūdhaj* was to remain a dish commonly found in anecdotes as an example of something extremely palatable.[19] Such luxury, though known, was rare until after the days of the Prophet; it was only after the great conquests of early Islam that the Arabs were regularly able to indulge in good food, especially in rich towns like Mecca and Medina. There is a tradition, deemed inauthentic by some but incorporated in one of the standard collections of Ḥadīth, according to which the Prophet was told by the archangel Gabriel about the luxuries in store for his world-conquering followers: 'They will even eat *fālūdhaj!*'. Mohammed asks, 'What is *fālūdhaj?*' When Gabriel explains: 'They will mix clarified butter and honey', the Prophet sighs deeply (*shahiqa shahqatan*).[20] The sigh may have a double meaning: regret at having missed this delicacy, or concern at the impending surfeit of worldly pleasures, so that the story may be used by ascetics and pious epicures alike. The change from austerity to luxury is illustrated in the famous 'Story of the Lie', told by ᶜĀ'isha, about her adventure during a raid of the Prophet many years before, when she was still a young girl: 'The women in those days tended to be light, for they ate only frugal meals and had not yet grown heavy, bloated with meat'.[21] The founder of the Umayyad dynasty, Muᶜāwiya (regn. 41-60/661-680), is depicted in many stories and anecdotes as being fond of good and rich food; from his daily routine, given in some detail by al-Masᶜūdī, the important role of food is immediately apparent.[22] When the governor of Medina offers him a large dish of *ḥays*, made of dates, curds and butter, a Christian doctor advises him against it: 'Don't eat from it, or I shall tear my clothes!' But Muᶜāwiya replies, 'I shall eat, even if you tear your belly'.[23] The Umayyad caliphs generally had a bad reputation in Arabic historiography - written under the Abbasids - yet Muᶜāwiya is usually praised for his wisdom, astuteness and tolerance. However, 'in spite of his generosity and liberality he was greedy and stingy in matters of food', says Ibn al-Ṭiqṭaqā (d. c. 709/1309) in *al-Fakhrī*, a popular compendium of history intended as a mirror for princes:

> He used to eat five meals a day, the last one being the largest. Then he would say to the servant, 'Take it away! By God, I have not eaten my fill, but I am bored.'[24]

The first four caliphs, by contrast, 'ate of the lowliest food of the poor'.[25] Even today Muᶜāwiya is considered by some as the first in Islam to indulge in good food, and his eating behaviour is contrasted, unfavourably of course, with the frugal and sensible diet of the Prophet and those nearest to him.[26] Worse than Muᶜāwiya was another Umayyad caliph, Sulayman Ibn ᶜAbd al-Malik (r. 96-99/715-717), who would not wait until a piece of roast chicken was cold enough to be picked up with one's fingers, and used the edge of his sleeve, who slept surrounded by baskets filled with sweets, and who would eat, we are told, vast quantities that stretch one's belief.[27] 'One day,' says al-Thaᶜālibī,

> he ate thirty chickens and one hundred boiled eggs, drank several pints of date wine and took pleasure with four virgins. Then he suffered from a surfeit, felt faint, and was felled by Fate.[28]

The contrast beween urban and Bedouin food is a common subject in literary sources. The Bedouins looked down, or pretended to look down, on luxury food. 'He taught his people to eat *khabīṣ* (a very popular sweet dish)', said al-Farazdaq in an invective epigram against the notorious governor ᶜUmar Ibn Hubayra.[29] *Khabīṣ*, basically a simple dish made of dates, flour and butter, is not listed among traditional Bedouin kinds of food; and, developing into more elaborate sweet forms, it became associated with luxury and non-Arab food. When someone told al-Aṣmaᶜī that he preferred '*shubāriqāt*, kinds of *khabīṣ* and *falūdhaj*', al-Aṣmaᶜī answered: 'The food of the Persians, Chosroes' way of life . . . A bad way of life! This is not the way of life of the family of al-Khaṭṭāb!'[30] In the rest of this anecdote al-Aṣmaᶜī criticizes several more of his table fellows in a similar manner, unfavourably comparing their luxury with the frugality of the caliph ᶜUmar and his kin, who, according to him, ate, as condiment with their bread, 'milk one day, oil one day, butter one day, dates one day, cheese one day, unseasoned bread one day, and meat one day', apparently on a weekly rota.[31] During the talks between Persians and Muslim Arabs before the battle of al-Qādisiyya (c. 14/635), al-Muthannā Ibn Ḥāritha is presented by a Persian commander with some *fālūdhaj*. 'What is this?', he asks his wife, who suggests, 'I think that his wretched wife tried to make *ᶜaṣīda*, without success.'[32] A mixture of mockery and admiration is implied in this and similar anecdotes: the Muslim Arab warriors were unsophisticated, almost boorish, yet in their simplicity superior to the effeminate Persians.

Just as among urban Arabs – al-Aṣmaᶜī among them – the old poetry was cultivated and ancient Bedouin virtues extolled, if not always put into practice, so we find a certain admiration and nostalgia for the simple tastes of yore. It is related that caliph ᶜAbd al-Malik (*regn*. 65-86/685-705) once asked a Bedouin, 'What is the best food?'. The Bedouin answers, 'A young camel with a firm hump, killed while healthy, not diseased, in overflowing cooking-pots, [cut] with keen knifes, on a chilly morning'. The caliph exclaims, 'By your father! You have given a nice description (*aṭyabta*)!'[33] From the verb used, it appears that ᶜAbd al-Malik implies that the food is tastily pictured; but this, one could argue, is largely due to the Bedouin's eloquence, for he employs *sajᶜ* or rhymed prose, with five relatively rare words ending in *-imah*. It is on account of its style and diction, not for its culinary interest, that al-Jāḥiẓ quotes this anecdote in his book on the eloquence of the Arabs. The following anecdote, again involving the same caliph and a Bedouin, is less ambiguous in this respect:

> ᶜAbd al-Malik Ibn Marwān once gave a rich banquet. He invited people, and they ate. One of them said, 'How nice is this food! I believe that nobody has ever seen more than this, or nicer food than this!' Then a Bedouin from the lower ranks (? or: standing aside, *min nāḥiyat al-qawm*) said, 'More, no! But nicer, well, I have eaten nicer things than this, by God!'
>
> They began to laugh at his words; but ᶜAbd al-Malik ordered the man to be brought near him and said, 'If you speak the truth, you must tell us to prove it!'
>
> The man answered:
>
> 'Yes, Commander of the Faithful! While I was living in Hajar, on a spot of soft red earth, in a remote place, my father died; I had to look after a family. He had owned date palms; among them was a palm tree such as no one had ever seen. Its dates were like the hoofs of camel calves born in spring. Never were dates seen that big and firm, with such small stones and so sweet. Every night a wild she-ass came, as I had noticed, to spend the night under that tree. She used to plant her hind legs against the lower tree, raising her front legs and pluck the dates with her mouth, thus leaving only a few scattered inferior dates. This annoyed me greatly. So I set out with my bow and arrows. I thought that I would be able to return after a short while, but I had to wait for a day and a night without seeing her. Finally, at daybreak, she came. I prepared myself, shot an arrow and hit her; I dispatched her. Then I looked for her navel-piece (*surratahā*) and cut it out. Then I looked for some thick pieces of firewood. I put this together with some heating-stones, looked for my fire-stick, lit a fire in that wood and put the navel-piece in it. Then I fell asleep like a baby (? *adrakanī nawm al-shabāb*) and was only woken up by the heat of the sun on my back. At once I went to it,

> dug it up, wiped off the dirt, coal and ashes that were on it. I turned over [the fat] like a white mantle and laid on it some ripe and half-ripe dates from the palm tree. I heard them crackling, it sounded like the mutual challenges of the tribes of ᶜĀmir and Ghaṭafān! Then I began to take a piece of fat or a piece of meat, putting it between two dates, and raised it towards my mouth. I swear that I have never eaten such food.'[34]

The caliph agrees that it must indeed have been a good meal. In the remainder of the anecdote the unnamed Bedouin, from the tribe ᶜUdhra, turns out to be an admirer of Jarīr's poetry. He leaves the party well-rewarded. In *Kitāb al-Aghānī* the story is told in the chapter on Jarīr; in this context all of the passage translated above merely serves as a rather gratuitous introduction – just as the information at the very beginning, on his situation in Hajar, has very little to do with what follows. However, if the anecdote is considered in isolation, food and its preparation are its main subjects. The man is described as eloquent, belonging to *fuṣaḥā' al-ᶜArab*, and describes himself as free from various speech 'defects' associated with various tribes; yet his story, though eloquent, is not adorned with the *sajᶜ*, assonances and parallelisms so often found in sayings ascribed to the ancient Bedouins. His speech is as simple as his meal, yet the implication is that both are somehow superior to the richness and refinement of a caliphal banquet.

A different version of the same story is given by al-Jāḥiẓ in the chapter on the food of the Bedouins in his *al-Bukhalā'*.[35] Here there is no mention of the caliph nor of a banquet. Al-Jāḥiẓ adds that he finds the story suspect 'because it contains things that no Arab who knows the ways of the Arabs would say'. This did not stop al-Iṣfahānī, nor his sources, from offering the story in the frame of a contrast between urban luxury and plain Bedouin delights.

One may compare a story that is given an earlier setting, a meeting between a Bedouin and the Sassanian emperor. When the Bedouin – brought in 'so that his uncouthness and ignorance could be marvelled at' – is asked, 'What is the best meat?', his answer is 'Camel meat'. The emperor replies, 'How could camel meat be better than duck, chicken, chicks, francolin or kid?'; whereupon the Bedouin explains that camel, cooked in water and salt, is superior to all the other kinds of meat when likewise cooked in water and salt.[36] This theme could be illustrated with many more similar stories and anecdotes about the Bedouins quoted in anthologies, some of which will be discussed below.

The place of the Bedouin is sometimes taken by rural villagers. In a common type of anecdote a caliph or king, while hunting, loses his way and is entertained by a villager. One such story mentions al-Mahdī and one of his courtiers who are regaled by a poor farmer, or 'Nabataean' as he is called in one version (a farmer of the rural area of Iraq), on a dish made of salted fish (*rubaythā'*), barley bread, leeks and olive oil. The courtier derides the man in an epigram, telling him that such a meal should be rewarded with two or three cuffs on the ear. The caliph, however, corrects him and his verse: two or three bags of ten thousand dirhams each; the Nabaṭī is rewarded accordingly.[37] The caliph's action was inspired, no doubt, first of all by a desire to reward his host for offering all the food he possessed, rather than to extol rural fare. Yet it is said that 'the two ate a lot, and al-Mahdī relished it and finished off everything, leaving nothing at all.'

Some non-Arabs, on the other hand, openly derided not only the Bedouin Arabs for their coarse feeding habits but all those of Arab descent on account of their ancestors' food.[38] Here are a few examples by Bashshār Ibn Burd (d. 167/783):

> never did my father (. . .) approach the colocynth, to pierce it for very hunger;
> nor approach the mimosa, to beat down its fruit with a stave;
> nor did we roast a skink, with its quivering tail,
> nor did I dig for and eat the lizard of the stony ground.[39]

*

> My daughter says, whenever a strange woman boasts to her, clad in a camel hair wrap and a patched cover
> (she has a father, a herdsman, who brings her in the evening some roast lizard hearts and livers):
> 'My father is the scion of kings (. . .)'[40]

*

> We, in our glory, used to eat white bread[41] and to drink from silver and gold vessels
> (. . .) You gnaw on the head of a 'praying' scarab[42] and are not concerned with house-grown francolins.

> At night you lurk for hedgehogs; hunting mice makes you forget glorious deeds.
> You envy someone who roasts a chameleon (. . .)[43]

One of the most famous lines of invective poetry is addressed by Abū Nuwās (d. c. 200/814) to the tribe of Tamīm. It is the first line of the invective section of a poem; a line that strikes like a bolt from the blue, since it follows abruptly, without transition, upon a seemingly peaceful Bedouin *nasīb* (elegiac introductory part):

> Whenever a Tamīmī comes to you, boasting, say: 'Never mind about that; but how is it that you eat lizards?'[44]

The following poem, ascribed to the late Umayyad poet Abū l-Hindī, is obviously a reaction to these anti-Arab sentiments:

> I have eaten lizards and did not loathe them, and I do like dried slices of cured mutton.
> I have put butter on dates: lovely food, lovely garnish!
> And clarified butter, and mushrooms from under *qasīs* trees, and camel's liver, best with the fat of the hump,
> And roast lamb, served to me sizzling hot on a cold day.
> But rice pudding (*bahaṭṭ*), and those big fish of yours always make me sick.
> I have had all that, like you have, but I have never found anything like an old lizard.
> There are no eggs like chicken eggs, and locusts' eggs are a cure for him who craves for meat.[45]
> And lizards' eggs are the food of the true Arabs: they are not to the taste of the non-Arabs.[46]

Abū l-Hindī, important precursor of Abū Nuwās as a bacchic poet, was not particularly noted for his bedouin habits; he lived part of his life in Khurāsān. The ascription of the poem, not found in all the sources, is therefore slightly suspect. If it is correct, however, this makes it all the more likely that the poem is polemical, anti-*Shuᶜūbiyya*. But even the staunchest anti-Shuᶜūbites had to draw the line somewhere. Al-Jāḥiẓ balked at some Bedouin eating habits: 'The Bedouin have the strange habit of eating beasts of prey and insects (*ḥasharāt*). Some pretend to like them, others even take pride in eating them.'[47] He cites an anonymous *rajaz* poem in which the poet, after a description of a jerboa (*yarbūᶜ*), continues:

. . . In hard times, when they happen, or afterwards,
I like it better than freshly picked dates.
White earthworms (*shaḥmat al-arḍ*)[48] are the food of the rich
and of every mighty man of wide renown.
Or a *haysha*,[49] which I pick up for breakfast
on a feastday and a day of vaunting.
Or anything that crawls in the dark,
such as a scorpion, a hedgehog or a hyrax (*wabr*),
or a snake that I cook in hot embers:
Those are my concern, the things I go for
at any time, whether I be rich or poor.
Everything goes to its destiny.
Every bird sitting on its nest,
every drone, every bee,
male hyena (*dhīkh*), *sim*ᶜ[50] or desert wolf,
dog, fox as well as cat,
lizard, fish, water fowl,
the squinting crow that speaks on a day of augury:
I eat them all, except the green chameleons
or the scarab that performs the afternoon prayer . . .[51]

Al-Jāḥiẓ is clearly skeptical about the poet's sincerity: 'he maintains that he likes all this';[52] and one must admit that the poem sounds like a piece of wilful eccentricity, or even a parody made by a Shuᶜūbī. It is possible, of course, that such tastes and preferences were acquired through habit. Abū Wā'il Shaqīq Ibn Salama, a contemporary of the Prophet, said, 'I'd rather have a roasted lizard than a fattened chicken' and there is no reason to disbelieve him.[53] More commonly the anti-Shuᶜūbites defend the eating of vermin on the grounds of necessity, which does not make it shameful. The early Muslim warrior al-Mughīra Ibn Zurāra admits to the Persian king Yazdagird that 'We used to eat scarabs, dung beetles, scorpions and snakes, considering this our food.' He adds that this state has now ended since the Prophet Mohammed has led the Arabs from misery to glory.[54] In a defence of the Arabs the great prose-writer al-Tawḥīdī (d. after 400/1010) quotes the Shuᶜūbite al-Jayhānī, who had reviled the Arabs for eating jerboas, lizards, rats and snakes; al-Tawḥīdī argues that any king, emperor or ruler of any nation would do the same if reduced to similarly harsh circumstances. The Bedouin Arabs, however, were adept at making the most of what nature offered them: 'when the heavens were generous, rain did not fail them, the earth adorned itself, fruit hung from branches, and river beds flowed, then they had plenty of milk, curds, cheese, fresh and dried dates and wheat.'[55]

A somewhat strange fragment of two lines seems to be transitional, since it shows that dwellers of the desert were not afraid to own that they relished urban dishes. Wa^{c}la al-Jarmī, a contemporary of the Prophet, said:

> It is no shame, that which you revile us for: roast chicks with *khabīṣ*.
> Crow's meat is not our fare, nor crab from the streams of al-Barīṣ.[56]

Wa^{c}la was a bedouin who, nevertheless, had apparently tasted sedentary delicacies and was not ashamed of it. It is unlikely that the revilers were urban themselves, yet bedouins would normally eat neither crab nor evil-omened crow.

In any case, the Bedouins were not alone in eating vermin: some non-Arabs had similar strange eating habits. To Khāqān al-Muflihī (late 3rd/9th century), a Turk judging by his name, meat was meat, whatever animal it came from: bear, hyena, or anything else.[57] Al-Jāḥiẓ relates that, during a banquet at the court of the Barmakī vizier al-Faḍl Ibn Yaḥyā, the host railed against eating lizards. Everyone followed him, except one Arab of the tribe of Hilāl. Subsequently, noticing that a dish was served that included wasps' grubs, he exclaimed,

> An uncouth non-Arab (*^{c}ilj*) who loathes lizards, wretched glutton that he is: but his dish contains flies' heads!
> If a prince screwed his mother in public, they would say, 'Decidedly the right thing to do!'[58]

The second line refers to another common topic in the *Shu^{c}ūbiyya* debate, viz. the matter of incest in Zoroastrianism, dwelt upon at length also in al-Tawḥīdī's defence of the Arabs. Thus the epigram combines two of the most common elements in intercommunal vilifying, gastronomical and sexual deviance. The reference at the end (to sura 38:20) seems to bring in a third element: religion, which of course encompasses sexual and eating behaviour. Whereas lizards are not forbidden as food according to Islamic law, wasps in their various stages are. In sura 38 it is Dāwūd or David – lord of everything that flies (see 38:19), therefore lord of flies and wasps – who is said to have wisdom and discernment; in the epigram another non-Arab is mockingly contrasted with David as someone lacking in taste, violating religion, and, in doing it openly, violating decorum. Bedouin ethos and Islam merge in this lampoon.

2. Satiety and Sin

Although rigorous abstention from good food is recommended neither by the Koran nor by the Traditions of the Prophet, Islam, like any religion or civilization, has its ascetic trends. The literary reflection of this trend is diverse; on the whole there are fewer sayings and stories extolling mortification and self-starvation than there are recommending moderation and condemning over-eating. Often it is less a matter of religion and ethics than of decorum. A letter attributed to the caliph ᶜAlī, included in the influential collection entitled *Nahj al-balāgha*, is addressed to a governor of Basra; he is sternly rebuked because he eagerly accepted an invitation to a banquet given by some of his subjects.[59] The same caliph says to another governor, 'I have been told that you eat much food and many different dishes (. . .). Why don't you fast a few days for God's sake (. . .) and eat seldom and frugally?'[60] A warning against overeating is justified by the austere caliph ᶜUmar on religious, ethical and medical grounds:

> Beware of overeating! It make one too lazy to perform the ritual prayer, corrupts the body and leads to sickness. Being moderate with one's food is less wasteful, healthier for one's body, and strengthens one's devotion. A believer will only perish when he favours his lust over his religion.[61]

His namesake, the Umayyad caliph ᶜUmar Ibn ᶜAbd al-ᶜAzīz (*regn.* 99-101/717-720), likewise was a paragon of austerity and frugality, someone who was admired in Abbasid times as the only godly Umayyad. Once, it is told, a guest of one of the Abbasid caliphs, al-Muhtadī (*regn.* 255-256/869-870) was served with bread, salt and vinegar. He took only a little, expecting better things to come. He was disappointed: the caliph explained that it would be a shame if the Umayyads could boast a pious ᶜUmar while the Abbasids could not offer anyone like him.[62] Abstention is a means to strengthen one's character, as is reported of the Būyid ruler ᶜAḍud al-Dawla (*regn.* 338-372/949-983). When on a diet, he had precisely those dishes served at his table that he was not supposed to eat. These he would contemplate intently by way of exercising his willpower and taming the 'power of passion', before he ordered them to be taken away. Thus, to the strong, the 'sweetness of abstention' may be greater than the pleasure of indulging oneself.[63]

Handbooks on ethics and pious behaviour offer much material on the close connections between piety, ethics and decorum, such as the chapter on 'The virtue of hunger and the condemnation of satiety (*shibaᶜ*)' in al-Ghazālī's *Revivification*,[64] which ought to be read in conjunction with his chapter on table manners.[65] Many books that could be classified as *adab* (on which see the following chapter) contain sections on the theme of hunger vs. eating one's fill, not rarely including conflicting and contradictory opinions.

In *al-Imtāᶜ wa-l-mu'ānasa* by al-Tawḥīdī a long section is devoted to food and eating.[66] The chapter is presented as being the proceedings of three nights' conversation with a vizier and others. The vizier asks, 'Before anything else, tell me which is better, to urge people to eat, or to refrain from doing so and let their eating take its course?' Two opposite opinions are quoted immediately: 'Food is too lowly (*ahwan*) a thing for anyone to be urged to partake of it', and 'Food is too noble a thing for anyone *not* to be urged to partake of it.' Both sayings are attributed to pious early Muslims; the latter is said to be the better opinion.[67] In the course of the chapter a lengthy piece provides 'definitions' of *shibaᶜ*, 'eating one's fill', attributed not to known authorities but to types: a mystic, a theologian, a cadger, a bedouin, a physician, a fuller, *et al.*[68] Each is asked the same question, *'Mā ḥadd al-shibaᶜ?'*, which means not only 'What is the definition of satiety?' but also 'What is the limit of satiety; or: When has one eaten one's fill?'. The word *shibaᶜ*, 'satiety', is itself somewhat ambiguous: it is in a sense the opposite of 'hunger', but according to one's attitude this means either excess (overeating) or moderation (eating just enough to still one's hunger). The first speaker, the Sufi, therefore answers, 'It has no definition/limit', because people differ in constitution, character, habits and circumstances (elsewhere, the Sufi defines its limit as 'death').[69] Ambiguous, too, is the answer of 'someone from Medina': 'The limit of satiety? I have never experienced it; how could I describe what I do not know?'[70] This could have been said by an insatiable glutton or by an austere ascetic alike. Taken as a whole the collection of sayings provides a good illustration of the range of attitudes towards food: from the ascetic (*zāhid*), who defines satiety as that which makes it possible to fast during the day and do pious works during the night, to gluttons such as 'the Turk' ('Satiety is: to eat until you are nigh death') and 'the man from Samarcand' ('When your eyes bulge, your tongue is dumb, your movements are heavy, your body teeters, your reason has left you: that is the beginning of satiety' – 'If this is the beginning, then what is the end?' – 'That you are split into two halves.').[71] In the middle we find the physician: 'Satiety is what rectifies nature, preserves the constitution, and leaves an appetite for other things.'[72]

'The first affliction that occurred in this community [of Islam] after the death of its Prophet (God bless and preserve him) was Satiety and its prevalence': a saying attributed to ᶜĀ'isha in a treatise on ethics in the famous encyclopedic *Epistles of the Pure Brethren*, written by an authors' collective contemporary with al-Tawḥīdī. The saying opens a section on 'The evils of Satiety (*shibaᶜ*)',[73] which are physical and spiritual. The stomach is a cooking-pot (the Pure Brethren are never at a loss for a catching analogy), heated by the fire of the liver; the surplus food is not cooked well and causes various diseases. In the long debate between the animals and Man, in the *Epistles*, the latter boasts of his sophisticated eating behaviour, his refined and variegated kinds of food, compared with the animals' coarse feeding habits.[74] Yet, the animals argue, he does not know that this amounts to being a punishment for mankind and the source of evils. People may boast of their tasty kinds of bread, but consider how bread is made! The laborious process of making bread from scratch, beginning with ploughing and sowing, serves as an example.[75] Similarly, in the story of Adam, as told by al-Thaᶜlabī (d. 427/1035), bread is presented as a mixed blessing. The angel Gabriel tells Adam what to do with a few grains of wheat, which after much labour produce a loaf of bread. At many stages Adam asks whether he can eat now, only being told that yet more work is needed: he is taught patience in the process.[76] Al-Ghazālī also makes good use of the example of food, in his chapter on 'Fortitude and Gratitude', in the fourth part of his *Revivification*. He not only describes the various stages of producing bread but also what human digestion involves, and indeed everything that precedes, such as the perception of and the movement towards things desired – all this in order to show the wonderful ways of God, who makes it possible, through myriad interconnected acts and processes, that man is able to perform such a seemingly simple act as eating.[77]

In the debate of man and animals the latter enumerate several dozen physical diseases and unpleasant consequences of human eating, of which animals are free, and which outweigh any gastronomical pleasures offered by food. In any case, the best kind of food by common consent is made not by humans but by bees, so Man has little to boast of. The conviviality of human banquets with their pleasures of conversation, mutual congratulations and greetings, dancing and music, is likewise offset by as many negative counterparts. Man has nothing to offer as a rejoinder and passes on to other subjects.[78]

The authors of the *Epistles*, for all their contempt for the base and earthly aspects of human life, have a keen eye for concrete illustrations of their lofty ideas. This is all the more justified because in their concept of the universe everything is strongly connected with everything else, the high with the low, the trivial with the cosmic. In their attempt to popularize esotericism, food and eating turn out to be useful. The habit of well-bred Muslims of eating with three fingers reflects the fact that knowledge, which is the food of the soul, is acquired through three roads: thinking, hearing, and seeing.[79] Man's opinions on the creation of the world are illustrated by means of an allegorical story. A wise man had several young children, some intelligent, others stupid. One day, they find in a container belonging to their father a quantity of sweets of various tastes and shapes. They wonder who it was that made them. The clever ones decide it must have been a wise maker, the stupid ones do not even perceive this. The brighter ones of the first group go a few steps further in their speculations. Finally they are told by some older brothers that the sweets are made by the confectioner (*ḥulwānī*) from sugar, oil and starch. The more persistent brothers, fewer at each stage, are told how these ingredients are used to produce the sweets, but they cannot grasp it completely. Various opinions are formed; the compassionate father, wishing to alleviate their bewilderment, instructs his eldest sons to tell the others that he himself made the sweets, from something unknown, in the way that he wished. These vague answers turn out to be more acceptable to the children than the strange concepts they heard of (confectioner, sugar, oil, starch, oven,[80] kettles etc.).[81]

In this allegory of God as the Wise Confectioner and Creation as a box of sweetmeats the boys represent different kinds of people: the more intelligent ones stand for the philosophers, the eldest ones who instruct the others at the father's instigation stand for the prophets, and the kind father is the Creator, as the added exegesis says. Interestingly, it is left rather vague whether or not this compassionate father and the wise Confectioner are identical. The children are told to believe it was their father who made the sweets, 'because knowing their father is closer to their understanding than knowing the Confectioner.'

Similar analogies using food are found in the *Epistles*. The digestive process of the body may be compared, in turn, to those of confectioners;[82] the world and its pleasures is allegorically likened at length, in what is called an Indian story, to a garden and its fruits, enjoyed by a blind man and a lame man (or body and soul).[83] Thus the appeal of food, or at least of food descriptions, is exploited as an educational tool, while at the same time food is depreciated: a rich diet is the source of sickness and evil, sweets are for children.

Craving for food, after all, is in a sense the root of all evil. As soon as Adam was created and his spirit entered his body, his very first wish was for food.[84] The Koran (20:120–21, cf. 2:35) tells the familiar story of how Adam and his wife were tempted by the Devil to eat from the forbidden tree of Eternity and Kingship, identified tentatively by the commentators as a tree producing wheat (bread being the archetypal food) or figs (the story of the fig-leaves used as covering was known) or grapes (wine being a source of many evils).[85] Abū Jād and Kalaman, two of the eponymous fathers of the alphabet, also ate from the tree, according to a curious report by Ibn ᶜAbbās; Abū Jād 'disobeyed (*abā*) . . . and ate with a will (*jadda*)'; Kalaman 'ate (*akala*) and was granted (*munna*) repentance'.[86] The story is curious because by all accounts Adam and Eve's offspring were born after they were driven from Paradise. Perhaps the eating ought to be interpreted allegorically: the alphabet, literacy and literature were nourished straight from the tree of Eternity, which is equated by some with the tree of Knowledge.[87]

CHAPTER IV

Adab, *or the Text as a Banquet*

1. *Adab* Anthologies

Much of Arabic literature after the coming of Islam is naturally permeated with Islamic ethics - which does not mean, incidentally, that all literature oozes with piety. The Bedouin ethos, with its insistence, not on piety vs sin but on honour vs shame, has by no means disappeared. Moreover, a new literature comes into being with food as its subject without any moral, ethical or religious connotation. To this category belong, for instance, scientific or practical works on food: cookery books or medical treatises on food. Here I shall restrict myself as much as possible to purely or mainly bellettristic works, even though the definition of this is not easy in classical Arabic literature.

A popular genre is the so-called *adab*-anthology or *adab*-encyclopedia: a more or less thematically arranged compilation of bits of prose and poetry, with or without commentary or connecting texts between the quotations; in short, a kind of literary banquet. Having discussed the concept of *adab* briefly,[1] it will be clear that there is a certain relationship with ethics and etiquette. The chapters in such a work deal with abstract concepts such as 'authority', 'war', 'friendship', virtues and vices such as piety, eloquence, intelligence, generosity and their opposites; but also with more concrete matters such as animals, women, or natural phenomena. Beginning with the earliest important *adab*-anthology a chapter on eating and food is almost always included.

The first anthology of this kind was *ᶜUyūn al-akhbār*, by the same Ibn Qutayba (d. 276/889) who was mentioned before. In his introduction the author fittingly compares his work to 'a table with different dishes of various tastes, according to the appetites of the eaters'.[2] This comparison is found elsewhere; the Koran itself has been called, reputedly by the Prophet, 'God's banquet (*ma'duba*)'; everyone is invited to partake of its many different courses, savoury, sour and sweet;[3] likewise, a 16th-century French writer wrote: 'Holy Scripture is like a dish of all kinds of foods'.[4] Ibn Qutayba's anthology is divided into ten parts, roughly going from the lofty to the lowly, by medieval Arab standards: it opens with *al-Sulṭān* ('Authority') and ends with a chapter entitled *al-Nisā'* ('Women'), which, incidentally, also deals with sex and bodily peculiarities of men as well as women. The penultimate chapter is *al-Ṭa*ᶜ*ām* ('Food');[5] thus one might say that the work ends with two chapters devoted to what is sometimes called *al-aṭyabān*, 'the two good things', viz. food and sex. In the chapter on food in his *Kitāb al-Ma*ᶜ*ānī l-kabīr* Ibn Qutayba restricts himself to the motifs found in early poetry; it is a collection of explanations of difficult expressions and obscure verses, not a complete survey of the theme of food in ancient poetry. In ᶜ*Uyūn al-akhbār*, on the other hand, Ibn Qutayba freely chooses from poetry and prose, ancient or modern. Accessibility rather than obscurity directs his choice. He does not once explicitly give his own words or his own opinion: his contribution is the selection and the presentation of the material, and possibly the wording of some of the prose passages. The chapter begins (iii, 197–213) with a motley collection of short sayings, by persons known and unknown, on particular kinds of food or dishes, recommended as wholesome or tasty. The persons quoted are early Muslims or the odd Greek sage, but above all Bedouins, admired for their eloquence and found strange because they eat such things as lizards. From the very beginning it is stressed that tastes may differ; yet not all preferences expressed should be taken at face value. In the first anecdote, the famous al-Aḥnaf Ibn Qays, when asked by the caliph ᶜUmar about his favourite food, answers 'Butter and truffles'. ᶜUmar explains: he does not mean that he likes them best of all, but they are an indication of fertility and abundance. The caliph is able to read between the lines, for it may be expected that the wise al-Aḥnaf does not merely give a personal answer to a trivial question, but utters a statement on the common good. After this lofty sentiment, personal preference takes over. In the following anecdote someone says: 'There is nothing that I dislike more than dates and butter'. The matter is clinched in favour of dates and butter in the next story, in which the Umayyad governor al-Ḥajjāj carries out a small poll, each person writing down his favourite food on a piece of papyrus. It turns out that butter and dates are unanimously preferred.[6]

Often the wording seems to be more important than the information, as when an anonymous Bedouin says, 'Our dates are smooth and snub-nosed; your teeth sink into them; their stones are like bird's tongues; you put a date into your mouth and you find the sweetness in your ankles'.[7] Another lovingly describes a dish of the common broth called *tharīda*: 'I long for a *tharīda* dark with pepper, speckled with chickpeas, with meat on two sides and two wings of bone, and me consuming it as a bad guardian consumes the property of an orphan'.[8]

Then there follows a similar series of statements on table manners and eating habits, mainly short, such as a saying by the Prophet Mohammed: 'Eating in the marketplace is vulgar'.[9] A long sermon by a father to his young son on the wholesome effect of eating little is taken over from *al-Bukhalā'*, 'The Misers', by an older contemporary of the author, al-Jāḥiẓ (d. 255/868 or 869), an important early source on food and eating. That al-Jāḥiẓ depicts the sermonizing father as a terrible miser cannot prevent Ibn Qutayba from quoting his words as a wise piece of advice.[10] Hunger and fasting are recommended in various sayings, followed by anecdotes about people who like tasty food and indulge in it. Ibn Qutayba refrains from making any comments, nor are the anecdotes explicitly condemnatory: the reader may draw his own conclusion, for instance when he learns that wise men like Luqmān or the Prophet Mohammed recommend moderation. By way of contrast, Anas Ibn Mālik tells of the very pious and godfearing Caliph ᶜUmar: 'I saw a gallon of dates being poured out next to ᶜUmar; he finished them all, even the bad ones'.[11] Extracting the point of the anecdote is left to the reader: it is either that even the most pious may at times indulge in gluttony; or that one should not be fussy and reject bad food. Many anecdotes are told merely because they are amusing. A Bedouin is asked, 'What do you call thick soup?' He answers, 'Hotpot'. 'And when it is cold?' 'We never let it get cold'. Another, called Hilāl Ibn Asᶜar, once ate a whole camel-calf; his wife did the same. Subsequently, carnal contact turned out to be problematical: he could not reach her. 'How could we', his wife exclaims, 'with two camels between us?'[12]

Ibn Qutayba continues with a long section on hospitality and its opposite,[13] and verses on cooking-pots and serving-dishes and bowls.[14] After these parts, on gastronomy and hospitality, he turns to health, dieting and other physiological or medical matters. Numerous aphoristical sayings on these subjects are presented, attributed to various authorities including the prophet Mohammed, Galen, and often 'the physicians' (*al-aṭibbā'*). The properties of many kinds of food are briefly mentioned: different kinds of meat, truffles and mushrooms, onions and garlic, leek, cabbage and other vegetables. Here the 'literary' element is all but absent, apart from a few short fragments of poetry and the occasional aphorism or saying with a form and content that are not so much instructive as entertaining, like the words of an anonymous bedouin: 'O God, I ask Thee to let me die the way Abū Khārija died: he ate a lamb, drank honeyed wine (? *muᶜassal*), slept in the sun and then met his Maker food-sated, thirst-slaked, and sun-bathed (*shabᶜān, rayyān, daf'ān*)'.[15] The chapter ends abruptly, with a recommendation by the Prophet to use olive oil as a remedy for hemorrhoids, and a recipe involving mustard, vinegar and ash from oak-wood, the purpose of which is, strangely, not given.

Ibn Qutayba's recipe for the *adab* anthology, a hotchpotch of the entertaining, the informative and the edifying, became popular. One who followed him, while trying to improve on his method, was the Hispano-Arabic Ibn ᶜAbd Rabbih (d. 328/940). The last chapter of his voluminous *al-ᶜIqd al-farīd* ('The Unique Necklace') is devoted to jokes and pleasantries (*al-fukāhāt wa-l-mulaḥ*); it is preceded by the chapter on eating and drinking.[16] That these are serious subjects is explained by the author at the beginning: eating and drinking preserve the human body and with it the vital spirits, *al-arwāḥ*. He quotes Christ in a surprising manner, to Christians at least: 'The Messiah has said of water, This is my father, and of bread, This is my mother. He meant that bodies are fed with these two, just as is done by parents.'[17] The beginning of the chapter, with its descriptions and naming of foodstuffs and dishes, does not differ much in method from Ibn Qutayba's book. Worthy of note is the inclusion of what is probably the earliest 'gastronomical' poem of some length (33 lines), by the 8th-century minor poet Musāwir al-Warrāq.[18] In it, he sets out to describe the pleasant things of life, singling out food and beginning with honey, with an allusion to the Koran. After that a banquet is depicted, with a few vivid lines when the servants bring the dishes: "Pick up!', 'Put down!' and 'Here!' and 'Take it!', 'Here you are!". Bread, sugar-loaves, sucking kid, chicken, marinated francolin, and *tharīda* are being served. Then the poet, apparently abandoning the banquet scene, digresses on the blessings of sucking kid, Mushān dates, Rāziqī grapes, and carps. Though rather unbalanced and showing some infelicitous or dull lines, the poem is important in that it breaks new ground. It is primarily descriptive poetry, yet, with its hint at the presence of a host (line 10: 'You called for me an attendant . . .') it possibly served to honour a patron.

Compared with Ibn Qutayba's *ᶜUyūn*, *al-ᶜIqd al-farīd* has a much longer section on medical aspects. Like the former, a series of separate anecdotes and sayings are given, but then there follows[19] a coherent scholarly treatise on digestion in general, followed by a systematic division of foodstuffs into rich or light, nutritious or harmful, 'hot' or 'cold', 'dry' or 'moist' food and its effect on bodies of different temperaments and humours. This scientific material looks almost like an alien element in these *adab* surroundings, were it not that *adab* easily accommodates nearly any strange body. The text might be by Ibn ᶜAbd Rabbih himself, because he gives no names or sources, apart from a lengthy quotation of a doctor from Qayrawān, originally from Baghdad, Isḥāq Ibn ᶜImrān, on what should or should not be eaten in certain months or seasons.[20] The rest of the chapter deals with wine and drinking and will not concern us here. The ethical component seems less strongly present than in Ibn Qutayba, but that is only apparent, since ethics dominates a preceding chapter, on 'false prophets, madmen, misers and parasites'; eating plays, of course, a main role when speaking of the two last-mentioned categories.[21] Moreover, the part devoted to 'knowledge and good manners' (*al-ᶜilm wa-l-adab*) includes a section on eating behaviour and table manners,[22] in which straightforward rules form a small minority compared with illustrative and entertaining anecdotes.

The *adab* anthology *Muḥāḍarāt al-udabā'* by al-Rāghib al-Iṣbahānī (d. probably in the middle of the 5th/11th century) is characterized by more extensive subdivision of chapters and sections, compared with its predecessors. The chapter on food[23] begins with descriptions of dishes and foodstuffs (*awṣāf al-aṭᶜima*), of which some fifty are enumerated without much system (kinds of fruit are grouped together). In cookery-books *ṣifa* is regularly used for 'recipe';[24] in the *adab* anthologies the word *waṣf*[25] does not imply information on the nature and preparation of the dishes in question, apparently presumed either sufficiently known or irrelevant to the reader. By way of illustration I give the section on two sweets, *fālūdhaj* and *khabīṣ*:[26]

Sufyān [al-Thawrī] said: A sensible person eats *khabīṣ* once every forty days: it preserves one's strength. – Every meal without a sweet is abortive. – A man once said in the company of al-Aḥnaf [Ibn Qays]: There is nothing I dislike more than sweets. Al-Aḥnaf replied: Many an innocent one is blamed.[27] – Al-Ḥasan [al-Baṣrī], hearing someone condemn *fālūdhaj*, said: finest wheat flour with bees' saliva and goat's butter: no Muslim has ever condemned it![28] – A Bedouin said: I wish that Death and *fālūdhaj* were wrestling on my breast![29] – When a man sent to Muzabbid[30] a dish of *fālūdhaj* of little sweetness,[31] he said, This must have been made before 'thy Lord revealed unto the bees.'[32] – It is said that the splendour of *khabīṣ* disappeared since it was made with honey.[33] – Yazīd Ibn al-Walīd was served a *fālūdhaj*. Al-Ghāḍirī[34] began to eat hurriedly. Yazīd said: Gently, for too much of it could kill you! Al-Ghāḍirī replied, I live on the road to the cemetery and I have not seen anyone being buried who was said to have died from eating *fālūdhaj*.[35]

Strikingly absent from this paragraph is what is surely the most often quoted anecdote involving *fālūdhaj*: someone, when asked which is nicer, *fālūdhaj* or *lawzīnaj*, answers: 'I cannot judge an absentee'.[36] But the compiler of *adab* is not compelled to be exhaustive.

The enumeration of foodstuffs and dishes closes with a few short sections of a different nature, such as on the 'filthy dishes of the Bedouins' (these include dogs, snakes, mice and lizards), on filthy things eaten by mistake or unawares.

Al-Rāghib's contemporary Ibn ᶜAbd al-Barr (d. 463/1071) wrote an *adab* anthology in his native Spain. Like that of his predecessor Ibn ᶜAbd Rabbih it is largely filled with material from the Arab East. The chapter on food[37] is a mere collection of aphorisms, anecdotes and epigrams; anything Andalusian, be it person or dish, is absent. More than earlier compilations it tends to moralize, recommending moderation, even frugality, and good table manners. There is no revelling in luxurious food descriptions, nor any medical information.

Much richer is the long chapter on food in *Rabīᶜ al-abrār*, the *adab* anthology by the great philologian and theologian al-Zamakhsharī (d. 538/1144).[38] In a shorter work, his *Maqāmāt*, he had used a typically literary form for moralistic and homiletic purposes. Indulging in rich food is condemned in rich and rhymed prose:

> It [the human soul that commands evil] invites you to eat the delicious and good * of all kinds of dishes and food: * fattened chicken from Kaskar[39] * and *rajrāj*[40] with butter and sugar * and all the titbits and sweet things * found upon the tables of princes and kings. * Beware! From its demands you must recoil, * its hopes you should thwart and foil! * Turn into pus all its lust * and eschew its distracting pleasures with vomiting and disgust.[41]

Instead of the tasty dishes described, he continues, two loaves of barley bread should suffice for a man's breakfast and supper: everything exceeding this only gives one a surfeit and makes one belch.[42] From the chapter in *Rabīᶜ al-abrār* al-Zamakhsharī's own voice is lacking, as is customary in *adab* anthologies; if he speaks at all, through his selecting and compiling, then his voice is far from loud and clear. It is true that the moralistic tone is firmly established by the opening *ḥadīth* attributed to the Prophet: 'Never did man fill a worse vessel than his belly', which is followed by a series of sayings in the same vein. But this is interrupted by other sayings that mitigate the sternness. Fuḍayl Ibn ᶜIyāḍ, an early ascetic and *ṣūfī*, when asked whether one should abstain from white bread, meat and *khabīṣ*,[43] replies: 'What about *khabīṣ*? I wish you would eat and fear God, for God does not mind your eating that which is allowed as long as you shun that which is forbidden.'[44]

Gradually the sayings and anecdotes shift towards the theme of hospitality, where frugality is of course to be avoided, then to the theme of gluttony, which brings back the moralistic tone of the beginning. Thus the themes follow each other in rapid succession through hundreds of brief sayings and anecdotes, without much order. While food is celebrated in many of these, the prevailing tone is still in praise of moderation and asceticism. Towards the end Fuḍayl is quoted again:

> 'What would you say about a man carrying dates, who sits down on a lavatory and throws in date after date?' – 'A madman', they said. – 'But he who stuffs his belly with them is more of a madman, for this lavatory is filled from that other lavatory.' Once he saw a table with much food on it. 'Do you

know why his table is thriving?', he asked his companion, 'It is because the prayer niche in his mosque is a ruin.'[45]

Religion and enjoyment are incompatible; just as dates are worthless because eating turns them into excrement, so earthly life is worthless because death destroys it. The two quotations from Fuḍayl, from the beginning and the end of the chapter, represent the two extremes of religious attitudes towards food. It does not matter that contradictory opinions are put into the mouth of one person, or that they are quoted with apparent approval by the same compiler. Consistency is not sought in *adab* anthologies, as long as the quotations are expressed eloquently and memorably.

The last[46] of the general encyclopaedic *adab* anthologies to be discussed here is *al-Mustaṭraf* by the Egyptian author al-Ibshīhī (d. 850/1446). Its chapter on food[47] is more systematic than that of al-Zamakhsharī. It opens with quotations from Koran and *Ḥadīth* and from the pious that recommend or at least allow the eating of good food, followed by a section with anecdotes involving food descriptions. These are all positive and celebratory, except for a short invective in prose by a certain Ibn Qur^{c}a (or Qar^{c}a) in the 4th/10th century on the aubergine:[48] 'Like the tails of cupping-glasses, bellies of scorpion, pods of the *zaqqūm* tree!'[49] Someone argued that when stuffed with meat it could be a palatable dish, but the first speaker replied, 'If it were stuffed with piety and forgiveness it would still be no good.'[50] By way of counterweight a section of abstemiousness follows. The remainder of the chapter, by far the longest part, is devoted to table manners, anecdotes about gluttons and the behaviour of guests and hosts. Rules of etiquette and good behaviour alternate with entertaining anecdotes, true to the various meanings of the word *adab*. The chapter as a whole is preceded by chapters on generosity and its opposite, in which food plays its usual important role.

A number of *adab* anthologies, more limited and specialized in scope than the general encyclopaedic ones, are devoted to the pleasures of earthly life. One by the poet al-Sarī al-Raffā' (d. after 360/970) is a collection of verses on love, perfume and drinking ('The Lover and the Beloved, What Is Smelled and What Is Drunk'); it offers nothing on food. A work by al-Tīfāshī (d. 651/1253) with the promising title *Surūr al-nafs bi-madārik al-ḥawāss al-khams* ('The Soul's Delight Through the Five Senses') is preserved in a shortened version which, unfortunately, seems to neglect the sense of taste. More rewarding in this respect is *Maṭāli^c al-budūr* ('Full Moons Ascending') by al-Ghuzūlī (d. 815/1412), which has chapters on fire, cooks, foodstuffs, dishes and meals, followed by short sections on washing one's hands, cleaning one's teeth, on water, sweets and soft drinks.[51] This sequence – itself nicely framed by fire and water – is, not illogically, preceded and concluded by chapters on the bath and the toilet.[52] Many anthologists are interested less in the technicalities of gastronomy than in the literary productions, in which food is often no more than a pretext. Al-Ghuzūlī, however, tries to balance literary pleasure and useful information. The several foodstuffs and dishes are dietetically described (in terms of their being 'hot', 'cold', 'moist' or 'dry'), their use is explained, and occasional stories, poems or traditions are added, rather eclectically. After a list of the useful nutritional and medicinal properties of garlic, for instance, an anonymous epigram is given that likens a head of garlic to a silken purse with pearls. The Prophet is mentioned only once: according to ^cAlī, he had recommended eating garlic and said, 'Even if the angel [viz., Gabriel] would descend upon me, I would eat it.'[53] It is very unlikely that al-Ghuzūlī was unaware of the several well-known and canonical Prophetic traditions in which eating garlic is condemned if one mixes with others.

Zooming in on food even more we encounter a few anthologies that could be called monographies, such as the books on parasites and misers: it is food that is always craved by the former and often refused by the latter. The typical miser (*bakhīl*) in Arabic literature is no Silas Marner who sits on his pile of gold, but a host who is stingy with food. As al-Tha^cālibī remarked, it is rare that one finds an epigram on someone who is stingy with drinks, for instance.[54] Al-Jāḥiẓ, who cannot of course be called a mere anthologist, wrote his seminal work *al-Bukhalā'* ('The Misers') which was used, directly or indirectly, by all later compilers, including al-Khaṭīb al-Baghdādī, who wrote a work with the same title[55] as well as a *Kitāb al-Taṭfīl* ('The Book of Gatecrashing').[56] Much later, Aḥmad Ibn al-^cImād al-Aqfahsī (d. 808/1405) compiled the rather derivative *al-Qawl al-nabīl bi-dhikr al-taṭfīl* ('Noble Words Concerning Being a Parasite').

In the anthologies hitherto discussed the material was, to a greater or a lesser degree, sifted and ordered. Table talk, in real life, is mostly far from systematic and well-ordered. There are several major collections of *adab* that mirror this perfectly in that their compilers renounce almost any attempt to arrange their material into chapters. In some of these works the setting is that of the *majlis* or session, either of teacher with pupils (as in the various book called *majālis* or *amālī*) or vizier with companions (as in al-Tawḥīdī's *al-Imtā*ᶜ *wa-l-mu'ānasa*). The format of the banquet or symposium, known in famous Greek and Latin examples - Athenaeus, Plutarch, Macrobius - does not itself serve as a frame for material on banquets and food in Arabic, as far as I am aware. Often there is no setting at all, as in al-Tawḥīdī's large unordered collection of maxims, anecdotes, poems and philological titbits enitled *al-Baṣā'ir wa-l-dhakhā'ir*, loosely to be rendered as 'Visions and Provisions', or al-Tanūkhī's collection of anecdotes, stories, gossip and miscellaneous entertainment called *Nishwār al-muḥāḍara*. This work has been partly translated by Margoliouth under the apt title 'The Table-talk of a Mesopotamian Judge'. The compiler tells us that all his material derives from oral rather than written sources; naturally one may assume that much of it literally was table-talk. The word *nishwār* (from Persian *nishkhʷār*) has in fact an alimentary sense indicating that the contents are food for thought: 'cud; food which a ruminating animal keeps in the mouth to chew'. Not surprisingly, both works include many anecdotes involving eating and food. It is possible that the word *dhakhā'ir* in al-Tawḥīdī's collection also hides a reference to food. More commonly, however, anthologists compare themselves, as in Western languages, with pickers of flowers, choosing titles such as *Zahr al-ādāb*, 'The Flowers of *Adab*' by al-Ḥuṣrī, or of fruit, with titles like *Thamarāt al-awrāq*, 'The Fruits of Leaves' by Ibn Ḥijja al-Ḥamawī, the leaves of which link literature with nature.

2. Dishes and Discourse: Food in Narrative and Poetry

Apart from poetry the most 'literary' genre in Arabic is doubtless the *maqāma*: a short, often narrative, text in ornate, mostly rhymed, prose interspersed with verse. Food is prominently present in some *maqāma*s of the earlier of its two most famous authors, Badīᶜ al-Zamān al-Hamadhānī (d. 398/1008). The protagonist of most of the *maqāma*s, Abū l-Fatḥ al-Iskandarī, is characterized by wit, a lack of scruples, and an excess of greed. His bad and good *adab* - bad manners and great erudition - are apparent in the *maqāma* called *al-Jāḥiẓiyya*, which is set at a banquet.[57] Abū l-Fatḥ sins against all rules of eating etiquette,

> seizing the choicest of the cakes and plucking out the centres of the dishes, pasturing on his neighbour's territory, traversing the bowls, as the castle traverses the chessboard, stuffing his mouth with morsel after morsel and chasing mouthful with mouthful.[58]

He is silent while the others discuss the merits of al-Jāḥiẓ. After the meal Abū l-Fatḥ has the effrontery of criticizing al-Jāḥiẓ for not being equally skilled in prose and poetry and not meeting with the rhetorical standards of the time of Abū l-Fatḥ, more than a century after al-Jāḥiẓ's death. The company is dazzled by his eloquence and they shower him with gifts. It is quite likely that the author, far from agreeing with his hero Abū l-Fatḥ and his narrator ᶜĪsā Ibn Hishām, is being ironical and wants to expose the shallowness of their literary taste. It is, in any case, fitting that a discussion on the great *adab* writer al-Jāḥiẓ should be set at a banquet where the dishes are varied ('viands of various hues, opposite a dish of something intensely black was something exceedingly white, and against something very red was arranged something very yellow') just as the subject and style of the works of al-Jāḥiẓ vary.

In what is perhaps al-Hamadhānī's best known and certainly most enjoyable *maqāma* food is in fact conspicuously absent and Abū l-Fatḥ, rather than sinning, is sinned against. It is entitled *al-Maḍīriyya*, after a popular stew of meat cooked in sour milk, *maḍīra*.[59] This dish is served at a banquet and is lovingly described, but is removed from the table at the instigation of the protagonist, Abū l-Fatḥ, who refuses to eat it. To explain his strange behaviour he tells his story. Once he was invited by a merchant to his house and promised a dish of *maḍīra*. On the way to the house, and for a long time after their arrival, he has to endure the endless chatter of his host, who is immensely pleased with himself and all he possesses. At a certain point Abū l-Fatḥ has had enough and, dreading the prospect of being told at great length and in great detail how the raw materials for the meal were produced, selected, and acquired, how the *maḍīra* itself was prepared, he despairs and absconds, on the pretext that he has to visit the lavatory. As Beaumont observed, the dish will apparently never be attained after the endless blether, just as Zeno's paradoxical arrow will never reach its aim. When the host assures Abū l-Fatḥ that the splendours of his lavatory would make it a fitting dining room, the latter runs off while his host cries out, 'But Abū l-Fatḥ, the *maḍīra*!' Boys in the street think that this is his name and start yelling. He throws a stone, hits an innocent passer-by, and spends two years in prison, having vowed never to eat *maḍīra*. The main point of this *maqāma* is the exposure of the boorish manners of some parvenus; its main technique is the motif of empty words instead of nourishing food. It is fitting that the street-Arabs' calls should turn Abū l-Fatḥ himself, in a sense, into *maḍīra*, for he and his story must take the place of the dish for the banqueting audience. The story resembles some of the countless tales about misers, even though there is no reason to believe that the upstart host was a true miser who did not intend, in the end, to have the food served for his guest.

It is striking that the narrator and his audience take it out on the dish: at the beginning, Abū l-Fatḥ refuses to eat the *maḍīra*, and the *maqāma* ends with the audience exclaiming that '*maḍīra* has of old sinned against noble people'. This is something of a paradox, for not only is the dish innocent of the host's behaviour, the word *maḍīra* could be translated (deriving it not from the root *MḌR* but from *ḌYR*) as 'wronged woman': the dish has not sinned but is sinned against, like Abū l-Fatḥ himself. The pun was exploited, and given an interesting twist, by Abū l-ᶜAlā' al-Maᶜarrī in a remarkable passage in his long *Risālat al-ṣāhil wa-l-shāḥij*.[60] The mule (the 'brayer' of the title), in an enigmatic monologue, says,

> In this land there was a judge who loved *fālūdh*; when he went to sleep, he put it near-by, when he woke up in the dark he would lick it. The *maḍīra*, when standing before him, would talk to him, her words being heard by those present as witnesses.[61]

The camel, hearing this, does not grasp the riddles and mocks their more obvious but absurd meaning at great length. Naturally, the word *fālūdh* misleads him into thinking of the dish rather than of 'wronged woman':

> . . . I have understood what you said about the judge who was addressed by a [dish of] *maḍīra*! He who is brave enough to lie will not be satisfied with only a little of it. If a *maḍīra* could talk, then surely a dish of *harīsa* could talk as well, and say to people when it is served, 'Gently, gently! Those humans have treated me strangely. First they concocted me from different parts, then they put me into a kettle. It wasn't

> enough for them to have heated me over a wood fire, so they stirred and beat me with a stick, as if I were a whore or a scold. Then they served me and ate me. «Swallowing with a will, but slow to pay the bill».[62] You humans, always eating, eating, drinking, drinking! Fate will eat and drink you; «Every term has a Book».[63]
>
> And if the *harīsa* can talk, then the *sikbāj*[64] can tell the Sultan's cook a story, about all the swindling and negligence that goes on in his kitchen. And if the *sikbāj* could do this, nothing could stop the *ṭabāhija* from singing, or the lamb from answering, when put on the table before the guests who ask, 'How was it in your oven?', saying 'Quite hot; I am well done!', and telling them how much salt was put on him, just right, too much, or too little. Then he would say to one of the dinner guests, 'Eat from this part of me, it is really tasty and well done!' He could tell whether the carving knife was hot or whether he felt its coldness in his jugular veins; he could tell how he felt while being scalded, and whether he who did it was gentle or rough.
>
> And if you maintain that *maḍīra* can talk, you will not find it strange if someone claimed that a dish of *jūdhāba* could compose poetry, and that a *fālūdhaj* could entertain people at soirées with amusing stories![65]

The absurdity of this fancy is subtly undercut by the fact that it is part of a work that is based on the idea that animals are gifted with speech and rational powers, precisely the same absurdity that is derided by the camel. This fantastic scene envisaged by the camel, stupid though he may be, nicely illustrates al-Maᶜarrī's method of creating worlds with language and its potential of ambiguity and amphibology. Two possible etymologies of a word for a dish trigger a world where dishes produce words. Although the camel is stupid, his words reveal something of al-Maᶜarrī's own attitudes. In the matter of dishes vs. discourse he stands wholeheartedly on the side of the latter. He was a glutton for words and an ascetic who abstained from meat and animal products such as milk and eggs, on the grounds that eating them was a form of cruelty to animals.[66] He would, therefore, have believed that the dish *maḍīra* was 'wronged' being made with milk, or that eating it was 'sinful'.

The substitution of words for food, in al-Hamadhānī's *maqāma* of the *maḍīra*, is both false and unmannered. It is a kind of torture, and the subject of another *maqāma* ('al-Nahīdiyya' or 'Fresh Butter') of al-Hamadhānī.[67] It is, in fact, a variation on an anecdote in which Ibn Simāk, hearing the description of a sweet ('What would you say of a *jawzīnaj* . . . very sweet, drowned in sugar and almond oil?'), exclaims, 'How hard to bear is a description when I do not see the thing described! If what you have mentioned were here, I would love the sight of it more than its description; if it is not here, I would rather forgo its description as I do without its sight.'[68] An extreme form of this torture is found in the *Tale of the Sixth Brother*, embedded in the *Story of the Hunchback* in the *Thousand and One Nights*, in which the hero is offered an ample but imaginary meal and is forced to pretend to eat it, while the host – a scion of the illustrious Barmakī family – kindly urges him to have some more.[69] The story of this 'Barmecide banquet' has left its traces in European literature.[70] In this story the hero takes it in good cheer and is rewarded by his repentant host with a real meal. In al-Hamadhānī's '*Maqāma* of Ṣaymara', however, such a happy ending is absent; it is a tale of revenge reminiscent of Shakespeare's *Timon of Athens*. Timon regaled his false friends with a banquet where the dishes turn out to be filled with warm water. The hero of the *maqāma* (not Abū l-Fatḥ this time, but the famous wit Abū l-ᶜAnbas al-Ṣaymarī) is a generous host for his acquaintances, feeding them with 'sucking-kids, Persian omelets, minced meat *à la Ibrahim*, pungent fried meats, kabob *à la Rashíd* and lamb . . .' After the fall of his fortune he is abandoned by them. When he is once more restored to opulence he invites his former friends to a banquet. Unlike Timon, he gives them real food and drink, but when they are all in a stupor, overcome by alcohol, he has a barber shave their beards, which is surely worse than being confronted with warm water. Timon's behaviour might well have been thought churlish by mediaeval Arab standards; Abū l-ᶜAnbas has preserved his own honour by providing food, but he has robbed his guests of their honour, or rather confirmed their lack of honour.

In the satirical story by the physician Ibn Buṭlān (d. 458/1066), *Daᶜwat al-aṭibbā'* ('The Physician's Dinner Party'), the torture is gradually increased during the first scene after the introduction, when the narrator, a doctor, is invited by an elder colleague. A sober meal of bread, vinegar and vegetables is served, but when the guest is about to eat the host stays his hand and expatiates on the danger of eating the foodstuffs in question, on medical grounds. This is repeated when more and more dishes are served, including roast lamb, *maḍīra* with beef, rice pudding and *fālūdhaj*. The poor guest can only abstain and the dishes are removed from the table. He expects relief after distress when a final plate is brought; but it contains a horrific collection of surgical instruments, which quite spoils his appetite.[71]

Sarcastic substitution of written words for food is the drastic and eloquent gesture of a poor scholar's mother, eking out a living while her son studies with the famous Abū Ḥanīfa: she serves a covered dish, which turns out to contain notebooks, and says to her son, 'Eat, this is what you have been working at all day!' When Abū Ḥanīfa learns of this he consoles his pupil and prophesies that one day he will eat *lawzīnaj* with pistachio nuts. Later, when the pupil has become the respected Abū Yūsuf al-Qāḍī, he is moved to tears when the prediction comes true in the company of the caliph Hārūn al-Rashīd.[72]

Maud Ellmann, in a study of starvation, posits a battle for supremacy between food and words, each striving for complete domination of the mouth, that interesting dual- or even multi-purpose orifice.[73] It is true that simultaneous speaking and eating are condemned, also in Arabic manuals on table manners (and by parasites, because talking distracts from eating).[74] To extend this into a struggle between eating and eloquence seems questionable, however, for it would seem that food and literature may happily meet on various levels, as indeed this study has attempted to demonstrate. Conversation during meals is generally recommended;[75] the banquet is a common literary setting.

One could, nevertheless, speak of a contest between speech and food in those cases, discussed above, where discourse serves as a substitute for dishes, or where a gift of food prompts a poetic response in which the poet attempts to surpass culinary art with artful imagery. One suspects that curiously crafted pieces of confection were made especially for the purpose of testing a poet's proficiency and provoking a corresponding epigram. The great poet al-Mutanabbī (d. 354/965) was given such a present, which included a fish made of sugar and almonds 'swimming' in honey. If this seems somewhat ludicrous to us, the poet, still in his youth, kept a straight face, to all appearances:

> People are preoccupied with great hopes,
> while you are preoccupied with great deeds.

They make comparisons to Ḥātim [al-Ṭā'ī]; if they were sensible

you would be the one to be proverbial as being extremely
generous.
Welcome to what you sent (enough!),
Abū Qāsim, and to the messengers.
A present – if you see its giver,
you see mankind combined in a man.
The least of the least of it is a fish
that swims in a pond of honey.
How can I reciprocate such a most noble favour
to him who does not even consider it a favour to me?[76]

According to the giver himself the present was merely a trifle, apparently. The sugar fish, though 'the least of the least of it', is the only item that is mentioned, perhaps because it was the most striking object. The poet merely mentions it, without doing anything poetical with it, even though, normally, a poet was expected to transform a real object into a poetic object by means of all the sophisticated techniques of fantastic and manneristic imagery. Here, however, the poet's ecphrastic art was forestalled by the confectioner's art, as if the poet was unable to add another level of artifice: the 'swimming' and the 'pond' are too obvious to count in this respect. The only way to partly redeem the poem is to read it as a kind of parody. The obscure giver of a sickly sweet is to be put above the proverbial Ḥātim, slaughterer of camels (it was of course a commonplace to say that So-and-so was superior to the proverbial So-and-so). The addressee is 'mankind combined in a man', another superlative that is rather trite after the famous line by Abū Nuwās on Hārūn al-Rashīd.[77]

There are some indications that Abū l-Ṭayyib may have been somehow embarrassed with the present. 'Enough! (*īhan*)', he exclaims in line 3, and not *īhin*, which he might have said had he wanted more, as the commentators point out (How subtle are the secrets of inflection!). Returning the empty bowl gave the poet an opportunity to write a true epigram, etymologically speaking, for we are told that he returned the bowl with another poem written on it with saffron, a poem resembling the returned bowl, since it is both empty and full: without importance but filled with paradoxes and antitheses.[78]

Food inspires poetry while, *vice versa*, poetry may inspire patrons to part with their food. Anecdotes such as this underline the fact that the connection between versifying and feeding is sometimes a very close one and that poets often depended on their patrons for their livelihood, no matter how al-Mutanabbī's pride would disdain to admit it. Even in pre-Islamic times, a poet like al-Nābigha al-Dhubyānī, with his panegyric odes for the Lakhmid king al-Nuᶜmān Ibn al-Mundhir at al-Ḥīra, 'earned a huge sum, so that he ate and drank from vessels of gold and silver'.[79] Originally, it is argued, poetry was a noble craft intended to preserve noble deeds; then it was debased and made into a *ṭuᶜma*, a means of earning one's bread.[80] The poet-critic Ibn Shuhayd describes how he helped the less talented to beg for food by means of verse:

> It happens that someone resorts to us asking for food in the name of poetry, someone who begs from high and low indiscriminately. It may happen that we have not much left to share with him and we excuse ourselves. Occasionally we provide him with a few lines of verse, with which he goes to grocers and butchers. When these lines strike their ears and mingle with their understandings, the milk of their generosity overflows, their minds open and this wretched person rises in their esteem. Then he receives, you name it: a fine loaf to put up his sleeve, a fat piece of shoulder to bury in his haversack, a jug of beer to pour into his mouth, a fresh fig to stuff into his gullet, a greasy pie (*sanbūsaqa*) to put under his tongue, a succulent *fālūdhaja* for his palate to taste. No sooner has this wretched man completed his round than he comes back to me, to kiss my hands, slavering over my fingers, imploring me to reveal the secret that may move the people so that they spend whatever they possess.[81]

Khālid Ibn Yazīd al-Kātib (d. 262/876 or 269/883), in his dotage, rewards someone who gave him dates and *harīsa* with the recital of a few lines of his verse – when asked for more, he declares that the gift was not worth more than that.[82] A poet may be reduced to beg for food in verse, not implicitly by praising a patron but asking for it explicitly, as did Abū Firᶜawn al-Sāsī (d. early 3rd/9th century) in a poem the facile rhyme of which (the pronominal suffix *-hum*) somehow reflects the poet's own poverty:

> Hear the complaint of young children and their mother,
> who have not eaten their fill, and their father like them:
> They have had some meat, but it did not fill them; they
> drank water for a long time.

> They mixed milk with water, but it was not enough. To chew – ah, that were a feast to them, if they could attain it!
> They do not know bread, except by name. Dates? Forget it, they haven't got any . . .[83]

A peculiar reversal of the normal procedure of rewarding praise with gifts is found in yet another tormented-dinner-guest story, related by a certain poet from Hamadhān. He had made panegyric poetry on a governor called al-Haytham Ibn Muḥammad; the latter told him, however, that it would have been more profitable if it had been an invective poem, 'because I am not one of those who give rewards for praise'. The unfortunate poet has to sit through a sumptuous meal, described in some detail, without being served anything and being teased at each new course with the words, 'If only you had made an invective poem!' Afterwards he is given some coarse food from a dirty plate and some sour wine. He sets out to make an invective poem, at first reluctantly but encouraged by a promise of fifty dinars for a poem of fifty lines. After he has quoted only a few obscene verses, the governor has had enough and rewards him with money and good food.[84] If there was a grain of seriousness in the governor's attitude, which is doubtful, it was an aversion from the mercenary nature of panegyrics. Whoever may have taken his point, it was not the poet from Hamadhān, who ended his story with the words 'So I left this most stupid and ignorant of all people'.

Although discourse is often metaphorically equated with edible things – 'Lick the honey [i.e. enjoy my talk] and do not ask [whether it is true or false]', says Abū Zayd, the trickster hero of al-Ḥarīrī's *Maqāmāt*[85] – the equation is false, as Abū Zayd says soon afterwards, when he eloquently dispraises eloquence:

> Can fresh dates (*ruṭab*) be bought for sermons (*khuṭab*)? Or dried dates (*balaḥ*) for pleasantries (*mulaḥ*)? Or fruit (*thamar*) for conversation (*samar*)? Or *ᶜaṣīda* for a *qaṣīda*? Or *tharīda* for a precious saying (*farīda*)? Or flour (*daqīq*) for a subtle motif (*maᶜnā daqīq*)?[86]

In a *maqāma* by Ibn Muḥriz al-Wahrānī (d 575/1179) in the form of a letter spoken by a mule, the animal complains to an *amīr* that he cannot live on books: 'if a mule eats a volume of *maqāmāt* he dies (*māt*) . . .; so would a camel (*jamal*) if he fed on the verses [quoted in the book] on sentences (*jumal*)',[87] and so on, in a series of intentionally atrocious puns; elsewhere al-Wahrānī says, in rhymed prose, 'Rhymed prose (*masjūʿ*) will never fatten someone or help against hunger (*jūʿ*)'.[88] Badīʿ al-Zamān al-Hamadhānī apologized to someone complaining about his lack of generosity in a letter:

> Erudition (*adab*) cannot be made into a bowl of *tharīda*, or turned into cash . . . I have urged the cook to make a dish out of the poem rhyming in *j* by al-Shammākh, but he would not. I asked the butcher to be paid by listening to *The Skills of the Secretary*, but he would not accept. Needing some oil in the house, I recited one thousand two hundred lines of the poetry of al-Kumayt, to no avail. If a poem in *rajaz* metre by al-ʿAjjāj could be added to the spices for the *sikbāj*, I would not be without them; but it cannot, so what can I do?[89]

Normally, then, in the life of ordinary people and animals, words cannot properly replace food. First comes food, then poetry and piety. An Arabic proverb, anticipating Brecht's maxim on *Fressen* and *Moral*, says it with puns: *Shaghalanī l-shaʿīr ʿan al-shiʿr wa-l-burr ʿan al-birr*, 'I was too busy with barley and wheat to bother about poetry and piety.'[90] But Abū Zayd is wrong, of course, in his depreciation of eloquence, because in literature everything is possible. Not only are poets often rewarded with food for *qaṣīda*s, we also see that the equation of food and words may be poetically true and laudable. Words may even be said to outvalue food. There is a story of Khālid Ibn Ṣafwān, who describes to Yazīd Ibn al-Muhallab, the Umayyad governor, a simple but delicious and unforgettable meal enjoyed by him in pleasant surroundings (a cool room in a water-sprinkled garden on his estate, with fragrant flowers and herbs). 'Then', continues Khālid,

> I was brought rice bread which was just like pieces of carnelian, *bunnī* fish, which have a white stomach, blue eyes, black sides, wide belly, thick neck. Thereto I had some seeds and different sorts of vinegar, mury and legumes. Then I was brought fresh, yellow dates, perfect with no blemishes, which were not worn in base hands nor bruised in the greengrocer's measure. Then I leaned back, eating now from this, now from that.

At this point the governor exclaims, 'Ibn Ṣafwān, a measure of your words is better than a thousand measures of corn!'[91] The meal itself is unforgettable for no one except Khālid Ibn Ṣafwān; but his depiction of it, like the food without artifice but attractive, makes it memorable and valuable.

An often-quoted saying is *Inna l-ḥadītha mina l-qirā*, 'conversation is part of a meal offered to a guest': pleasant words and food should be inseparable.[92] In the chapter on table manners in the *Iḥyā' ᶜulūm al-dīn*, the great handbook of daily spiritual and practical life for the ordinary Muslim, al-Ghazālī (d. 505/1111) recommends that one should not be silent during a meal, 'for that is the custom of non-Arabs'; naturally, distasteful topics are to be avoided.[93] Non-Arab, i.e. Sāsānian Persian court etiquette is offered by *Kitāb al-Tāj*, a text formerly attributed to al-Jāḥiẓ; it prescribes silence during meals in the presence of the king.[94] Al-Masᶜūdī (d. 345/956) relates that it was the mythical Iranian king Kayūmarth who first ordered silence during meals, on physiological and psychological grounds rather than for reasons of decorum.[95] The Arabs, at least in the past, thought otherwise, for although moderation in talking or even silence is sometimes recommended,[96] al-Ghazālī's opinion is supported by other writers on table manners, such as the Egyptian poet and butcher Jamāl al-Dīn (Ibn) al-Jazzār (d. 669/1270 or 679/1281) in his *Fawā'id al-mawā'id*,[97] and by numerous anecdotes. Talking is no waste of time, according to al-Ḥasan Ibn ᶜAlī Ibn Abī Ṭālib, who is reported to have said: 'Sit long at the table and have much conversation, for those times are not counted as part of your lifetime'.[98] Conversation, too, may be exploited in the agonistic context of the meal in which the host must offer as much as possible and the guest decline as much as is decent. Thus Diᶜbil (d. 246/860), rather crudely, boasts in a poem:

> I cheat my guest with conversation at the table until he has indigestion.[99]

It is at the table that the two main senses of *adab* come together: good manners and literary erudition. Ideally, they go together, but a lack of the former may be compensated by the latter. Very telling is the anecdote told about the philologian Abū Riyāsh (d. 339/950) and the vizier al-Muhallabī. Abū Riyāsh was a greedy and messy eater:

> During the meal he blew his nose in his napkin and spat in it. Then he took an olive from a bowl and kneeded it violently, so

> that the stone jumped out, hitting the vizier in the face, who was amazed at his bad manners (*adab*). But he tolerated him because of his erudition (*adab*).[100]

The closest possible association of food and literature is of course the poetical description of food, dishes and banquets. Among the various minor genres in Arabic literature we find the 'flower poem' (*zahriyya*) or 'garden poem' (*rawḍiyya*) and of course the bacchic poem (*khamriyya*, hardly a minor genre). Although I have not yet come across the term 'food poem' (**ṭaᶜāmiyya*), there is no doubt that gastronomic poetry is a minor genre in its own right. How it could function is well illustrated in the famous passage in al-Masᶜūdī's *Murūj al-dhahab* ('The Meadows of Gold'), written in the first half of the tenth century. It relates at some length how the Caliph al-Mustakfī (*regn.* 944–946) arranged a banquet at which gastronomic poetry played a large part.[101] Poems by famous poets are recited: by Ibn al-Muᶜtazz (d.296/908), Ibn al-Rūmī (d. 283/896), Kushājim (d. 350/961) and others. After the recital of the first few poems, on *kāmakh*, roast kid, *ṭardīna*, *sanbūsaj* etc., the caliph orders the particular dishes to be brought in; but after a while there is no more mention of real food being served, only more poems on food: on *harīsa*, *maḍīra*, *jūdhāba*, *qaṭā'if*. To give just one example I quote Arberry's rhymed translation of Kushājim's poem on *jūdhāba* or *gūdhāba*, a kind of sweet:

> *Jūdhāba* made of choicest rice
> As shining as a lover's eyes:[102]
> How marvellous in hue it stands
> Beneath the cook's accomplished hands!
> As pure as gold without alloy,
> Rose-tinted, its Creator's joy;
> With sugar of Ahwaz complete
> In taste 'tis sweeter than the sweet.
> Its trembling mass in butter drowned
> With scent the eater wraps around;
> As smooth and soft as clotted cream,
> Its breath like ambergris doth seem;
> And when within the bowl 'tis seen,
> A star in darkness shines serene,
> Or as cornelian's gold is strung
> Upon the throat of virgin young;

It is more sweet than sudden peace
That brings the quaking heart release.[103]

Here, it seems, the poems have taken the place of real food, perhaps because the banqueters have gorged themselves by now.[104] On a different level, such 'ecphrastic epigrams' also take the place of what in other cultures would take the form of still-lifes and other visual representations of food, which are not absent in Arabic culture but less prominent.

Al-Mustakfī may have been inspired by his father, the caliph al-Muktafī (*regn.* 289–295/902–908), who also let poets recite appropriate and appetizing poems at a meal, as again al-Mas^{c}ūdī tells us.[105] One of these poems was by Ibn al-Rūmī (d. 283/896):

A roast [chicken], yellow, dinar-like
in value and colour, like a bride led by a lad,
Enormous, almost a goose; so fat[106]
that her skin all but bursts.
A *jūdhāba* generously gives herself, melting,
in which sugar mingles[107] with almonds.
What a fine sky was there, steadily pouring its showers,
and what a fine earth, steadily being rained upon!
How beautiful upon the table, its daughter[108] before her,
its molten fat bubbling.
We peeled its skin from its flesh, and it was
as if gold was being peeled off silver.
Before this came broths (*tharā'id*)
like gardens, rightly given precedence,
And mincemeat balls,[109] all garnished
with eggs shaped like tongues and dinars.[110]
Then came fine pastry (*qaṭā'if*)
that pleased the palate and the gullet:
Laughing faces of sugar-candy, with eyes on top
from which tears of oil were pressed.[111]

At the caliph's table and for the anthologists these ten verses were sufficient. In Ibn al-Rūmī's original poem they form the introduction to a following panegyrical section of another eleven verses, in which the host, a certain Abū Bakr al-Bāqiṭā'ī, and his brothers are praised:

. . . From the possession of a high-souled man, whose fingers
are like the gushing channels of the Euphrates,

Who gives much and deems it little,
whereas a little of it would be deemed much from others;
A sun on whose right and left hands
sit heaven's full moon and bright Jupiter:
What a noble triad of brothers, of fine appearance and good nature!

In the rest of the poem, which ends with a reproachful reference to an unfulfilled promise, there is no more mention of the meal. The function of the gastronomic prologue is obvious: ecphrasis serves as praise, both metonymically and metaphorically. Metonymically, because a rich meal honours the host, just as the bedouin hero is honoured in verse for the meat he provides; and metaphorically, because the host and his brothers are themselves, like the dishes, 'of fine appearance and good nature'. Understandably, it was the beginning of the poem that lived on as an independent ecphrastic epigram of varying length: six lines in the oldest source, Ibn Abī ᶜAwn's monograph on poetic similes, ten lines in al-Masᶜūdī's story, two lines in the *adab* anthology of al-Rāghib al-Iṣbahānī. That the poet himself shaped the piece as an epigram rather than a mock-*nasīb* is evident from the first line, which has no internal rhyme and begins with *wa-* (often, but not here, to be rendered as 'many a'), a particle not normally introducing formal *qaṣīda*s. Yet the very fact that such an epigram takes the place of a more traditional prologue such as an amatory *nasīb* inevitably draws attention towards the parallel between food and love, especially since the chicken is described as a lovely bride.

Ibn al-Rūmī, who was fond of good food,[112] made several gastronomical epigrams. An extended vignette on *lawzīnaj* is incorporated in a long poem (92 lines) in which he congratulates a patron on the birth of a son.[113] Here food does not take the place of a *nasīb*, which is usually absent from a congratulatory poem, but follows the main part of the poem after an old-style transition or *takhalluṣ*: 'Leave this [subject] and pass on to something else' (vs. 66). This is no doubt meant as a parody, for one would expect the poet to embark, after such a formula, on the main theme. It is as if Ibn al-Rūmī finds his request of a sweet dish, lovingly depicted, more important than the preceding congratulations and praise of his patron. At the same time he manages to suggest that the new-born son is as sweet and splendid as the *lawzīnaj*.

The fact that food descriptions may occur in longer poems, even if they are sometimes quoted as if they were independent compositions, should not convey the impression that this is the rule. The great majority of descriptive epigrams are what they pretend to be and a panegyric element is usually absent or only implied. Among the specialists in ecphrastic pieces was Abū Ṭālib al-Ma'mūnī (d. 383/993), whose epigrams have been edited, translated and studied by Bürgel.[114] The food – including various kinds of sweets, fruits, bread, egg dishes, *jūdhāba*, *harīsa*, *lawzīnaj*, *khabīṣ*, *fālūdhaj* – is, as always, primarily described as visual, the taste and effect receiving far less attention. The objects are compared to inorganic natural phenomena, often precious stones and minerals: dates as rubies, sweets as stars, white candy as hailstones, pomegranate seeds as jewels, *jūdhāba* or eggs as silver and gold, a fish is roasted from silver into gold, *harīsa* as pearls. Often anthropomorphic similes are used, which are already present in names of sweets such as *aṣābi*ᶜ *Zaynab*, 'Zaynab's fingers';[115] other sweets (candy, *lawzīnaj*) are also likened to fingers; a round loaf of bread is like a pock-marked face of a Turk – a tasteless comparison by our standards, as Bürgel observes, but not necessarily intended negatively.[116]

A cascade of comparisons, in a poem of eight lines,[117] is inspired by the simple combination of cheese and olives: 'son' of a blessed (tree, linking Koran 24:35 and 28:30) and 'son' of the udder, pressed by Time; then a silver hand with black fingertips; Byzantines or Blacks, or pupils of the eye; two opposite friends, darkness and daylight; a pale, love-bitten cheek covered by a black hairlock. That the imagery is minimally unified, by personification being dominant, is less important than that the reader's or listener's mental eye is dispersed and his concept of the homely plate of cheese and olives fractured geographically (from Byzantium to Africa), temporally and cosmically (from day to night and back to the primeval Koranic tree containing the luminous and numinous image of God's light, here identified with Moses' burning bush). The dish is a happy conjunction of opposites, associated with friendship and amorous petting.

Al-Masᶜūdī's *The Meadows of Gold* is a mixture of history and geography, specializing in the anecdotal and entertaining digression, a typical work of *adab*. Rich though the work is, we can only regret that his *Akhbār al-zamān* is lost, because he refers to it for more information on banquets, food and drink 'and all the etiquette of cookery (*ādāb al-ṭabīkh*), everything that the courtier ought to know and the literate should understand about modern inventions, such as the knowledge of various dishes and the quantities of spices and condiments'.[118] How useful such knowledge could be, on occasion, is evident from another story told by al-Masᶜūdī about an Abbasid caliph. Al-Muᶜtaṣim (*regn.* 218–227/833–843) organized a cooking contest between his courtiers, at which the well-known judge Ibn Abī Du'ād should act, appropriately, as judge. While the dishes are being consumed, the conversation turns around great eaters of the past: the Umayyad caliphs Muᶜāwiya and Sulaymān Ibn ᶜAbd al-Malik, and the Umayyad governors ᶜUbayd Allāh Ibn Ziyād and al-Ḥajjāj and others.[119] The story is suspiciously similar to another told by al-Masᶜūdī about al-Muᶜtaṣim's older brother and predecessor, al-Ma'mūn (regn. 198–218/813–833). Here a commoner is asked to taste and judge the dishes made by the caliph and his companions, including al-Muᶜtaṣim and the well-known *qāḍī* Yaḥyā Ibn Aktham.[120] In a third story of such a contest, also instigated by al-Ma'mūn, his brother Abū Isḥāq spoils his own dish by the addition of pickled capers (*kabar*), maliciously suggested by the jester ᶜAbbāda al-Mukhannath (the son of one of the caliph's cooks and himself an expert). The caliph mocks his brother for his stinking broth; the victim, unable soon to forget this loss of face, has his revenge, for when he reigns as caliph al-Muᶜtaṣim he at first orders ᶜAbbāda's death but, on second thoughts, has him banished instead.[121]

A rich source of gastronomical poems is of a different nature from that of *The Meadows of Gold*, but shows clearly that culinary expertise and being literate may be combined in one person or even one book. It is the cookery-book, *Kitāb al-ṭabīkh*, by Ibn Sayyār al-Warrāq, who wrote in the second half of the tenth century. This is a very valuable and interesting work, not merely because it is the oldest preserved Arabic cookery-book, but also because it contains so many poems, which are perhaps the equivalent of the luscious colour photographs of modern cookery-books. As far as I can judge this is by no means normal. The only poetic features of other cookery-books that have been preserved, such as *al-Wuṣla ilā l-ḥabīb*, *Kanz al-fawā'id*, or *Fuḍālat al-khiwān*, are their titles and sometimes their preambles, the recipes themselves being written in a factual and unliterary style – fortunately, at any rate, for culinary historians. It may be that some of the older cookery-books, now lost, were at least partly of a literary character, because several well-known men of letters wrote books on culinary matters: Ibrāhīm Ibn al-Mahdī (d. 224/839), prince, poet, musician and cook, wrote a *Kitāb al-ṭabīkh*;[122] Ibrāhīm Ibn al-ᶜAbbās al-Ṣūlī (d. 243/857) wrote a *Kitāb al-ṭabīkh*;[123] ᶜAlī Ibn Yaḥyā Ibn al-Munajjim (d. 275/888) was the author of a *Kitāb al-ṭabīkh*;[124] Jaḥẓa (d. 324/936) wrote a *Kitāb al-ṭabīkh* (called 'nice', *laṭīf*) as well as a *Kitāb faḍā'il al-sikbāj*, on the excellence of a famous meat dish;[125] Kushājim, cook and poet (d. c. 350/961), may have written a *Kitāb al-ṭabīkh*.[126]

Ibn Sayyār (Abū Muḥammad al-Muẓaffar Ibn Naṣr Ibn Sayyār al-Warrāq) is not known as an *adīb* (or as anything else, for that matter), but his (or his grandfather's) profession, 'the bookseller' at least suggests a familiarity with books and literature. The title of his cookery-book, *'Cookery-Book'*, is factual and unliterary, whereas he used rhyming prose for most of the 132 chapter-headings, a tour de force which is unusual even in works of a literary nature.[127] The text is a mixture of three different styles: the non-literary technical style, used for the recipes; the literary style in the parts on good behaviour at the table and other matters of etiquette that are part of *adab*, and finally the poetic style in numerous poems, some of which are versified recipes. Prominent among the poets are again Kushājim,[128] and Ibrāhīm Ibn al-Mahdī, who was an Abbasid prince, an accomplished singer, a poet, and a famous cook, creator of many dishes some of which are preserved in Ibn Sayyār's book. Here is a poem by him, a versified recipe for a dish called *narjisiyya*, 'narcissus dish', obviously on account of the egg on top:

> You who have asked me about the best of dishes:
> You've asked today someone who is not ignorant!
> Now take, my friend, some ribs of meat,
> And after that some meat of leg, and fat,
> And chop some fat and succulent meat
> And rinse it with sweet and clear water.
> Put it into the frying-pan on the fire,
> Then fry it with oil and herbs
> And when the contents have become red-brown,
> Cut up some onion bulbs over it,
> And fresh green chives,
> And add to it some rue and coriander.
> And pour on it some pickling brine[129] and ginger
> And afterwards a little pepper.

And after that, put some asparagus on top.[130]
Then break an egg on it, like eyes,
Like shining stars of the firmament
Or round narcissus flowers,[131]
And sprinkle bits of rue on it,
Some of it standing upright (?)
Now serve the dish in a covering
Or in a wicker basket made of osier.
Then mention God's name and *bon appetit*!
A wholesome and delicious dish![132]

Although Ibn al-Mahdī was a competent poet, he did not have any exalted literary aspirations when making this poem. Unlike the typical ecphrastic poem it is all but devoid of tropes and figures; in the nexus of comparisons 'eyes/narcissus/eggs/stars' only the eggs, here the *primum comparationis*, are extraneous in the sense that they do not belong to conventional poetic diction. The name of the dish is already 'poetic' in providing the basic comparison. This versified recipe is a kind of unpoetic didactic poem, as is corroborated by the prosody: paired rhyme and *rajaz* metre, usual for such poems, although one also finds the occasional recipe in monorhyme.[133] Ibn Sayyār's book contains several other versified recipes, one of them attributed to Ibn al-Rūmī, on a *muṭajjana*:

You who loves delicious food
before the date wine is served:
Take a Kaskar chick[134]
and a fat turtle-dove chick from ᶜAskar [Mukram].
Mix them, my friend, after scalding them,
with the meat of a duckling.
Carve up all of these,
limb for limb, cutting them into many pieces.
Then gather the pieces in a stone pot
and pour on them a measure of olive oil.
Mix sesame oil with it, to make it tasty;
it will render it delicious and palatable.
Fry it with vegetable oil, until it is brown,
and when the meat is brown it is finished.
Cut fresh meat in slices,
then roast it over a charcoal fire,
When it is well-cooked and the skin is crackly,

take some *murrī* and sprinkle
From this over it a sufficient quantity,
and cinnamon, in good measure.
Then scoop it out into a dish,
flat, thin and round.
Then deck it with flowers of rue
and surround it with a ring of kebab.
Then begin eating it, as a first course:
it is one of the tastiest quick dishes.[135]

This poem shows none of the characteristics of Ibn al-Rūmī's style and is not found in his *Dīwān*, which contains, nevertheless, a somewhat similar poem, also in *rajaz* metre with paired-rhyme; it is in fact another poem recited at the banquet of al-Mustakfī.[136] This latter poem however, although it resembles the other versified recipes in some prosaic lines, is more poetic in other lines, as when almonds and nuts are said to be aligned on the bread-and-chicken-meat as lines of writing, while cheese and olives are the diacritical dots, mint and tarragon form the vowel signs, and salt is sprinkled like the sand that dries the ink. Unusual, too, in a recipe is an adhortation to look at the result:

. . . and let your eyes roam over it for a moment,
for the eyes must have their share of it.
Feast your eyes upon it for a while,
then take the bread in your hand and *bon appetit!*

An ordinary recipe might have stopped here, like Ibn al-Mahdī's poem cited above. Ibn al-Rūmī, however, ends the poem, after a few similes, on an mock-elegiac note:

. . . Alas! Your teeth - biting, biting -[137]
soon destroy what you have built.
Ah, how I long for it, while I am the spokesman
of a stomach whose Satan is cursed![138]

Only a handful of the more than seventy poems in Ibn Sayyār's cookery-book are versified recipes: the great majority are ecphrastic poems, quoted in the appropriate sections and very often concluding a chapter. Exceptionally a poem does not neatly fall into either category, such as a poem of 19 lines by Ibn al-Mahdī in which he sets out to tell us about his own preference for stewed dishes prepared with vinegar, after which the poem turns into a recipe. It concludes with a pun on *maghmūma* ('stew' or 'grieved'):

> So there's your stew in a sad stew for you,
> But it has never seen any sadness!
> Itself glad, it gladdens the hungry when it appears
> in a dish like the full moon in the black night.[139]

It should be mentioned here that the form of the recipe, medicinal or culinary, is occasionally used jestingly, or in a combination of jesting and moralizing, using the technique of the incongruous genitive metaphor, known in Arabic since Abū Nuwās.[140] 'Take the leaves of poverty,' says ᶜUlayyān Ibn Badr the Madman,

> the root of endurance, the emblic of humility, the myrobalan of knowledge and the agaric of reflection. Pound it thoroughly with the mortar of remorse, put it into the casserole of piety, pour on it the water of modesty, light under it the firewood of love until the foam rises. Then pour it into the bowl of contentment, fan it with the fan of praise and put it into the beaker of thought, pound it with the spoon of apology. Then you will never sin again.[141]

Two other versions of this recipe are ascribed to the same ᶜUlayyān, one being a recipe for a spiritual kind of *fālūdhaj*, the making of which involves intuition (*maᶜrifa*) rather than ordinary knowledge (*ᶜilm*):

> Take the honey of sincerity, the sugar of fidelity, the clarified butter of contentment, and the flour of certainty. Throw it into the casserole of piety . . . (etc.)[142]

Unlike the poetic recipes in Ibn Sayyār's book his prose recipes, or those of his colleagues for that matter, are never mixed with literary ingredients.

In view of the literary slant of Ibn Sayyār's book it comes perhaps as a surprise that, in a chapter on eating etiquette, he should recommend 'little speech and silence at the table, and no conversation'.[143] He makes it clear that he is mainly concerned about the unsightly consequences of eating with one's mouth full; he mentions that others approve of conversation during meals, particularly as a means for the host to put his guests at ease, in accordance with the maxim that says that conversation is part of hospitality.[144]

Many of the poems in Ibn Sayyār's book, like the poems that were recited at the banquets described by al-Masᶜūdī, are fit to be served during meals, or as a pre- or post-prandial pastime. Among the oldest poems of the genre is one by al-ᶜUmānī, who died at an advanced age during the reign of Hārūn al-Rashīd. After a meal with Muḥammad Ibn Sulaymān Ibn ᶜAlī, a member of the ruling Abbasid dynasty, the host commands the poet, 'Now make a poem on what you have eaten.' Al-ᶜUmānī responds with 22 lines of *rajaz*, mentioning as the first dish to be served a loaf, soaked in butter and stuffed with sugar; followed by various hot and cold dishes: ribs (*sharāsīf*), *ṭurdīn* (a Kurdish dish according to the editor), veal served with the skin (*hulām*), marinated meat, goose, chicken, then sweet dishes including *jawzīnaj*, *khabīṣ*, *lawzīnaj*, followed by fruit: grapes, figs and various kinds of dates. The last part of the poem is an apostrophe to the host:

> Muḥammad, Sire of sons,
> (. . .)
> Listen to this artless description,
> Moving from one thing to another:
> Talking about you is a multifarious affair.[145]

As in Ibn al-Rūmī's poem on the roast chicken, the descriptive poem is turned into a panegyric, in which the rich meal is metonymically and metaphorically related to the addressee: the host is himself likened, as it were, to a series of courses which could form the subject of a long poem. The same poet, it is said, also made a poem for Hārūn in which food description is a substitute for real food, at a time when the caliph was waging war against the Byzantines, far from Baghdad. 'Then al-ᶜUmānī recited a poem, mentioning the good life in Baghdad, with all its luxury and pleasures', for which he is richly rewarded:

> . . . Then they brought in chicken meat,
> Dried or roast and well-cooked,
> And fresh meat, uncooked,
> Minced as if by [the hooves of] a plodding hack,[146]
> Stuffed as sausages in skin from guts.
> Then he said to the singing-girl, 'Pour and mix the wine!'[147]

A description of a meal, sometimes presented as a more or less ordered sequence of courses and events in a narrative, may be incorporated in a longer narrative. An example in poetry is offered by the *urjūza* (in paired rhyme) by the 12th-century Egyptian poet ^{c}Alī Ibn al-Ḥusayn al-^{c}Aqīlī, entitled 'In praise of drinking in the morning' (a popular theme since the late ninth century when Ibn al-Mu^{c}tazz wrote his long poem against drinking in the morning). Eating and drinking are not normally done together: the latter customarily follows the former.[148] Al-^{c}Aqīlī therefore begins his poem with a meal that presumably takes place through the night, with a succession of kid, gosling, *jūdhāb*, a dish of *narjisiyya* likened to a bride or a garden, two kinds of cheese, eggs, etc. Music follows; then the cook enters before daybreak, loaded with more food: bread, eggs, cheese and condiments. Finally the drinking begins.[149] As we have seen, the sequence of eating followed by drinking is reflected in thematically ordered works such as Ibn Qutayba's *Kitāb al-ma^{c}ānī al-kabīr* or Ibn ^{c}Abd Rabbih's *al-^{c}Iqd al-farīd*. It is amusing to see how a modern Muslim scholar believes, or wants to believe, that wine was absent: 'some special drinks [were] taken after the meal, but no alcoholic drink was included.'[150] It should be obvious that wine is very often drunk in stories. It is true that irregular and dissolute behaviour, by puritan Muslim standards, tends to be highlighted and exaggerated in literary representations of the good life; but to assert or to imply that all this is fiction without counterpart in reality is naïve or disingenuous. The narrative sequence may be extended, as will be shown in the next chapter, with a further element: love-making and sexual intercourse.

When meals and banquets are described in prose, this is usually not done gratuitously. Literary self-display and panegyric often combine; the difference from poetry is made less by means of poetic imagery and the use of rhymed prose. Thus it almost comes as a surprise when Ibn al-Khaṭīb (d. 776/1374), a great master of rhymed prose, inserts a long, highly rhetorical but rhymeless meal description in his travel account in North Africa when invited by a local chief of the Jabal Hintāta region in Morocco. The very absence of the expected *saj^{c}* lifts the piece out of the ordinary, as if to stress the normality of the lavishness of the food and the pleasantness of the conversation, which turned around local history.[151] Meals unusual in their lavishness may not need any special literary embellishment: a mere enumeration of the extravagances and foodstuffs is enough. In the year 312/924 Mufliḥ, the black eunuch, invites the caliph al-Muqtadir and his retinue to his garden, in which he has arranged rivulets of water and *sharāb* (apparently wine) sweetened with sugar and cooled with 50,000 pounds of ice. On the banks of these streams food is set down in decorated containers; lamb and poultry are hung from the trees. The eaters are provided with fruits, flowers and various kinds of perfumes and incense, altogether 'a memorable day with all its beauty and splendour'.[152]

In the accounts of some very famous feasts the food is hardly mentioned at all, pushed into the background by all the paraphernalia of the banquets, as in the case of what al-Thaᶜālibī calls 'the two feasts of Islam', one being given on the occasion of al-Ma'mūn's marriage to Būrān, daughter of his vizier al-Ḥasan Ibn Sahl, in 210/825-26 - their names live on in the several dishes called *ma'mūniyya* and *būrāniyya* - and the other celebrating the circumcision of al-Mutawakkil's son al-Muᶜtazz.[153] More food is described in a circumcision banquet given by another Ma'mūn, of the Dhū l-Nūn dynasty in 5th/11th-century Spain. In a description attributed to a certain Ibn Jābir the pots and bowls are said to be brimful, the bread in various shapes in harmony with the food taken with it, the dishes combining opposites of hot, cold, sweet and sour, the precious dishes corresponding to the worthy people attending the banquet, for which 'animal nations' were slaughtered, the trotting, the flying and the swimming. The prose uses assonance and rhyme in which the vowel *ā* is strikingly dominant, as if to indicate that mouths were opened wide both in admiration and in eating.[154] Most of such descriptions, particularly quantities, should be taken as literature, not necessarily literally, although this is not rarely done when the luxuries and extravagances of mediaeval Arab civilization are to be depicted, admired or condemned. Hyperbole is recommended in factual and fictional description. The latter type is nicely illustrated in a pair of contrasting *maqāma*s by the 6th/12th-century Aḥmad Ibn Abī Bakr al-Ḥanafī, on two banquets, one given by a miser and the other by a model host.[155] The latter provides one thousand tables, on each table one thousand golden bowls, one thousand silver bowls, one thousand dishes from Qāsān and one thousand beakers from Isfahan, and so on. Every reader knows that a *maqāma* is fiction, yet this is not said explicitly and the descriptions in fact and fiction are not essentially different.

Among the more elaborate literary food descriptions is a letter of invitation written by Abū l-Ḥasan ᶜAlī Ibn al-Ḥusayn al-Karkhī to a singer and lutenist called Abū Naṣr.[156] It offers, in rhymed prose, a list of dishes with short similes: 'minced meat (? *mufarrakāt*) like vowels minced by singing girls or the melismas (*layliyyāt*) of the effeminate; asparagus green like emeralds . . .', interrupted by longer sections on the preparation of a kid and a sheep. A touch of cannibalism is present since the kid is described as an *amīr* who is felled, skewered and grilled,

> a poor forbearing fellow, one of those in distress 'and adversity, who restrain their anger and forgive people';[157] . . . 'and being generous with one's own life is the highest generosity.'[158] When brought to the table he appeared in purple cloakes . . . When you rob him of his clothes and tear away his skin he shows a snowy-white colour and reveals a brightness like dawn; as the slave of the Banū l-Ḥasḥās said: 'I may be a slave, but my soul is noble; of black appearance, I am white of character.'[159]

Gastronomical purple patches are a common ingredient of popular stories. For the flow of the narrative they may be unnecessary or even impediments to it, yet most audiences, not merely childish or hungry ones, would relish descriptions of food. Moreover, though the narrative may require nothing more than the mention that some people were eating, the seemingly superflous details on what they were eating, how the dishes were prepared and what they looked like often provide useful information that may be relevant to the interpretation of the story. Particular dishes are associated with particular social strata or ethnic groups; the semiotic role of a specific kind of food may be either confirmed in a story or not, as when a rich man eats simple fare, or when a bedouin eats urban food.

Sometimes the purple patches seem to take over the story to the point of pushing themselves into the foreground. The *Tale of the Sixth Brother*, mentioned above, is one of a series of six stories about persons who all show a bodily defect, the result of a mutilation. One might expect that the point of the stories is the explanation, and possibly the justification, of this mishap. But in more than one case the mutilation comes in fact almost as a gratuitous afterthought. The sixth brother, introduced as the one with his lips cut off, loses his lips, and, it turns out, his male organ as well, at the end of his story; but the main part of the tale is the imaginary meal offered, which could have been told in a few sentences but is spun out with a succession of dishes: white bread, *harīsa*, *sikbāj* with fattened duck, chicken stuffed with pistachio nuts, *ṭabāhajāt*, sweets, pastry, and *khabīṣa* with almonds.[160] It is only after twenty years that he loses first his lips, when a bedouin tries to extort money from him, and then his penis, when the same bedouin, apparently on another occasion, punishes him for fondling his wife. This latter punishment strikes us as somehow fitting, if harsh. One is tempted to connect the labial loss with the eating scene of twenty years earlier, but the link is not supported by the text of the story or by a comparison with the other stories in the set.

In other stories the narrative hinges in some way or other on the presence, the preparation, or the consumption of food. The motif encountered at the beginning of al-Hamadhānī's *maḍīra maqāma*, in which a story is triggered off by a character who swears that he will never eat such and such a dish, is echoed in other stories. Al-Hamadhānī's story itself in fact sounds like an echo of an anecdote about Ashᶜab, famous greedy fool from the 2nd/8th century, who swears that he will never again eat *maḍīra*, after his greed for it is about to land him in jail.[161] A banquet is the setting of the eighteenth *maqāma*, entitled *al-Sinjāriyya*, by al-Ḥarīrī.[162] His hero, Abū Zayd, in a partial emulation of al-Hamadhānī's *maqāma*, swears that he will not eat the sweets that are served in a splendid glass bowl, since glass, he maintains, is a 'slanderer', revealing all, and he hates all slanderers. His fellow banqueters feel compelled, out of solidarity, to abstain as well. His apology must take the place of the food, as he says in verse after telling his story (which is not concerned with food at all):

> Do not blame me, after my explanation, for your having been deprived of your pastries;
> My excuse for what I did is obvious. But I will make amends from all my possessions, old and new:
> The pleasantries I have fed you with are, after all, more delicious than sweets, to those who know.

The host rewards him with sweets served this time in opaque bowls;[163] his friends get a second chance.

In a story found in al-Tanūkhī's works, in *The Thousand and One Nights* and elsewhere,[164] a man refuses to eat a dish of *zīrbāja* (or, in other versions, *dīkbarīka*)[165] before he has washed his hands forty times in succession. It appears that, on the day of his wedding, he failed to wash his hands properly after eating a tasty dish at the caliph's palace, thus offending his bride; they are reconciled after he swears that henceforth he will always wash his hands forty times over before eating that particular food. This innocent story is given a gruesome touch in the *Thousand and One Nights* version, where it is incorporated in the mutilation-ridden series of tales that make up *The Story of the Hunchback*. Here the bride, olfactorily oversensitive, is angered by the strong smell of cumin with which the dish was spiced. She has her husband flogged and cuts off his thumbs, after which, amazingly, they make up again.

Another man, in a story told by al-Tanūkhī and others,[166] swears upon a sudden impulse that he will never eat elephant meat. A storm is threatening the ship in which he travels, and by swearing oaths he and his travelling companions attempt to avert the danger. His fellow travellers do not think much of this good intention; yet it turns out that it will save his life, whereas the others, their more sensible oaths notwithstanding, will all perish. Stranded on an island, the hungry travellers catch and eat a young elephant and are subsequently killed by its mother, who spares the abstemious hero. Swearing oaths is a serious matter; in pre-Islamic times oaths of sexual or alcoholic abstinence were sworn before embarking on grave undertakings such as blood revenge. Even in Abbasid times such oaths may occasionally be found: the *kātib* al-Ḥasan Ibn Wahb swore to abstain from 'tasty food' (*ṭaʿām ṭayyib*) and cold water as long as his brother was in prison.[167] When the substance of the oath refers to food, especially of a particular and peculiar type, this may convey an element of comedy and curiosity, suitable for amusing tales.

An amusing short tale is 'ʿAlī the Persian', in *The Thousand and One Nights*; here two persons, each claiming to be the rightful owner of a certain bag, describe its contents in an extraordinary and farcical enumeration ('farce' or 'stuff-and-nonsense' is an apt term here) in rhymed prose.[168] The cosmic proportions are inflated when the bag is opened at the order of the judge, and it turns out to contain a loaf, a lemon, cheese and olives. The real versus the imaginary, simple fare contrasted with an imaginary collection of almost anything in the world: it is fitting that basic foodstuffs should be found in the bag. Naturally, in the *Thousand and One Nights* there are also containers that do have magical properties and limitless resources. In the story of Jawdar and his brothers, Jawdar meets a man with a saddlebag containing rather more than the bread and cheese that the modest hero suggests: twenty-four hot dishes are produced, though its owner insists that a thousand, if required, would not pose any problem.[169] As Mia Gerhardt has remarked, the story of Jawdar is preoccupied with food;[170] even in Jawdar's fall – for, exceptionally, this fairytale has a sad ending – is food instrumental: he dies after eating poisoned food.

3. Food and filth in al-Azdī's *A Day in the Life of Abū l-Qāsim*

The story of a day and a night in the life of Abū l-Qāsim from Baghdad by the early 5th/11th-century Abū l-Muṭahhar al-Azdī is unique in classical Arabic literature. It describes a fictional person's behaviour at a party in Isfahan. He enters and leaves the scene as a seemingly pious man who upbraids the other guests for their sinful deeds and words. Between entry and exit, however, he presents himself as one of the most foul-mouthed and blasphemous characters in Arabic literature.[171] In the course of the narrative (146 pages in the edition by Mez) food is an important theme. Al-Jāḥiẓ is quoted in the author's introduction, where versatile Man is called

> a Microcosm, as it is said, offspring of the Macrocosm, because he shapes with his hand every shape and copies with his mouth every sound; because he eats herbs like cattle, meat like beasts of prey and grains like birds; and because he combines traits of all kinds of animals.[172]

The protagonist is introduced like a microcosm of paradoxes: '. . . erudite, marvellous . . ., full of praise, full of slander, witty, silly, near and far . . . sincere, hypocritical, . . . actively and passively pederast, . . . pious, heretical, ascetic, murderer . . .';[173] on the last page he is sent off and called 'the bright blaze of his time, Satan's equal, meeting-point of good and bad qualities, transgressor of every limit and boundary, paragon of jest and earnest.'[174] Soon after his arrival this Abū l-Qāsim – not so much a realistic character as a protean mouthpiece of everything that undermines itself – depicts the other guests as greedy parasites: 'You wretched pimps . . . followers of grilled and roast meat, slaves of wineglass and pint, friends of sweetmeats and fried fritters!'[175] In the course of his monologue he quotes epigrams on spongers:

> If they cooked a pot in an underground oven
> in Byzantium or at the furthest front line,
> While you were in China, you would find it,
> You supernatural diviner of pot-luck.[176]

When he, determined, sees a table spread
He grasps the table firmly by its edge
And lets a shower of fried bits descend,
with fat sucking kids.
He only relishes bread
with meat and fat together;
He relishes *khabīṣ* only
when it is *fālūdhaj*-like, with saffron:
You may see him, without henna,
with dyed hands and fingers.

At banquets he prefers to stand near the tables and to rummage about the *tharīdas*, to forage amongst the titbits, giving particular attention to exotic dishes and going straight for those best things that are most artfully made, are the nicest to gobble, are the most expensive on the market and go down most smoothly:

He falls upon the fine fat shoulder-pieces,
paying no attention to endive or lettuce,
his heart like a brisk and nimble ambler,
with determined canines and frantic molars . . .[177]

A substantial portion of the story is taken up by a comparison between Baghdad and Isfahan in which food is also discussed. Isfahan, argues Abū l-Qāsim, is no place for gastronomy. There follows a long and difficult passage describing food in a breathless enumeration, roughly following the course of a banquet:

> I can see no table amongst you with legs of Khurasanian *khalanj* wood, unbroken, out of one piece (. . .) so beautiful that one would be distracted from eating from it; with on it *jarmāzaj* (?) bread, like full moons speckled as if with stars, baked from high-quality *Hawīdī* (?) and *Ṭansīrī* (?) flour,[178] ground in Bedouin-style, white with some yellowness, its dough like resin, malleable like mastic, sticking to the fingers; a cupful of it could absorb the River Tigris; flattened by the rolling-pin, producing a wheat loaf like *amīrī* gold clippings; bread that crackles under the teeth, chewy to the point of hurting one's jaws; merely looking at it would satisfy your appetite and if a mouthful of it reached the heart it would be the end of its longing. And china and metal platters, white, azure-blue, wine-red, yellow, red, filled with strong Dīnawarī

> cheese which stimulates one's appetite and stirs the stomach. And smoked Daqūqī[179] olives mixed with peeled almonds and thyme: cut one olive through over the loaf and it will soak it in oil, then roll away like an amber pellet. And baked Greek cheese looking as if it had been made with cow's butter, so pungent that it makes the tears run from the eyes as though one had parted from one's loved ones, white, with shining yellowness, smooth, young; one could eat a whole cheese with bread without feeling bloated or thirsty; it has no foul smell; it cleans the stomach and laps up the phlegm . . .[180]

Many appetizers follow, among them turnip, cucumber, aubergine, various juices, salted nuts and seeds such as almonds, pistachio nuts, 'grain of the green (plant)',[181] hemp seeds, sesame seeds, cumin; then poultry: Kaskar chicks, chicken livers, duck's breast etc.; carp-like fish such as *shabbūṭ* and *bunnī*, salted fish (*ṭirrīkh*, from Greek *tarīchos*); *sanbūsaj* made with chicken and francolin breast. Next the roast dishes are mentioned and described: duck, kid, chicken, lamb, fattened chicks, supported by *jūdhāba*, rice with various additions. The breathlessness increases at various intervals where description is omitted and names of dishes are merely strung together:

> And other dishes follow, like *ma'mūniyya, rukhāmiyya, ibrāhīmiyya, muᶜtaḍidiyya, khālidiyya, fustuqiyya, simsimiyya, mishmishiyya, ḥabashiyya, ᶜinabiyya* made with the juice of big *rāziqī* grapes, and *miskiyya, summāqiyya*, yes, and *nūbiyya, ṣaᶜtariyya, narjisiyya, khashkhāshiyya, fākhitiyya, ḥummāḍiyya, ᶜanbariyya, ṣāᶜidiyya, ṣuᶜdiyya, dīkbarāja, mamqūriyya, isfīdhbāj, zīrbāj, darūnāj* . . . [182]

After the sweets, which include various kinds of *lawzīnaj, fālūdhaj, khabīṣ, ᶜaṣīda, qaṭā'if*, and *zalābiya*, there is incense; hands are washed. 'These are the descriptions of Iraqi meals,' says Abū l-Qāsim, 'of which I find nothing here with you'.[183] This is the starting-point for the counterpart, an invective passage on the eating habits of his hosts. They eat tripe, fit only for dogs and cats;

> and I can see pots in which big chunks of beef are being boiled. These are snatched from them as if by leopards and eaten as if by wild beasts, the meat not being divided into little bits by the hands but tugged between the hand and the teeth,

so that one's face, beard and clothes are bespattered. The meat is mixed with broth in which a barge could move about, in which one plunges one's arm as far as the elbow in order to find the meat. The smell of boiled lettuce, artichoke, beetroot, cabbage and turnip wafts over the dishes that are being served like the smell of a fart of a feverish person, or the belching of a dyspeptic . . .

The unpleasantness of the following is somewhat redeemed when Abū l-Qāsim names the delicious fruit which he does not find in Isfahan, together with a few epigrams on plums, watermelons and figs. After this the theme of food is abandoned for the time being. The protagonist, who has done most of the talking for some ninety printed pages, falls asleep. Waking up during the night he demands breakfast from the host. 'What would you suggest?' asks the latter, 'for you have quite frightened us by your scornful words.' – 'Do not fear, I shall not make things difficult for you in matters of food, God forbid!', answers Abū l-Qāsim, who then states his modest wishes in straightforward verse, quoting a poem from al-Hamadhānī's brief *maqāma Sāsāniyya*:

I want from you a loaf on top of a clean table.
I want coarsely milled salt. I want strong vinegar.
I want well-done meat. I want freshly plucked vegetables.
I want a sucking kid; or else a young ram.
I want water with ice, in a brimful exquisite beaker . . .[184]

When the host begs his guest to be more moderate (the poem also mentions a horse, singing-girls, a pretty boy and clothes), Abū l-Qāsim responds with more poems and some prose which only add to the host's distress, then settles for some bread and cheese with some condiments, though not without uttering invective lines:

Cheese only makes the body sick
and distresses the heart with hallucinations.
Give me instead two mouthfuls of *sikbāj*,
or some roast meat taken from the bones!

Grey is my head and bent my bones because
I have so long eaten cheese and sour sauce:
It is as hateful to me
as the poison of a black snake.[185]

Later more food is served, which gives Abū l-Qāsim the opportunity to expatiate on culinary comparisons, anecdotes and descriptions.[186] In the rest of the story, in which Abū l-Qāsim reverses his judgment on Isfahan and Baghdad but annoys the company with his behaviour and scurrilities, food plays no part.

Abū l-Qāsim is a subversive character in several ways, in his obscenity which is difficult to surpass, his cynicism, greed and blasphemy ('I have undone the Koran with poetry, broken the teeth of God's apostle, robbed his grave, erected a mangonel in front of the Kaaba and pelted it with menstrual rags, shat in the well of Zamzam . . .').[187] One could argue, as does El Outmani, that the text itself is subversive.[188] A distinction ought to be made, however, between the character and the composition as a whole, even though most of the text is put into the mouth of the protagonist. Abū l-Qāsim is described as a microcosm and a mixture of good and bad, but it is obvious that he is, on balance, a thoroughly bad character, of the same type as, but surpassing, the anti-heroes in the *maqāmāt* by al-Hamadhānī and al-Ḥarīrī. As a genre the *Ḥikāya* may be exceptional, yet its constituent elements are found in many works that belong to polite literature, enjoyed by the literary, scholarly and often even the religious élite. It would be wrong, therefore, to speak of a subversive text, unless one means by it that even the establishment likes to be subverted by way of titillation and as an occasional outlet.

The most direct way in which the theme of eating itself can be subverted is its digestive counterpart: excretion. The excremental theme in the *Ḥikāya* is at least as strong as the alimentary. Like Ibn al-Ḥajjāj, the specialist in scurrilous poetry very often quoted in the *Ḥikāya*, the author prefers to combine the excremental and the sexual. The text is redolent with scatology and coprology; not rarely this is expressed by means of images taken from food. The protagonist is described in the introduction in a verse as 'a follower of Mālik [i.e. someone practising anal intercourse] whose prick daily churns milk in the space of arses'.[189] Abū l-Qāsim describes a woman in another line: 'I pierced her dung with my cock so that the meat mixed with the *tharīda* broth';[190] of another it is said, 'the marrow of her arse is greasy, not like the oil of *harīsa* on plates';[191] a woman lying on her back is compared to a chicken being roasted.[192] An epigram goes:

Umm Razīn shat one day into the flour.
We asked her why. She said, 'It is the leaven in the dough.'[193]

Examples could be multiplied. Coprophagy, as in the epigram quoted, is the ultimate connection between the alimentary and excremental themes. It was celebrated by the minor ninth-century poet al-Faḍl Ibn Hāshim, who apparently specialized in filth.[194] One example of his verse must suffice:

> If you saw me, eating stinking faeces,
> when people have roasted for me a rat,
> so fat that its eyes are bulging,
> while I was eating shit and, like an addict,
> sipping thin shit,
> drinking pus like others drink milk,
> then you would think that God
> did not create anyone like I.[195]

The poet shocks with his language, even with his grammar (the solecism at the end is in the original: *ka-anā*). A brief anecdote is told about al-Wāthiq or another caliph ordering the poet to live up to his verse in his presence; it turns out that once more poets 'say what they do not do', as the Koran has it. In an extraordinary poem al-Faḍl, after thirteen lines of self-description in which he explains his perversion as the result of an unhappy life since childhood, ends with three lines in praise of al-Wāthiq: 'Leave this, and praise the Pure Commander . . .!'[196]

Abū l-Qāsim's juxtaposition of the high and low, the delicious and the revolting, thus stands in a tradition of tolerated subversion, admitted in the presence of caliphs and in literary anthologies by high officials like Ibn al-Jarrāḥ, whose ephemerous vizirate ended together with the equally brief caliphate of the princely poet Ibn al-Muᶜtazz.

CHAPTER V

Food for Satire and Parody

1. Cacophagy

Food has always been a topic favoured by satirists and parodists. We have seen in chapter III that eating desert fare was a topos in anti-Bedouin and anti-Arab satire. In pre-Islamic poetry eating lizards was, of course, not mentioned as shameful. In invective poetry only bizarre kinds of food can be encountered: there are some poems in which individuals or tribes are accused, rightly or wrongly, of cannibalism, or eating dog meat or donkey's penises, for instance. The Banū Asad were said to eat dogs, hence al-Farazdaq's line:

> When an Asadī suffers from hunger one day in one place or other, and he has a fat dog, he eats it.[1]

Sālim Ibn Dāra addressed a man from Faqᶜas (a clan of Asad) who was blamed for eating dog meat:

> You Faqᶜasī, why did you eat it, why?
> If God had been afraid [that you would eat it], He would have forbidden it [explicitly]
> And you would not have eaten its flesh and blood.[2]

Abū l-Muhawwish, an early Islamic poet from the same clan, was addressed by Shurayḥ Ibn Aws:

> You have reviled us for eating the dates and wheat of Iraq,
> While your food is dog's prick, roasted on the embers.[3]

The unfortunate tribe of Fazāra were forever branded as eaters of donkey's penises, after one of its members unwittingly ate one, tricked by his companions. Poets exploited the anecdote without mercy:

> Which would you like better, Fazāra, a Ṣayḥānī date with some clarified butter, or a donkey's prick?
> O yes, Fazāra prefers a donkey's prick and its balls to Fazāra itself.[4]

> Do not trust anyone from Fazāra when you are alone with him, after that man baked an onager's prick in the hot ashes.[5]

If one mishap of one individual may stigmatize a whole tribe, why not blame half of all the Arabs as well? Abū Nuwās used the motif in his poem against the 'Northern' Arabs, to which Fazāra belonged; a poem in which also the Banū Asad are mentioned again for their alleged craving for dog meat.[6]

In invective verse culinary obscenity may be combined with cannibalism, as in a gruesome poem on a clan of the tribe of Hudhayl, that was said to have eaten a man from a friendly clan in a time of famine:

> You have eaten the fat parts of Ḥubaysh Ibn Mukhadh-dham's back; now nobody is safe from you any more.
> They gathered around him after seven plus four nights, when his nails had fallen off and his skin was scorched.
> They had buried his penis for their chief, Muᶜāwiya Split-lip – ah, what a nice present!
> (. . .) If, one day, they would find food on their mother's clitoris, they would leave nothing to come back to.[7]

Ḥassān Ibn Thābit referred to a similar incident in a poem which he recited at the battle of Uḥud:

> Have al-Ṭābikhī's balls and prick not distracted the Banū Shijᶜ, those jackals' heads, from us?
> Each summer the testicles of friendly neighbours look, in the hands of their virgins, like hare's heads.[8]

Because once, as it is told, an Arab of the tribe of Tamīm mistakenly thought food was being prepared when he noticed the smell of burning human flesh, the Tamīm were mocked for their craving for food:

> When someone of Tamīm has died and you would like to see him revived, then bring some food:
> Bread, or dates, or meat, or that thing wrapped in a striped cloth (*bijād*)![9]

The last expression evoked some different interpretations. In view of the burning corpses in the story, cannibalism is suggested, for *bijād* is a piece of clothing for people. Perhaps in an attempt to remove the shocking insinuation the famous Tamīm leader, al-Aḥnaf Ibn Qays, gives a more innocent explanation of the 'thing wrapped in a cloth': it is the dish called *sakhīna*;[10] the philologist al-Aṣmaᶜī thinks it means milk in a skin.[11]

Not every reference to 'eating people' or 'eating the flesh of people' should be taken literally, for the expression is a common idiom for slandering people. The Koran (49:12) employs this strong metaphor in order to stress the repulsiveness of slander. When Ḥassān says, 'They urge one another, all of them, to eat their neighbour; their best man is like a billy-goat',[12] it is possible that he does not literally accuse them of cannibalism – billy-goats, after all, are not carnivorous. Al-Jāḥiẓ, however, seeing that the line is addressed to Hudhayl, connects it with the above-quoted lampoon and has a different second hemistich that leaves little doubt about his interpretation: '. . .for sheep, or dog, or human are alike (to them)'.[13] The philologian al-Aṣmaᶜī (d. c. 216/831) did not know how to interpret a line by the pre-Islamic poet ᶜAmr Ibn Qiᶜās: 'Some meat there was that people had not tasted before me: I ate it, alone, taking the choice parts'. An unnamed commentator said that the poet, when drunk, had slaughtered and eaten his son, but according to another the poet had made lampoons on a king who had never been the subject of lampoons, therefore it was 'as if he had eaten his flesh'.[14] Human flesh – more tasty than any other kind of meat, according to a reliable authority [15] – stands for what is man's most precious possession: his honour.

Religion and food come together in a report on the pagan tribe of Ḥanīfa 'who had an idol made of *ḥays* (dates with curds and butter), revered it for a time, then ate it during a period of famine'; a poet mocked them:

> Ḥanīfa have eaten their god at a time of drought and hunger;
> They feared not their god's reprisal nor his anger.[16]

One wonders if this refers to one particular occasion or whether the epigram makes fun of the Eucharist, Christianity being known to some extent among the Banū Ḥanīfa.[17] J.G. Frazer, had he known it, would naturally have included the report in his chapter 'Eating the God'.[18] It somehow found its way into *The Thousand and One Nights*: in the story of ᶜAjīb and Gharīb, a heathen opponent of the latter, Jamraqān, says that he adores a god made of date-paste, butter and honey, which he eats after a certain time and then makes a new one. Gharīb falls over backwards with laughter, but soon converts him to the true religion. Then he asks the new convert, 'Have you tasted the sweetness of Islam?'.[19]

If eating one's god is ridiculous to Muslims, the thought of eating pork is repellent to them. Although pork, as al-Jāḥiẓ says, is in fact rather tasty,[20] to most Muslims it has always been abhorrent. Eating pork is explicitly forbidden in the Koran; pigs are a source of ritual impurity and they are associated with legends about their being metamorphosed Jews.[21] Another kind of metamorphosis can be observed in a recurrent motif of invective poetry against eaters of pork: they become what they eat. One of the three great Umayyad poets, a great portion of whose verse was devoted to the exchange of *naqā'iḍ* or 'flytings', was al-Akhṭal (d. c. 92/710) who was a Christian. In many poems his opponent Jarīr exploited the Muslim aversion to pig and pork (which in Arabic are expressed by the same word). In the following selection, al-Akhṭal and his people eat pigs and are pigs:

> Go on pilgrimage to the Cross, make your sacrifices, and take your share of pork![22]
>
> Little Akhṭal is a pig, a disaster feared wherever he goes round.
>
> (. . .) They [al-Akhṭal's people] laugh with lust when seeing a pig; may God make these mouths ugly when they grin!
>
> They cast dice, playing for the portions of pork: how awful such a slaughtered beast, how awful the players![23]
>
> (. . .) Pig meat, cooking in wine, has given the dark-toothed woman from Taghlib [al-Akhṭal's tribe] a big belly.[24]

> Little Akhṭal's mother, drunk, jumps at every swine, thinking it to be a gazelle.[25]

> Little Akhṭal's mother is a mother who bears no noble sons: she lays in wait for [?][26] a grey snorting [swine] with tusks of different size.
>
> (. . .) The piglets and the beans that she has eaten rumble in the guts of a farting dungbag at night.[27]

> A tame she-pig got pregnant by a grey [swine] in al-Kunāsa;[28] thus they gave birth to another swine.[29]

The pigs of the Peninsula want to fight us, but their dogs are hiding in their holes from the roaring of a lion.
(. . .) How can a slave boast to us when his mother is from Taghlib, her teeth dark from eating piglets,
With thick-skinned nostrils, stinking, her veil fastened over a pig's snout![30]

The early Bedouin poets prided themselves on feeding others and abstaining themselves. If abstaining is a virtue and eating its opposite, then in a sense eating is a dishonourable act, when one thinks in polarities. Few lines of invective were thought to be as damaging as al-Ḥuṭay'a's line:

Never mind noble deeds! Do not go and look for them!
Stay; you are someone who (merely) eats and gets dressed.

The story goes that the addressee complained to the Caliph ᶜUmar, who at first saw, or pretended to see, no harm and said, 'Don't you like eating and getting dressed?'. But when the poet Ḥassān Ibn Thābit was asked for his opinion, he pronounced it to be the worst kind of insult.[31] In Islam there are no injunctions against enjoying food, but moralistic satirists and ascetics have always blamed epicures. An epigram ascribed to Ṣāliḥ Ibn ᶜAbd al-Quddūs, a moralist of the eighth century, condemns the people of those days:

If you talk of fish and vegetables,
you are in their view a superior man;
But if you talk of topics of real knowledge,
you are in their view a killjoy and a bore.[32]

In ancient Latin literature, a description of a rich meal is as often as not intended as a satire - think of *Satyricon* (Trimalchio's Banquet) or the satires of Horace (II, 8) and Juvenal. I can think of few Arabic equivalents. It is true that food plays a part in some satirical poems;[33] but usually it is the bad behaviour of the guests that is mocked or condemned, not the fact that they eat good food. On the contrary, descriptions of sumptuous banquets and appetizing dishes are usually free of any moralizing or criticism of luxury and the good life; at most one may detect a subdued and implicit form of moralizing, as when straight after the celebration of food at al-Mustakfī's banquet, mentioned before,[34] al-Masᶜūdī remarks that the caliph later came to a sorry end. There is no explicit moralistic link between the pleasant life and the unpleasant death of the caliph. More explicit is Ibn Shuhayd (d. 426/1035) in his 'Treatise on Sweets' (*Risāla fī l-ḥalwā'*),[35] where a 'gluttonous jurist' lovingly describes sweet dishes but is then himself rather less lovingly described while he eats:

> while his eyes gleamed like two live coals, protruding from his face like two testicles . . . he belched, and a 'withering wind' blew from him, whereupon we became sure of the 'painful punishment'. It scattered us hither and thither . . .[36]

Of course there have always been ascetics who made poems in praise of abstention or moderation, but they do not describe food, wisely perhaps, so as not to raise an appetite in the audience, as Ibn Shuhayd's prose might do. One will look in vain for banquet scenes in the poems of Abū l-ᶜAtāhiya (d. 210/825), poet of death and anti-worldliness, who with grim humour makes man a banquet for maggots and worms: 'I have seen those who taste what they crave/ While they themselves will be food for earth's layers/saucers (*aṭbāq*).'[37] In anthologies there is often a nice balance between poems and anecdotes in praise of food and in praise of moderation.

Gluttony is scorned in an anonymous poem reputedly made on the death of the famous ninth-century sponger (*ṭufaylī*) Bunān:

> You dead one, despised by near and distant people:
> Who will now take care of the dishes of *harīsa*, now you are dead, and of *tharīda* and *ᶜaṣīda*?
> And attending banquets, sitting at tables,
> Eating anything you could lay your hands on, hot or cold?
> You used to swallow sheeps' heads when alone or in company;
> You used to wreak havoc on your friends' money, as if you had inherited it from a father.
> Did you really think that you would live forever? No human lives forever![38]

Although the poet employs a motif of *rithā'*, elegiac poetry, ('Who will now take care of . . .?'), the poem cannot be called a true parody of elegy, unlike the much longer poem (36 lines) on the death of another parasite by a certain Abū ᶜAbd Allāh al-Bunānī – a colleague, judging by his *nisba*:[39]

> I weep because I miss you at every luncheon, and your hearty appetite at every dinner:

> Ah, unrivalled master of eaters, if only you could hear or answer my call!
> If decked tables could ransom you, they would do so. But ransom can no longer be offered.
> Who will now take care of dishes of *jūdhāb*, of fine bread, milk-bread and water-bread,
> Of cold dishes that quench a burning thirst so fine, like a garden that laughs because of heaven's tears . . .
> I weep for you because of a fat lamb; another time I weep for you because of a fat-tailed ewe;[40]
> Also, because of a suckling kid brought forward, followed by golden orioles (? *ṣafā'ir*), next to the roast meat . . .

Many other dishes are enumerated, some of them personified and sharing in the universal grief:

> Your loss has struck all earth and all people with all-encompassing gloom and darkness . . .
> Who will now provide an exegesis for every gastronomic problem that perplexed all table-companions and fellow-eaters?
> The eyes of the *narjisiyya* are sore, now that he is dead, from longing for a green *kashkiyya*;[41]
> They both vie in sorrow and grief for you; that, too, is the condition of your scattered associates.
> Banquets stumble[42] since you have been felled; parasitism is a hostage of sorrow and weeping.
> You have left in the hearts of the *qaṭā'if* pastries a distress that is unremitting, morning and evening . . .
> The table slaps its face, consumed by burning grief, having heard of your death . . .

The mock elegy even contains a few lines that parody the conventional topoi of the *qaṣīda*, in which kitchens and ladles take the place of abandoned camp-sites and camels:

> Abandoned are the kitchens and the cauldrons; gone are the cooks in them, after being busy for so long.
> You have left the lean ladles limping, grieving from being worn out[43] and exhausted.

The poem ends with customary exclamations and appropriate blessings:

> Do not leave us! But you have left. Every near one is bound to go far away one day.
> May a thunderous incontinent cloud drench the earth of your grave with a downpour of clarified fat;
> And may your tomb be enlarged with a fully loaded hamper, brought by the hands of servants;
> And may geese and rice be your friendly companions, protected from dirt and dust . . .

That the poet mocks the conventions of genre with his parody does not necessarily mean that he is mocking the deceased sponger at the same time: it is possible, even likely, that in this case humour and sincere grief are combined. Another example of the conventional motifs of the *qaṣīda* being given a parodistic culinary twist is a poem quoted more than once in *The Thousand and One Nights*, beginning:

> Turn aside with the cranes in the abode of the *sikbāj* maker, and mourn for the fried meat and the *ṭabāhajāt*;
> and mourn for the daughters of the sand-grouse – I still mourn for them, together with the fried chicks.
> Ah, my heart craves for two kinds of fish served on two loaves of *maᶜārīj* bread . . .[44]

The alienating effect is in line with the fact that the poem is recited at a king's table by an ape (in reality an educated human transformed by a sorcerer).

Serious and respected genres could be parodied without impunity. The poem by al-Bunānī quoted before is perhaps amusing but not particularly subtle. Parodying religious beliefs and discourse naturally demands far more circumspection and subtlety in an Islamic environmment. Both may be found in the remarkable and diverse works of al-Maᶜarrī (d. 449/1058).

Abū l-ᶜAlā' al-Maᶜarrī, poet, prose-writer, philologist, moralist, pessimist, misanthrope and ascetic, mocked and parodied the beliefs of his contemporaries in a scene, part of his 'Epistle of Forgiving', in which the Hereafter is described as a kind of Land of Cockayne. There is a heavenly banquet[45] for a number of deceased poets and grammarians. A peacock passes along and Abū ᶜUbayda, famous early ninth-century scholar, expresses a wish to have it as a marinated dish. Instantly it appears on a golden plate; a similar fate befalls a goose as big as a Bactrian camel, which is first partly consumed as a roast, then revived and subsequently turned into several other dishes, while the diners have an interesting conversation on the morphology of the Arabic word for goose.[46] Al-Maʿarrī's parody may not have been recognized as such by his some of his contemporaries, who believed such things; see, for instance, the *ḥadīth* in which the Prophet speaks of birds in Paradise that land on people's plates, and have a different kind of food under each feather, whiter than snow, softer than butter, sweeter than honey.[47] One may note here that al-Maʿarrī, who stresses that the animals slaughtered in Paradise do not suffer any pain,[48] was himself a vegetarian, or even a vegan, since he abstained from meat, fish, milk, eggs and honey, not wanting to harm any animal, as he says in a poem.[49] He was forced to defend his vegetarianism against a bitter and potentially dangerous attack by a leading theologian of the Fāṭimids, Abū Naṣr Ibn Abī ʿImrān, who accused him of heresy and unbelief: had not God allowed eating meat? Is not vegetarianism a blasphemous attempt to be more compassionate than the Merciful, the Compassionate?[50]

Al-Maʿarrī has also been accused, unjustly, of parodying, or rather trying to surpass, the Koran, both equally sinful in orthodox eyes, with his *al-Fuṣūl wa-l-ghāyāt*. True parodies of the Koran are, naturally, all but absent in transmitted texts. Some preserved specimens of the 'holy book' of Mohammed's rival, the 'liar prophet' Musaylima, almost read like such a parody:

> Frog, daughter of a frog! ✡ Croak! What are you croaking? ✡ Your top half in the water soaking, ✡ your lower half in the mud poking! ✡ The drinker you rile not, ✡ the water you soil not.[51]

The agrarian background of Musaylima and his following[52] may be seen in another fragment:

> By the women sowing seed ✡ and the women reaping crops ✡ and the women winnowing wheat ✡ and the women milling flour ✡ and the women baking bread ✡ and the women sopping bread broth ✡ and the women gobbling morsels ✡ of fat and butter: ✡ You are deemed better than the dwellers in tents of hair ✡ Nor do the village dwellers take precedence over you . . .[53]

It is unlikely that Musaylima, if he produced it, consciously mocked the style of Koranic passages such as sura 51 ('By the swift scatterers ☼ and the burden-bearers . . .'), sura 79 ('By those that pluck out vehemently ☼ and those that draw out violently . . .') or sura 100 ('By the snorting chargers, ☼ by the strikers of fire, ☼ by the dawn-raiders 7. . .').[54] If not Musaylima but one of his Muslim opponents composed the passage, the butt of the parody is of course the Liar prophet and not the Koran; yet to non-Muslims it seems to make fun of the Holy Book, not only by using a series of feminine participles that refer unambiguously to women of flesh and blood instead of vaguely to rather obscure, almost eschatological beings and objects (clouds, horses, camels, angels?),[55] but also by making food, its production and consumption, its theme.[56]

More common than parodying or imitating the style of the Koran is the wilful quotation of passages out of context and inappropriately and therefore, to some critics, improperly and irreverently.[57] It is frequent in many kinds of jesting texts (*hazl*). In one story a man keeps begging for yet one more piece of *lawzīnaj* using Koranic verses: 'Your God is One God' (2:163), 'When We sent unto them two' (36:14), 'So We sent a third' (36:14), and so on, jumping finally to 'Then We sent him unto a hundred thousand, or more' (37:147).[58] Bunān, the parasite, tells how some of his table companions, 'shameless buffoons' (*qawm mujjān*), quarrelled over food while exchanging Koranic quotations:

> . . . One of them took a mouthful, dipping it in the butter [from a well in the middle of the platter], saying, 'They shall be pitched into it, they and the perverse (26:94).' He then drew the butter towards himself. Another said, 'When they are cast, they shall hear its bubbling and sighing (25:13, 12).' He drew the butter towards himself, so that [the butter] ran away. Then I said, 'How many a ruined well, a tall palace! (22:45)', and I pierced[59] [the well, directing the flow of the] butter towards myself. Another said, 'Thou hast made a hole in it so as to drown its passengers? Thou hast indeed done a grievous thing (18:71)'. . .

The fight goes on until Bunān mixes what is left of butter and food, exclaiming, 'And it was said, "Earth, swallow thy waters; and, heaven, abate!" And the waters subsided, the affair was accomplished, and [the Ark] settled on El-Judi, and it was said: "Away with the people of evildoers! (11:44)"'[60]

Such apt but improper quotations out of context, that seem to debase the holy text, may in turn be quoted by respected scholars such as al-Khaṭīb al-Baghdādī or Ibn al-Jawzī, as long as they themselves cite them in their proper context of *hazl*, even though many authorities condemn such frivolous playing with God's word.[61]

2. Ibn Sūdūn's Sweet Nothings

The theme of food can easily serve to debase any text. In the preceding examples the Koranic passages were affected by the context which acts as a parasite, yet remained unchanged as to their letter, if not spirit. Less sacred but equally serious texts could with less danger be changed and debased. A few interesting minor poets from later periods made pastiches or *contrefacta* of famous serious poems, turning them into poems on food: a form of light verse practised in Persian literature by Abū Isḥāq (or Busḥāq) around AD 1400.[62] This great pioneer of alimentary parody compiled his works in a *Dīwān* which earned him the sobriquet 'Edibles Busḥāq' (Busḥāq Aṭ^cima). It contains poetry of various types: many *ghazal*s and other short forms, longer narrative poems such as 'The Story of Pilaf and Pastry', and some prose, like the account of a dream about food (*kh^wāb-nāma*). Busḥāq had some followers in Persian literature; in Arabic he had an early follower in Ibn Sūdūn (d. 868/1464), who in turn may have inspired a later poet, ^cĀmir al-Anbūṭī (d. c. 1171/1758). The word 'follower' means, first of all, that Ibn Sūdūn came after Busḥāq: there is no evidence that the latter's work was known to Ibn Sūdūn.

Ibn Sūdūn, the son of an Egyptian mamluk, possibly of Circassian origin, tells us in the introduction to his collection of prose and (mainly) verse called *Nuzhat al-nufūs wa-muḍḥik al-^cabūs* ('The Recreation of Souls That Raises Laughter in Him Who Scowls')[63] that originally he did not bother to arrange his material, mixing panegyric, love lyrics and bawdy 'libertine' themes (*mujūn*) indiscriminately, but in the end preferring to separate the serious (*jidd*) from the jesting (*hazl*).[64] It is not possible to determine whether he is telling the truth here or whether he is merely making some concession to a common attitude towards the topic of jest vs. earnest, *viz.* approval of a certain mixture, but not to the point of confusion (even though part of *hazl* lies in its confusing effect).[65] The first section, on serious subjects, has been dismissed as little more than 'insipid jingles'.[66] Its seriousness is somewhat undermined by the preamble to the book as a whole, where the alimentary element is already present when God is praised as 'He Who protects those who have entered into the darkness of hunger and brings them out into the light by sating them; He Who makes fresh dates from dry sticks, gourds from mud, and birds from eggs.'[67]

The second section, on *hazliyyāt* ('pleasantries'), opens with another preamble that is at the same time pious and parodic, thanking God for his many favours to those who appreciate good food. Three similar preambles in rhymed prose are interspersed among the poems, such as the following which begins:

> Praise be to God the Almighty, Who bestowed upon His servants various niceties (*laṭā'if*). He taught man what he did not know [cf. Q 96:5] and inspired him when He taught him to make, as he was taught, from sugar stuffed pastry (*ḥashw al-qaṭā'if*). He made sellers subservient to swallowers, those who sit in their shops and those who are ambulant. He made the kernels of pistachio nuts, having been cracked, whole. He made streams of sugar syrup descend from the firmly anchored mountains of sugar, down into the bellies of the wadis of syrups . . .[68]

These mock doxologies set the tone for the following poems, the first of which begins with 'You who describe food, may you be spared criticism! Repeat to my ears delicious words!' and goes on to describe kinds of food – a *ma'mūniyya*[69], sugar syrup (*qaṭr al-nabāt*),[70] bananas – as if they were beloved women that ought to visit the poet, if only as a nightly apparition or a dream (*wa-law bi-l-ṭayfi ʿinda l-manām*).[71] One poem begins with tautological nonsense:

> The river[72] is a river and palms are palms,&
> the elephant is an elephant and a giraffe is tall
> The earth is earth and the sky is its opposite;
> Birds fly around between the two.
> When the wind blows in a garden
> The earth stands firm and the twigs sway. . .[73]

But the poem ends with food followed by hashish:

> How sweet are peeled bananas
> On which sugar syrup and honey[74] are poured!
> Ah, you *kunāfa*s seasoned (*tubbilat*) with sugars,
> My heart is madly in love (*matbūl*) since it misses you.

> You who have 'killed' hashish,[75] you are killed yourself, you wretched fellow: killer and killed . . .

The glaring incoherence of this poem is apparently intentional: with the contrast between the first half and the second Ibn Sūdūn seems to imply that nothing meaningful can be said about the world, or that meaningful things can no longer be said in verse, except when the subjects are food and intoxication.

Pride of place among food is given to bananas with sugar syrup or honey. This may simply mean that Ibn Sūdūn had a sweet tooth, or no teeth at all, being unable to chew. Five centuries after Ibn Sūdūn a literary critic would be deemed unacceptably naïve if one was not tempted to look for sexual innuendos behind the banana and the sticky substances, especially given the fact that the word *ᶜusayla* ('sweet little honey') was, according to Tradition, used by the Prophet as a euphemistic expression for sexual intercourse.[76] Being tempted, however, does not mean being convinced. A sexual interpretation is only possible here in psychoanalytical criticism which takes no account of the poet's intentions and the literary conventions of his age. Sex in Arabic obscene poetry or prose is always clearly to be recognized even when it is veiled in allusions and metaphor, as when, for instance, a heterosexual girl says to a lesbian one, 'There is nothing in the world that is nicer than bananas'.[77] Ibn Sūdūn's alimentary verse is free from such unmistakable pointers; if any obscene allusions may be extracted from his poems, the poet did not put them in consciously.

The second part of the section on *hazl* contains 'trumped-up stories' (*ḥikāyāt malāfiq*). Food plays an important role again; and once more almost all the food is sweet. It has been observed that this may well be connected to the consumption of hashish, which is another prominent theme in Ibn Sūdūn's text: it is well known that addicts of hashish crave for sweets.[78] In some stories, however, the sweetness may have nothing to do with hashish and is simply, it would seem, the sweetness that is found in fairy tales and children's stories. In the first story a man who is seen to sleep a lot explains that once he dreamed of a Hansel & Gretel-like house: bricks of *qāhiriyya*[79] and *qaṭā'if*, roof of *mumashshak*[80], windows of *mushabbak*,[81] etc. Inside, a meal is served. Just as he is about to take a first bite of a chicken leg he wakes up. Since that time he sleeps as much as he can, hoping to bring his dream to a happy conclusion.[82] A rich man, in another story, is summoned by an invisible caller (*hātif*) to give alms to the poor. He summons one thousand confectioners who make pastry in plenty for the poor and the rabble. Then he dreams of an edible castle in edible surroundings and is told that this is the heavenly reward for feeding his poor brothers.[83]

Hashish and sweets go together in another story, in which an insomniac swallows 'something greenish making the white of the eye red' (obviously hashish, often called *al-khaḍrā'* 'the green one'), given to him by his father.[84] This induces a dream in which he finds himself near a sea of syrup, its bottom made of *ṣābūniyya*,[85] its sides of *ma'mūniyya*, its fish of peeled bananas and *zalābiya* on its coast. He plunges into the sea and, after seven days of swimming and eating, he reaches an island with mountains of *kunāfa*, wadis of pastry, etc. He is about to have a pleasant time with the inhabitants of this land of Cockayne but stumbles, falls for ten nights and plunges into a pond of salted lime juice. After swimming for a day and a night he reaches his home and scolds his father.[86]

Thus the whole world is transformed into edibles, as in a two-liner (*dūbayt*):

> If the sun, the stars and the moon
> are reflected in the river's water,
> then the sun is a loaf, the little stars are eggs,
> and the full moon a fresh buffalo cheese.[87]

In this transformation the status of food is raised, while at the same time the whole cosmos is lowered. Paradoxically, the cosmic status-enhancing powers are outdone by the debasing effect of the humble food theme. Something similar happens, too, when the low and the lofty are combined in panegyric. A letter by al-Wahrānī addressed to al-Qāḍī al-Fāḍil strikes a high note of praise in the beginning by comparing the addressee's virtues with those of the heavenly bodies, but the jesting (though not disrespectful) character of the letter becomes apparent when al-Wahrānī lets Capricorn (the kid), be slaughtered in one of the lunar mansions, Pisces (fishes) be fried, Aries (the ram) be roasted, or Taurus (the bull) be cooked into a *sikbāj*, all for the sake of his patron.[88]

This section in Ibn Sūdūn's collection contains more than just stories. The following prescriptions are variations on the mock recipe genre:

> He who performs the last evening prayer and remains thereafter one hundred and twenty times four minutes, and then eats five hundred eggs without salt, half a hundredweight of *nayda*[89] from Upper Egypt, fifty-seven pints of the dregs of sesame oil, seven beakers of the stalks of sycamore figs . . . will never find himself hungry during the night; if he lives till morning he will not be free from various diseases and he may be confident that he will not be healthy.[90]

> He who eats in a night in Ramadan two pounds of *kunāfa*, two pounds of *qaṭīfa*, eats before daybreak five pounds of peeled bananas with refined sugar syrup, then, at the feast (at the end of the fasting month), 45 almond bread buns with sugar icing,[91] giving the shells as alms to his poor neighbours, keeping this up as long as he lives, then the worms will never eat his heart, as long as he stays alive.[92]

The following sections contain poems which 'parody the insipidity and inanity of the poetry of his time and the triviality of the (strophic) *muwashshaḥ* poems', as Kern said.[93] Inevitably food is a vehicle for parody again; Ibn Sūdūn makes *contrefacta*, poems using the rhyme and metre of existing poems, indicated by their first line: 'On the manner of *Bless the bringer of good tidings* I said: *With peeled pistachio nuts . . .*'[94] The numerous poems on sweets and the ubiquitous bananas with syrup, after a while, may be found cloying by the reader: Ibn Sūdūn himself may be accused of insipidity. The point is, it would seem, that this insipidity itself is part of the parody; the monomaniacal insistence *ad nauseam* on sickening sweets is obviously intentional. It is possible that the individual *contrefacta* would seem wittier if we knew the texts of the poems on which they are based, but this is not very likely. In any case, it seems to me that all too often it is taken for granted that parody is necessarily subversive, that it always exposes and denounces its model. This is surely mistaken and misunderstands the nature of much of *hazl*. It is perfectly possible that Ibn Sūdūn, *pace* Kern, did not find any 'insipidity and inanity' or 'triviality' in the poetry of his contemporaries. The amusing mock letter of appointment in which a certain ᶜAlīkā, a notorious sponger, pompously nominates a Lieutenant-General of Parasites was not composed by Ibrāhīm Ibn Hilāl al-Ṣābi' (d. 384/994) with the purpose of subverting his own profession, that of chancery official.[95] If the Persian Busḥāq parodies the great Ḥāfiẓ, or twentieth-century writers and film-makers parody Shakespeare or the Gospel it is not always in order to debunk and deny the greatness of their models: rather, the parody springs from the sheer fun of making parodies, or what is debunked is excessive and humourless veneration. Similarly, the mock doxologies of Ibn Sūdūn may be called irreverent but not impious or anti-religious. Ibn Sūdūn's is, in a sense, a 'marginal' voice, since 'it reflects the existence and the activities of beggars, thieves, vagabonds, rogues and other figures of low life'.[96] But although the content may be marginal, this does not necessarily marginalize the text or its author. Since the time of al-Jāḥiẓ the intellectual élite has had a lively interest in the consumption and production of such themes. Thus that paragon of pornographic poetry, Ibn al-Ḥajjāj (d. 391/1001), even though his verse was kept out of schoolchildren's hands, came from a respectable family, was popular with leading members of the ruling class and even served as a *muḥtasib* or 'market inspector', charged with supervising public moral behaviour.[97]

Deservedly popular was another kind of parody, given at the beginning of the last section of Ibn Sūdūn's *Nuzha*: a mock commentary of several pages on what appears to be a line of children's verse.

> Abū Qurdān sowed an acre
> with Jew's mallow and aubergine.[98]

In the commentary ingenious fantastic explanations are given for the obvious. On the etymology of the words *mulūkhiyyā* (Jew's mallow) and *bādinjān* (aubergine) one learns that the former was coined by the said Abū Qurdān, who exclaimed, in the course of a story told at some length, *yā mulūkhī yā . . .!* ('O, my pulled-out bits, o . . .!'). The word *bādinjān* consists of

> *bā*, which is B-A: any young schoolchild will know this. *Din* is (the same as) *dann*: a big jug made of earthenware. As for *jān*, that is a Persian word meaning 'spirit', although I prefer to interpret it here as 'heart', since a heart, like an aubergine, is red and elongated.[99]

Again, this may be read as a caustic exposure of traditional glossography with its combination of the abstruse, the obtuse, and the trivial; or it is mere irreverence on Ibn Sūdūn's part, without seriously subversive intentions.

Eloquence and learning may be displayed in the genre of the *maqāma*. Ibn Sūdūn includes in his book a short *maqāma*, in which the narrator and his companions, on a tour in Gizeh, meet a man who offers a good meal to those who can answer some questions on matters of philology. The words discussed are *maᶜrifa* (knowledge), *mighrafa* (ladle) and *mijrafa* (scoop). The last two words have more diacritical dots than the first because, as the narrator explains to the host's satisfaction, one spatters *nuqaṭ* (drops, dots) when using a ladle or a scoop. The *maqāma* then ends with a banquet scene.[100]

The gastronomo-parodical method of Bushāq and Ibn Sūdūn was followed by the Egyptian poet ᶜĀmir al-Anbūṭī (d. c. 1178/1758),[101] who accepted bribes from contemporary poets in exchange for his promise not to maltreat their poems in his wonted manner. However, deceased poets, no longer bribable, were not exempted from his parodies. He made *contrefacta* on famous *lāmiyya*s (poems rhyming on the letter *l*) by al-Ṭughrā'ī and Ibn al-Wardī. He is also said to have made a *rajaz* poem of a thousand couplets on food in imitation of the famous versified grammar, *al-Alfiyya* by Ibn Mālik. Where Ibn Mālik had said,

Kalāmunā lafẓun mufīdun ka-staqim
wa-smun wa-fiᶜlun thumma ḥarfuni l-kalim

Our *Speech* is Useful Words, like 'Teach!'
Noun, Verb and *Part'cle*: *Parts of Speech*,[102]

al-Anbūṭī says,

Ṭaᶜāmunā l-ḍānī ladhīdhun li-l-nahim
laḥman wa-samnan thumma khubzan fa-ltaqim

Our food consists in tasty mutton:
Meat, butter, bread: tuck in, you glutton![103]

The grammarian's useful, but rather indigestible words on discourse are thus turned into more digestible though distinctly less useful discourse on dishes.

3. Warring Edibles, High and Low: Ibn al-Ḥajjār's *Delectable War*

In the genre of the literary debate (for which *munāẓara* is one of many names),[104] different kinds of food may appear as the contestants: figs *vs* grapes,[105] or dates *vs* grapes,[106] cheese *vs* olives,[107] etc. Among the more interesting texts, certainly from a culinary point of view, is the 15th-century Mamluk *Kitāb al-ḥarb al-maᶜshūq bayna laḥm al-ḍa'n wa-ḥawāḍir al-sūq* ('The Lovely War between Mutton and the Refreshments of the Market-Place'), by a certain Aḥmad Ibn Yaḥyā Ibn Ḥasan al-Ḥajjār, partially translated by J. Finkel in 1932–34,[108] and recently edited by Manuela Marín.[109] It is not a debate but the story of a regular, or rather irregular, war between King Mutton and his followers on the one side, and on the other King Honey and his host, which includes vegetables, fruits, milk, cheese and fish.

The basic plot is fairly simple. King Mutton, a powerful monarch, respected by every Caliph and Sultan, reigns supreme, helped by dignitaries such as his vizier, Goat Meat, his commander, Beef, and his chamberlain, Scalded Meat. The king hears about the growing power and pretensions of Honey, who has won the allegiance of many paupers, foodstuffs from the market. He orders a wise man, Fat Tail, to go to his rival and demand his obedience. Fat Tail travels (in a frying-pan) to the other side, but prior to appearing before King Honey he secretly visits many of the latter's servants, including Sugar, the vizier, cleverly canvassing for his own sovereign by means of promises and intrigues. Having secured sufficient support, he addresses King Honey, whose reply is intransigent. Who could compare Honey, mentioned in the Holy Book, with Mutton, who abides in filthy places and begins to stink after a short time? Battle on the table is inevitable. Troops are rallied on both sides. After fighting has commenced, the outcome seems uncertain for a time. The defection of part of King Honey's army, carefully prepared by Fat Tail, is decisive. 'This turned the encounter into a picnic', as Finkel translates racily.[110] King Mutton is victorious in the end, after the enumeration and description of countless dishes (many of them omitted in Finkel's translation), and the tale ends fittingly with a banquet at the court of the Mamluk sultan, where the various edibles and dishes, now depersonified, are being consumed with relish. That not only the conclusion but in fact the whole battle is one great banquet is obvious, for instance from the recurrent expression *maydān al-khiwān*, 'battleground of the table' as the place of action.[111] The equation of table and battleground is helped by etymology (*mā'ida/maydān*); hence to dream interpreters a table – whatever else it stands for – may denote strife and battle.[112]

The endless lists of dishes, especially in the rallying of troops and the description of the battle, 'seriously obstruct the flow of the narrative', according to Finkel, who is, however, not blind to the fact that they are in a sense the raison-d'être of the experiment and that the author should not be blamed.[113] The inclusion of the lists is not merely an advertising device, it is a powerful literary element: lists may have a comic effect, and the surfeit of dishes is here extremely appropriate. Other effective literary techniques include the use of rhymed prose, the quotation of poetry or Koranic verses, at times deliberately out of context, at other times so well integrated that they are easily overlooked.[114] The main technique is of course the personification of inanimate objects and substances, here rather more striking than in the average literary debate because there is far more action. The main actors, the two opponents and their viziers, emirs and chamberlains and messengers may stand for real persons at the Mamluk court, but this is difficult to prove.

Finkel calls the story 'utterly devoid of a moral'; it cannot be considered a fable, he says, 'since no didactic element is discernible. To impute to it a symbolism would also be unwarranted'.[115] The battle is between rich and poor food, or food of the rich versus that of the poor, and Finkel surmises that it was made in praise of the lavish kitchen at the Sultan's court, 'as the most literary food-register that ever issued from the pen of a writer'.[116] Although one is reminded of the European theme of the battle between Carnival and Lent,[117] it seems to me that Finkel may well be right. High and low cooking, to borrow Jack Goody's expressions,[118] are contrasted, but not at the moral expense of the high.

The contrast between high and low, or rich and poor, in the story of King Mutton should not be taken too strictly, however. Although King Honey's followers are described as 'paupers' (*mafālīs*),[119] and it is true that on the whole dishes with meat would have been more difficult to obtain for the poor than sweets and dairy products, yet it turns out that on King Honey's side there are countless meatless dishes that seem rich and luxurious enough. Many literary debates are peacefully concluded by the demonstration that the opponents may be reconciled and mutually assist each other. Here, too, it is obvious that the aim of the composition is, at least partly, to show that at the Sultan's court both kinds of food are found and consumed in great quantities. After all, Meat and Sweet do not merely appear at the table in successive dishes but are very often combined in recipes, as may be ascertained by anyone who cares to look up recipes of dishes described in *al-Ḥarb al-ma*ᶜ*shūq* in the contemporary cook-book *Kanz al-fawā'id*. Appropriately, when Fat Tail tries to win over some of King Honey's subjects, he promises Sugar that King Mutton will make him lord over dishes such as *lubābiyya* (*Kanz*, p. 39, contains honey and chicken), *khashkhāshiyya* (p. 23, includes 'red meat' and sugar or honey), *sitt al-nūba* (pp. 32, 35, 57: chicken and sugar or honey), *asyūṭiyya* (pp. 55, 104, 106 combining Fat Tail, *alya*, himself and honey, dates and sugar), *ḥubayshiyya* (not found),[120] *qishmishiyya* (not found),[121] *fustuqiyya* (pp. 17, 32–33, 36; it may involve chicken and sugar) and *bunduqiyya* (pp. 33, 39, 266–67, may combine chicken and honey).[122]

Our knowledge of Arab food, at least from Abbasid times onward, is inevitably biased towards the high side. The cookery books tend to represent haute cuisine and neglect simple fare. Even though everyday dishes figure freqently in anecdotes, popular stories enjoyed by the masses commonly prefer to relish in the depiction of precisely the rich and costly food that is beyond the reach of the audience. Recipes for 'low' dishes - who, of those who would need them, could read them? - are exceptional. In the chapter on food in al-Ghuzūlī's *Maṭāli*ᶜ *al-budūr*, the entry on the popular dish called *kishk*, made of wheat and milk, consists of a mere six words: 'Galen said, 'Noble parents, low offspring''.[123]

4. From *Falūdhaj* to *Fūl*: Different Food for Different People

The awareness that particular kinds of food are associated with different groups or classes of people is ubiquitous in Arabic literature, and reference has been made to it in the present study on several occasions. A particular kind of woman of easy virtue, who makes her victims believe that she is an innocent girl from the countryside, carries to that end a bag filled with *kishk*, chickpeas, lentils and eggs.[124] Everyone eats bread, but 'princes eat *samīd* (semolina bread), the élite eat *ḥuwwārā* (white bread), the populace eat *khushkār* (bread made of coarse flour), and ascetics eat barley bread', it is stated.[125] Only exceptionally may such divisions be broken down: when Sulaymān/Solomon is said to have fed the people on white bread while himself eating barley bread, it is in order to stress his asceticism and his wealth.[126]

> Kebab is the food of vagabonds (*ṣaᶜālīk*), water and salt is the food of bedouins, *harīsa*s and (sheep's) heads are the food of those in power (*al-salāṭīn*), roast meat is the food of immoral people (*duᶜᶜār*), and vinegar with oil is the food of people like ourselves,

said a certain Yazīd Ibn Rabīᶜ.[127] His classification of people is rather odd, as is the division of foodstuffs. One may compare a remark in the brief but interesting autobiographical introduction of *Aḥsan al-taqāsīm* by the traveller and geographer al-Muqaddasī (c. 380/990):

> I (. . .) consumed *harīsa* with the Sūfis, *tharīd* (broth) with the cenobites, and *ᶜaṣīda* (flour, butter and honey pudding) with seamen (. . .) At Makka I have drunk *sawīq* (ptisan) from the public fountain, I have eaten bread and chickpeas in the monasteries . . .[128]

In the two preceding passages, *harīsa* is associated with two very different groups of people, rulers and Sufis. It is, of course, possible that the use of the same word is misleading and that *harīsa* came in various forms, simple and luxurious. The cookery books tend to give the latter variety: one should not believe that the '*harīsa* of the Sūfis' was identical with the *harīsa* described in the 'Baghdad Cookery-Book' translated by Arberry, for instance.[129] The same is valid for a great many other culinary terms.

One can only conclude that one should not jump to conclusions on the basis of such cryptic statements as those quoted above, by Yazīd Ibn Rabīᶜ and al-Muqaddasī. Sufis are supposed to be moderate, abstemious, even ascetic in their eating habits, a picture confirmed in countless anecdotes and stories and, naturally, in works written by and for Sufis, such as Abū Ṭālib al-Makkī's great *Qūt al-qulūb* ('Food of the Hearts').[130] They have even been condemned for their mortification of the body, witness the attacks by Ibn al-Jawzī (d. 597/1200).[131] Yet one may read elsewhere that 'the eating of Sufis is proverbial: one may say, 'eating more than the Sufis' or '. . . more than a Sufi'. This is because it is their profession to eat a lot. They take big mouthfuls . . .'[132] Such statements derive from a combination of anti-mystical prejudices and the existence of 'false', or at least hedonistic, Sufis.

If 'true' Sufis or pious people abstain from good food for the sake of religion and the Hereafter, there were other people who made life difficult for more earthly, non-religious reasons, by being extremely particular in their choices. The 'refined people' or *ẓurafā'*[133], according to al-Washshā' (d. 325/937), would not eat offal such as kidneys, tripe, spleen, lungs; nor dried meat (*qadīd*), *tharīd*, or the greens in the soup. They should not eat locusts, prawns (*irbiyān*), or any pulses or grains that cause flatulence. They must avoid, among many lesser known edibles, endive, dodder (*ukshūth, Cuscuta*), turnip, cress, leek, onions, garlic, lettuce, cucumber, asparagus, anything with stones including olives and dates, apricots, peaches, figs, plums, watermelons and pomegranates.[134] This remarkable passage, which employs rhyming prose and other literary techniques, almost reads as a satire on the ultra-fussy and finical, but it is not meant to be. Al-Washshā' uses the descriptive mode, although it is obviously at least partly intended to be prescriptive. It is difficult to determine how widespread such restrictive eating habits were; one can be sure that most of the numerous persons called *ẓarīf* are merely being described as 'witty' or 'elegant', without any implication that they adhered to the strict behavioural rules outlined by al-Washshā'.

There are few persons whose eating habits are described in any reliable detail. The habits attributed to the Prophet should, of course, be classified not so much as description as prescription *par excellence*. To a lesser degree the reports about other famous and pious people are naturally embellished in order to conform to what must be expected of them. Michael Cooperson has written, in a comparative study of the reports on two famous men, Aḥmad Ibn Ḥanbal, the jurist and theologian (d. 241/855), and Bishr al-Ḥāfī, the mystic (d. c. 226/840):

> The reader will have noticed the importance of food in the biography of both men, who seem to have practiced a sort of competitive anorexia for the sake of their souls - justified, perhaps, in view of Adam's fall from Paradise for the tasting of a fruit.[135]

There is a report on Bishr's abstention from food even in Paradise,[136] whereas another story tells how Ibn Ḥanbal, still on earth, is mysteriously presented, probably by an angel, with a big hamper containing twenty milk loaves, peeled almonds whiter than snow and more fragrant than musk, a hot roast lamb with saffron, together with salt and vinegar, fruit and sweets made from sugar. He does not refuse the gift.[137]

Convincing on account of its details is the description of the table manners and diet of the famous historian and Koranic exegete al-Ṭabarī (d. 311/923).[138] His behaviour while dining was impeccable and elegant (*kāna ajmala l-jamāᶜati aklan wa-aẓrafahum ᶜishratan . . . mā ra'aytu aẓrafa aklan*). He kept the common dish as clean as possible. At every bite he would say 'In the name of God . . .' and cover his beard with his left hand to protect it against dripping and spilling. His diet was inspired by medical considerations: he did not eat fat, 'which soils the stomach', but only meat without fat, cooked with raisins. He avoided sesame seeds and honey ('they corrupt the stomach and cause bad breath'), and dates ('they pollute the stomach, weaken eyesight and cause dental decay'). It is surely remarkable that this pious scholar, steeped as he was in the Tradition of the Prophet, did not slavishly follow his Sunna and refrained from eating dates and honey, both beloved by Mohammed. His preference for semolina bread (*khubz samīdh*) had a partly religious background: it involved washing the wheat, which would remove impurities (*tuṭahhiru najisan*) not removed, in his opinion, by sun, fire and wind. Mention is made of a dish specially made for him from condensed sheep's milk made into a broth with thyme, poppy seed and olive oil. He was fond of *isfīdhbāj*[139] and *zīrbāj*.[140] After a meal he slept in a ventilated room,[141] wearing a short-sleeved chemise (*qamīṣ*). The rest of the day is spent in prayer, writing and teaching. 'Thus he divided his night and day between the well-being of himself, his religion, and mankind'.[142] In this sentence, 'of himself' is expressed by means of the usual Arabic idiom, *nafsihi*, literally 'his soul', but it is clear that the bodily self is meant above all: one does not have to be an ascetic to be a great and pious scholar.

5. Peasant Fare: al-Shirbīnī's *The Nodding Noddles*

In spite of the numerous recommendations of moderation in eating and condemnations of saturation (*shibaᶜ*), there are remarkably few satirical texts where people are upbraided for their luxurious eating habits, as they often are in medieval European literature.[143] One is chided and mocked on account of gluttony and overeating, but enjoying good food is not usually condemned. The victory of King Mutton and his troops over the less costly edibles is seen as a good thing. Fullness and satiety are to be preferred to leanness and dieting. To some people a rich diet is compulsory:

> Ḥamdān said: 'I once said to a slave-girl I wanted to buy, a nice soft-bodied plump girl, 'What did you eat at your master's place?' She said, '*Mubaṭṭan*.' I asked, 'And what is *mubaṭṭan*?' 'Rice saturated with milk, with *fālūdhaj* saturated with honey, and *khabīṣa* saturated with oil, sugar and saffron'. 'The right thing for you,' I said'.[144]

The Bedouins were sometimes derided for their meagre and repellent food, as we have seen. Unlike them, peasants are almost wholly invisible in Arabic literature, with one prominent exception. Peasant fare is ridiculed at length in the famous satire by al-Shirbīnī (*fl.* 1098/1687) on the Egyptian *fallāḥīn*, *The Nodding Noddles*, or *Jolting the Yokels* (*Hazz al-quḥūf*).[145] It must now surely count as one of the politically most incorrect pieces of Arabic literature. At the beginning, in the *laudatio*, the author praises God for having ennobled mankind, at the same time having made people's natures divergent; 'He has distinguished a man with good taste through subtlety of essence and sweetness of tongue; whereas he has characterized his opposite by a bad disposition and a coarse nature, like common rustic people'.[146] The book consists of two parts. In the first al-Shirbīnī describes life in the Egyptian countryside in general; the second and longest part contains a detailed mock commentary on a poem in the Egyptian dialect by Abū Shādūf, a spurious poet (who, amusingly, has been taken to be a real person by some benighted critics).[147]

Al-Shirbīnī presents his text as an exercise in nonsense, 'stupid trifles, depraved stuff, shameless things; something that resembles the work of Ibn Sūdūn.'[148] It is true that before this, on the first page of his text, he has already explained that the stupidity and depravity of his work are a consequence of its subject matter. But passages such as the one just quoted seem to make it clear that al-Shirbīnī is not only vilifying and abusing the peasants but also deliberately degrading and abasing himself and his own text, thus considerably undercutting his attack on the fellahs. Undermining oneself is part and parcel of *hazl*.

In this text food is a prominent element; in the poem and its commentary it is even dominant. Of the 47 lines of the poem, the majority (lines 10–42) deal with peasant fare.[149] The first, general, part only mentions food in passing, as in the description of a wedding meal (pp. 9–10). A recurrent topic is the theme of 'peasant goes to town', in order to contrast rustic squalor and ignorance with urban or courtly luxury and sophistication. In one story the caliph Hārūn al-Rashīd treats a country bumpkin (*qiḥf min quḥūf al-rīf*) to buns of *khashtanānak*,[150] a kind of rich pastry. (13–15). The peasant, first taking the buns to be balls to play with, exclaims,

> All my life I have eaten lentils, *baysār* (or *bēsār*, mashed beans),[151] *kishk* (cakes of bulgur with sour milk)[152] with *fūl midammis* (cooked broad beans with oil). I have never seen anything like this. But I've hear Umm Mi^{c}ēka, my granny, say that 'the hammam is Paradise on Earth'; now I know that this must be the hammam that they're always talking about.[153]

Another peasant in town is given a dish of fried fish and thinks it must be *kunāfa*, a well-known sweet pastry. Boasting of this to his fellow villagers he produces some fish bones, kept in his skullcap, which hard evidence silences their initial scepticism.[154] But even in his village there is a distinction between the relatively good food the villagers are forced to provide for the tax farmer (*multazim*) on his round with his *mushidd* or steward and his *naṣrānī* or Christian tax collector:

> They are obliged to provide for the steward and the Christian and all the tax farmer's retinue when they arrive, to give them food and drink and all they need: fodder for their animals, all the food they need, such as meat and poultry. Even if one is poor one is forced to comply, or else one is apprehended by the steward and beaten painfully. It happens that someone flees, not finding anything else that he can do; then the steward sends for his children and wife and threatens them, demanding from them whatever he needs. The woman may have to pawn some of her jewellery or her clothes in order to buy poultry or meat so that she may feed them, while depriving her own children out of fear for herself, in case it should not be enough for them. Sometimes a peasant raises chickens without eating them himself or giving them to his family, for fear of being beaten or imprisoned. Likewise he saves his clarified butter and his wheat flour for such dire occasions, while he cooks his own food in sesame oil and eats barley bread.[155]

In this passage, and there are a few more like this, there is no trace of the mockery and the satire that dominates the text: like many works of *adab*, the author assumes many voices, which makes the text a heterophonic, or cacophonic (rather than polyphonic) composition. The term polyphonic I adopt from Mikhail Bakhtin, who introduced the term into literary criticism, and through whom it has gained some popularity. Heterophony should be distinguished from it, as it is in musicology; it refers to the simultaneous sounding of two or more versions of basically the same melody, for instance a plain one and a more embellished one. This is the normal technique of Arabic music, where true polyphony is unknown; as a literary counterpart one could mention the usual relationship between a text (*matn*) and its commentary (*sharḥ*). The word polyphonic refers to a texture of several different parts that are relatively independent yet go well together, in principle. Cacophony, of course, is the simultaneous sounding of disparate and discordant parts. Musicologists seem to dislike it;[156] but it could be applied to literary texts such as *Hazz al-quḥūf*, in which the several voices are far from harmonious and concordant, and where the commentary on the poem deliberately jars with the poem itself. We ought to be wary, however, of necessarily attaching a pejorative sense to the term cacophony, for in literature, and especial in marginal and parasitic modes such as invective and parody, ugliness and discordance may be intentional. Much of *Hazz al-quḥūf* is a study in ugliness, bad taste, coarseness, and distortion.

Abū Shādūf's poem is a mock complaint which parodies the rather more heroic complaints found in popular epics and romances such as that of the Banū Hilāl.[157] Food is conspicuously present in the poem because the poet sings of its absence: he sees it or imagines it, but to him it is unattainable. Words have to do instead of real food, even though he only mentions simple fare: *kishk*, *fūl midammis*, *bēsār*, *bilīla* (stewed wheat with milk and sugar), *qulqās* (Colocasia, taro root), *mishsh* (milk-based liquid with lumps of fermented cheese), onions, leek, sour milk, *umm il-khulūl* (freshwater mussels), *mishakshik* (a dish containing fish skins, onions and oil, according to the commentary), *gilbān*[158] (vetch), lentils, bread, rice pudding, *hayṭaliyya* (broth of wheat and milk), salted fish, pigeon and tripe.[159] The commentary is a mixture of the ludicrous and the serious. A running gag is mock etymology, just as it was in Ibn Sūdūn: thus the word *kishk* is a palindrome because if one turns over a cake of *kishk* it looks the same; it is called *kishk* because it shrinks (*yakishh*) when it dries; possibly it is derived from saying *kshksh!* when one throws a piece of kishk to a dog, or from *kushk* (kiosk, pavilion), or from *kuss*, because it may resemble a female pudendum, the word having been changed for reasons of euphony, etc.[160] Sheer nonsense is alternated with plain and informative passages. Thus the author provides many recipes for dishes, revealing an intimate knowledge of his subject. On several occasions he compares two or more varieties of one dish, one of them being the coarse rural variety, and other ones being more refined versions. Several recipes for making *kishk* are given, with regional differences, that are said to be good to eat; especially the kind made by those of Turkish descent, prepared with lamb or poultry and rice, is delicious, according to al-Shirbīnī.

> As for the bad kind, which upsets the stomach, mentioned in the verse [by Abū Shādūf], that is the *kishk* of the villagers and rural parts. They do not care too much about washing and purifying it well when they cook it. They put it into a pan or cauldron or kettle and put it on the fire. They add some bruised broad beans and cook it until it is ready. Then they add a chopped onion and a little bit of sesame oil and fry it in it. They scoop it into bowls or earthenware vessels. They crumble some durra bread or barley bread on it. Each person eats one or two bowlfuls, chewing and guzzling . . . This is their most precious dish . . . They do not cook it with rice or meat, for they rarely have rice, and meat they eat only once a year[161] . . . Another kind they make without broad beans, just *kishk* without adding any condiments, which they call *nayrab*.[162] This and the preceding kind cause flatulence and upset the stomach . . . The people of Upper Egypt cook it without purifying it. As a result it resembles nothing as much as bran cooked merely with vinegar. It is neither nutritious nor tasty . . .[163]

Similar contrasts are given for *midammis* (151-52), *bēsār* (153-55), *bilīla* (158), *khubbayz* (mallow, 165), lentils (168-69), rice pudding (172), *qaṭāyif* (179), salt-cured fish (*fisīkh*, 188), pastry (*fiṭīr*, 192) and tripe (198). As Baer observed,[164] the dishes made by the Turks are particularly praised. Between the recipes and other factual passages, which are always derogatory towards the peasants, implicitly by means of the contrast with urban luxury or explicitly by references to their unrefined manners, there are anecdotes and titbits of nonsensical learning. Not unexpectedly, al-Shirbīnī makes the most of the scatological consequences of the digestive process: references to excrement, colic or flatulence abound, culminating in a lengthy tract on farting.[165]

In the course of the discussion of rice pudding the author inserts a sermon of his own composition on foodstuffs.[166] In this parody the preacher praises God

> with the praise of one who eludes hunger in uncanny fashion; whom Allāh has blessed with a bowl of flour-gruel and a thin sheet of unleavened bread; and who, filling his belly thereof, in consequence thinks well of his maker, and then reclines by His grace in restful slumber.

He goes on to lambast his flock in rhymed prose:

> O ye people! Why do I see you forgetful of yellow rice seasoned with honey and abstaining from mutton with peppered rice, from almond cakes served on trays, and from fat geese and roasted chickens? O, brethren, it behoves none but paupers to act in such wise.

To poor peasants he recommends rice pudding as an excellent dish, describing the homecoming of the 'great sheikh' while the food is served:

> And you see nothing but hands cutting (bread), and hear naught save the gulping of the gullets and the crunching of the jaws. The big lumps they swallow bring tears to their eyes, and their insatiate bellies grow yet keener (with greed).

Whereas coarse food such as lentils, beans or peas should be avoided, the rich ought to eat rich food, especially mutton, the lord of all foods, but also many other dishes savoury and sweet, the latter headed by Sultan Sugar-Candy, son of Cane. At this point an element of personification enters the sermon, together with some of the martial metaphors that informed Ibn al-Ḥajjār's *al-Ḥarb al-maʿshūq*, in which King Mutton defeated King Honey. Here, the enemy is paupers' food: 'O my God, kill the three rascals, the lentils, the pea and the bean.' The only gluttons mocked in the mock sermon are the pauper peasants, as quoted above, who are, by way of a final vilifying flourish, taunted in the last sentence with a veiled reference to their sexual habits involving mules.[167] In

Europe such mock-sermons had their place in the ecclesiastical year, particularly during Shrovetide;[168] one might expect that al-Shirbīnī's sermon and similar compositions were associated with Ramadan, but if this is so, the text itself contains no unambiguous allusions to this.[169]

Towards the end of the poem (lines 39–46) the spurious peasant poet expresses his desire to go to town, where it his utmost ambition to glut on lupin seeds (*tirmis*) and baked beans. Even though the last line of the poem (47) is a straightforward prayer to the Prophet, the 'commentary' soon closes with a last bunch of ribald jokes, both irreverent and irrelevant, for they are not concerned with peasants. Finally al-Shirbīnī, in a poem in *rajaz*, once more describes his book in deprecatory terms ('like a piece of dung on a stream' etc.) and mentions a scholar, Aḥmad al-Sandūbī, as the one who urged him to compose it.[170] For once, this information seems to be true, for unlike Abū Shādūf this al-Sandūbī was a real person, like al-Shirbīnī himself of rural origin.[171] The book has been taken to be an exercise in veiled subversion, by those critics who have read the text as an indictment against Ottoman government; it could with some justification be read, rather, as an exercise in repression. To exclusively believe the former is a delusion, to argue only the latter would be misleading, for either reading imposes a one-sidedness and a seriousness alien to the mood and the mode of the work, which, for all its uniqueness, shows a very familiar mixture of the serious and the jesting, where true facts alternate with perfect nonsense and gross lies, in which blatant contradictions are rife and perfectly acceptable, and where bitter mockery and compassion are not incompatible. That food is so prominent in *Hazz al-quḥūf* is scarcely surprising. It offers rich possibilities for texts dealing with extremes, since it lends itself to themes ranging from utmost luxury and delight to utter filth and loathing.

CHAPTER VI

Alimentary Metaphors

1. Two Good Things: Food and Sex

Food and coition, or consumption and sexual consummation, are obviously linked, for instance in the Arabic expression *al-aṭyabān*, 'the two good (or nice) things'. But for these, life is not worth living and one might as well be dead: 'If those two good things have eluded you, you should not care/when that day comes upon you that you used to fear.'[1] Al-Ghazālī deals with them together in one of the forty 'books' of his *Revivification*, entitled 'Breaking the Two Lusts' (*Kasr al-shahwatayn*).[2] Food and sex are two of the three 'fleshly delights' of this world in a saying attributed to the pre-Islamic poet Ta'abbaṭa Sharrā and others: 'I have never enjoyed anything as much as three things: eating flesh, riding on flesh and rubbing flesh against flesh'.[3] Ibn Zuqqāᶜa (d. 816/1414) describes in a short poem that, when ill, he was revived by the combination of a female visitor and food, '. . . because I am a man who loves women and a loaded table' - perhaps with an arch allusion to the fourth and fifth suras of the Koran (entitled 'Women' and 'The Loaded Table', respectively).[4]

The literary interactions of food and sex are manifold: they may supplement each other or be substituted for each other, on the level of imagery as well as the level of themes and motifs. Chaste lovers are conventionally uninterested in food and are consequently wasting away. Active lovers, too, are sometimes praised for their modest eating habits. One of the women praising or criticizing their husbands in the famous 'story of Umm Zarᶜ' berates her spouse for eating and drinking much but neglecting her in bed; a commentator adds: 'the Arabs pride themselves on eating and drinking little and copulating much, for therein lies an indication of their virility and manliness.'[5] This may reflect not merely the attitude, or presumed attitude, of women towards men's alimentary and sexual behaviour, but also, it seems, the old Bedouin heroic ideal of abstemiousness and being able to cope with hunger. In other reports active love and a good appetite are deemed perfectly compatible. The famous ᶜĀ'isha Bint Ṭalḥa (a granddaughter of Abū Bakr) is impressed by ᶜUmar Ibn ᶜUbayd Allāh, one of her several husbands, and says to him admiringly, the morning after their wedding night, 'I have never seen anyone like you; you have eaten as much as seven men, prayed as much as seven men, and fucked as much as seven men!'[6] Just as some foodstuffs have an aphrodisiac effect,[7] so literary descriptions of rich food may act as a stimulant preparing scenes of love and lust, an obvious example being the bawdy tale of the Porter and the Three Ladies in *The Thousand and One Nights*, in which the porter is regaled by the three ladies on a rich diet of food and sex; the tale is introduced by a shopping expedition to the fruiterer's, the butcher's and the grocer's.[8] Admittedly, it is wine rather than food that more commonly serves this purpose in stories and poems since Abū Nuwās; the combination, or rather succession, of food and wine is so frequent that the sequence eating - drinking - love play could be called a narrative formula. The identical sequence is found, on a smaller scale, in expressions such as 'edibles, drinks, and sex *(al-ma'ākil wa-l-mashārib wa-l-bāh)'* or 'food, drink, and women *(al-ṭaᶜām wa-l-sharāb wa-l-nisā')*'.[9] The elements are nicely contained in the story of an extraordinary reception of a company of people, including the narrator, by a mysterious host, as told in al-Tanūkhī's *Nishwār al-muḥāḍara*.[10] The liberal and libertine host mentions 'food, drink, and sex' as 'all that a guest needs and is entitled to'.[11] These three basic elements are linked together by other sensualities: erotic temptations are offered, but resisted, during the bath that precedes the meal; erotic anticipations are present during or after the meal, when young boys massage the guests, and during the drinking, when beautiful girls sing and play. A cyclic pattern is suggested because sexual intercourse should, strictly, be followed by a ritual ablution preferably to be performed in the bath: a cycle of sensual pleasure that could last forever, it would seem, but for the lack of sleep.

In the bawdy short story of the Slaughterhouse-cleaner and the Noble Lady in *The Thousand and One Nights*,[12] we find the same sequence: bathing, eating, drinking with music, and love-making; but here the pleasantness is subverted by the liberal addition of excremental elements. The lady, who wants to revenge herself on her unfaithful husband, has sworn to have an affair with the filthiest man she can find. The hero is called a *ḥashshāsh*, usually translated as 'slaughterhouse-cleaner'; this is in fact his job, as he describes himself. Yet the word *ḥashshāsh* is surely derived neither from *aḥshā'* ('innards') nor from *ḥashīsh* ('hashish') but from *ḥushsh* ('privy, latrine') and means 'privy-cleaner'. The cloacal associations are rubbed in by the concluding poem uttered by the hero, in which he says that he would like to kiss the lady's left hand (which is used for cleaning oneself after defecation), rather than her right hand (used for eating). Here kitchen-humour and privy-humour are inextricably intertwined; it is only appropriate that the lady should have looked for her husband first in the privy, but found him *flagrante delicto* in the kitchen, rogering a kitchen-maid.

Conversely, the absence of food is sometimes linked to the absence of sex. There are, it appears, different attitudes. Fasting is sometimes recommended against inappropriate sexual urges. Ibn Qayyim al-Jawziyya, in his book on love, quotes lines by a slave girl, addressed to al-ᶜUtbī (d. 228/842) who was enamoured of her:

> If you are stirred by carnal lust (*ghulma*), then cure your lust with fasting.
> You suffer not from love: you only want to copulate.[13]

Hunger, whether voluntarily induced by fasting or the result of unsought poverty, may dispel lust and even love. That food may take the place of sex was expressed by an anonymous poet, who was apparently not sorry for the substitution:

> Make your camel kneel down and dip a piece of bread in oil if passion overcomes you: it may compensate the loss of your beloved!
> When painful hunger and passion come together you will forget the union with full-breasted girls.[14]

However, this runs counter to the conventions of literature. It is no coincidence that Abū Tammām (d. 231/846), the compiler of the famous anthology from which these lines are taken, placed them in a short chapter of 'pleasantries' (*mulaḥ*), with similar jesting violations of decorum and received opinions. An anonymous one-liner from the same chapter illustrates the fact that love often acts through the stomach:

> She shot at me the arrows of love: tips of dates, feathers of barley gruel.[15]

He means, the commentator says, that she fed him with such dainty morsels 'and therefore he fell in love with her'. Al-Tawḥīdī tells a story of a man in love with a Byzantine slave girl, who keeps asking her to prepare rich meals for him and his friends. Exasperated, the girl finally sends an epigram that ends with: 'Once, love was in the heart; now it has settled in the stomach.'[16] A good meal greatly restores and revives poor Shāhzamān in the frame story of *The Thousand And One Nights* after the awful and sexually frustrating shock of witnessing the unfaithfulness of his wife ('he was himself again, or even better').[17]

As everyone knows, a true lover, in the style of the ᶜUdhrites, fasts and wastes away because his love distracts him from all trivial things such as hunger. This very common topos, which needs no illustration, was commented on in a satirical epigram attributed to the most famous ᶜUdhrite poet, Jamīl (d. c. 82/701):

> Jaᶜfar surprises me! He avidly eats my loaf of bread, while shedding tears because of Juml [a girl's name]:
> If your attachment were ᶜUdhrite you would not eat your belly full: love would have made you forget gorging yourself.[18]

Only in unserious poetry may one prefer bread to a beloved. A certain Abū l-Mukhaffaf, minor poet from Baghdad around the time of al-Ma'mūn (d 218/833) who specialized in poems on bread, does this by playfully rejecting the traditional *nasīb* or amatory introduction of *qaṣīda*s:

> Please, no abodes abandoned in the wastelands!
> Spare me your lines about expensive wines;
> No virgin girls with narrow waists and waistbands.
> Describe a noble loaf: a sun that shines,
> Or like the moon when it is full and round;
> For only then my poetry is sound.[19]

> I've given up all contacts with attractive girls.
> I've sobered up: no more consorting with all those
> Who please the eye until you die from love.
> Leave those campsite remains to stupid people
> Who cry at all abodes abandoned.
> Don't praise in poems beardless youths
> Or servants, or those pretty girls,
> But praise a loaf of bread, embellished with a crust
> Transcending all description.

It leaves a sober man madly in love, out of his wits,
So that he bungles his devotions.
The pattern on the loaf: like stars that rise at night.
Withholding such a loaf is insolence,
To grant it is a true donation.[20]

To call this jesting poetry is not to deny that part of it may have been meant seriously: perhaps the poet detested traditional *nasīb* – which hardly makes him subversive, since producing anti-*nasīb* was fashionable in his day. It is not at all unlikely that he did indeed prefer bread to romantic love. He used to roam the streets of Baghdad, riding on a donkey and begging bread from 'those with authority, merchants and artisans' (and keeping a little list with the names of his benefactors). It is not without significance, perhaps, that he made a girl (*jāriya*: slave girl or daughter?) ride with him. Abū l-Mukhaffaf's theme is occasionally found in later times. A Hispano-Arabic poet known for his *hazl*, Abū ᶜAbd Allāh Muḥammad Ibn Masᶜūd,[21] renounces love for food:

Keep lovers' habits far from me; no more passion and meetings;
Give me less weeping over traces, do not grieve over the departure in the morning!
A sensible person is not gladdened by a lover or by cheeks and glancing eyes:
Feeling like a king is rather having a dish of *tharīd* made of *tafāyā*[22] with fattened first-quality chicken.
If you ask me with whom I am in love and why my eyes pour forth tears,
I say: a *sikbāj*, dishes of *jamalī*,[23] tender roast meat, together with loaves of bread.
Bruised white flour[24] is sweeter to me than the saliva of the beloved who is embraced.[25]

In a story about the famous early Abbasid wit, Abū l-Ḥārith Jummayn (or Jummayz),[26] he makes a show of love to a girl who invites him for a meal. When the food is slow to come he complains. The girl says, 'Isn't it enough for you to look at me?' He answers, 'Dear lady, if Jamīl and [his beloved] Buthayna sat together from morning to evening without eating any food, they would spit in each other's faces.'[27] That good food may be a way to win someone's heart is suggested by the title of the cookery book by

Ibn al-ᶜAdīm, *al-Wuṣla ilā l-ḥabīb fī waṣf al-ṭayyibāt wa-l-ṭīb*, which I have loosely rendered before as 'The Way to the Heart Is Through the Stomach'. Literally, it means 'Union with the beloved: on the description of things nice [to eat] and perfume'; at the same time the word 'beloved' may be taken as a metaphor for the nice food itself that the book offers. Food and beloved have merged.

On the level of imagery, the beloved may be described in terms of food, or *vice versa.* Both are common and illustrations may be found in preceding parts of this study, such as the Prophet's comparison of his beloved wife ᶜĀ'isha to a dish of *tharīda*. The caliph ᶜUmar, comparing the virtues of marrying a virgin with those of marrying a non-virgin, likened the former to 'wheat that may be milled, made into dough and baked as a bread' and the latter to 'a traveller's ready snack: dates and cottage cheese'.[28] An anonymous line from the chapter of 'pleasantries' in Abū Tammām's *Ḥamāsa* runs:

> She has eyes of cottage cheese and dates; the rest of her is made of *tharīd*.[29]

The line, which has been ascribed to Diᶜbil (d. 244/859 or 246/860),[30] may be ironic, on a girl with an ugly face, as al-Rāghib al-Iṣbahānī seems to think.[31] But although the poet is obviously not altogether serious, attractiveness rather than ugliness is suggested.

There is something slightly daring about such imagery. One of the basic oppositions between sex and eating is that the former is normally a private and secret act, and the latter communal and public – not just in Arab society, but practically universally.[32] Expressing the attractiveness of a woman in culinary terms in poetry will thus make her, as it were, common property; doubly so, for poetry is a communal rather than a private medium. Conversely, when a dish is compared to a bride the poet seems to stress his appropriation of the food with the exclusion of others. Both acts, the communalization of the private and *vice versa*, are shameful. However, the power of poetry, or poetic techniques such as metaphor and simile, is such that it takes away the shame or at least mitigates it. Nevertheless, such imagery is usually close to *hazl*, 'jesting' if it is not straightforward jesting. In a humoristic form first found in al-Jāḥiẓ the idiom of several craftsmen and professionals is shown to be heavily influenced by their occupations, when they describe a trivial incident or make love poetry. Al-Jāḥiẓ includes a baker whose love-poem begins with 'Absence has kneaded the flour of passion in a bowl made of the wood of rejection', and a cook who turns his beloved into a range of delicatessen.[33]

Names of dishes are put to a peculiar, rather obscure use in a story told by the famous literate vizier al-Ṣāḥib Ibn ᶜAbbād (d. 385/995). A visitor saw in his company a dishy boy and looked at him 'almost eating him with his eyes'. The vizier said to him, '*Sikbāj*!'; the visitor replied, '*Kashkiyya*!'. Al-Ṣāḥib expressed his surprise at the quick repartee, since the names of both dishes hide intricate puns involving the reading of the letters with a different punctuation, a not uncommon literary pastime called *taṣḥīf*.[34] I must confess that I am unable to solve the riddle, but one can be certain that it is obscene.[35]

Besides specific comparisons of a woman or boy with something edible there are blanket equations of women with food. An attitude that is not only rather woman-unfriendly but gastronomically insensitive is evinced by the early prosaist and practical moralist Ibn al-Muqaffaᶜ (d. c. 139/756) when he warns against being infatuated with women, particularly other men's wives, since, as he maintains,

> all women are alike (. . .). He who prefers other men's property to his own is like someone who would rather have the food in other people's houses than that in his own. But women are in fact even more alike than one kind of food is to another; the various kinds of food of different people are more diverse in quality and kind than their women.[36]

This image is echoed in a story from the cycle of 'The Wiles of Women' in *The Thousand and One Nights*: in order to demonstrate that there is little to chose between women and that the king should not covet, David-like, another man's wife seen on a rooftop, the women in question (the wife of the vizier) prepares ninety different dishes for the king, all tasting the same. When the king expresses his surprise, she explains: 'You possess ninety concubines in your palace, all of different colours (*alwān*, also 'dishes'), yet of the same taste.' The king, ashamed, repents, even though he might have argued that preparing ninety different dishes that differ in taste is surely easier than making them all taste the same.[37]

For food lovingly described as the beloved, one may refer to some of the 'banquet poems' or Ibn Sūdūn's verse, quoted before. A dish of *narjisiyya* is like a bride, as is the cook who serves the food.[38] Al-Thaᶜālibī's *Siḥr al-balāgha wa-siḥr al-barāᶜa* ('The

Magic of Eloquence and the Secret of Excellence'), a collection of literary expressions and idioms gleaned from his contemporaries and predecessors, offers several similar examples in the chapter on food: an apple combines the blush of the beloved and the paleness of the lover; a table on which food is served is like a bride on the wedding night – consumption and consummation are approaching – or like the face of a beautiful boy.[39] The fact that most names of dishes in Arabic are feminine facilitates the equation of gustatory and sexual attraction, even where no similes are made. 'She dazzles the eyes of the beholders with her light / and shows you the light of the full moon even before the evening has arrived' could have been a line of *ghazal*, but the subject is a dish of rice pudding.[40] However, masculine nouns can play the part equally well. Bananas (*mawz*) are, according to Ibn al-Rūmī,

> voluptuous (*khurramī*) food that flirts with one's bowels:
> Sweet smell, lovely taste, adding delight to delight:
> As it glides into where it goes, you imagine it is like deflowering virgins or like a slumber.
> If food ever lodged in the heart, hearts would contend with bowels over it.[41]

A watermelon (*biṭṭīkh*) is likened by Abū Jaᶜfar al-Baḥḥāthī al-Zawzanī (d. 463/1071) to

> A visitor, proud in her mantle, amazing me with her thick skin,
> Heavily built, short, her cheeks appearing pale –
> A fragrant smell went before her, that revived the soul of a lover whose passion has died –
> I got up quickly, deflowered her, and tasted her delicious sweet little honey.[42]

'Tasting' someone may be a straightforward euphemism for sexual intercourse: 'I should like to taste you (*an adhūqaki*)', says a man to a prostitute, 'to see whether you are nicer (*aṭyab*) or my wife'.[43] In exceptional cases, one may even fear that perverse and inhuman minds will go as far as to turn the metaphor into reality and combine consummation and consumption, as when princess Fakhr-Tāj, in the 'Story of ᶜAjīb and Gharīb', is afraid that a man-eating demon (*ghūl*) will take her maidenhood and eat her.[44]

In all this the connections between food and sex are explicit or at least obvious. However, literary texts have a habit of harbouring things that are not obvious at a first or second glance, particularly to critics from distant cultures and centuries. Does food stand for something else at all in Arabic literature, even if there are no unmistakable markers? If Emily Gowers is to be believed, references to food in Roman literature abound with hidden allusions, notably to sexual matters.[45] It is possible that it is no different in Arabic literature; I have already speculated on the nature of Ibn Sūdūn's obsession with bananas and syrup. Yet I am under the impression that, very often, the description of food in Arabic literature is just that, with little or no ulterior design apart from a naïve delight in describing delightful things in delightful ways.

Nor is there, I believe, much sex concealed in Arabic food descriptions. Freud, whose popularity in circles of literary critics still lingers on, has been turned upside down by some, for instance by Maud Ellmann who, in a context very different context (she is talking of self-starvation by prisoners)[46] reverses Freud's priorities by suggesting that food, not sex, is the source of desire and identity, and that the genital drive might be a substitute for the oral drive, rather than *vice versa*; a suggestion that should be taken seriously, but is, in the end, unconvincing.[47] If she were right, we ought to look for food hidden in love poetry and erotic or pornographic verse.[48] The results of such a research - admittedly cursory and provisional in view of the vast material - turn out to be somewhat disappointing. This might mean merely that it is hidden well. Only when one strains the limits of interpretation can anything be unearthed. Consider the following lines from a short love lyric by al-ᶜAbbās Ibn al-Aḥnaf (d. between 188/803 and 195/810):

> My heart calls me to what harms me and will give me sickness and pain.
> How can I be on my guard against an enemy when the enemy is lodged between my ribs?
> If you keep away from me, you who possess me, people will soon announce my death.[49]

Abū l-Ḥārith Jummayn provided an 'analysis': the poet must have been enamoured of a pretty female cook. The enemy inside the ribs is obviously the poet's stomach, or his heart or appetite which drives him to eat and drink things that will make him ill, waste his fortune and make him miserable. If his beloved stays away, he will die of hunger.[50] Of course, this jocular interpretation is wholly nonsensical, although it does not differ in principle from some of the extravaganzas of serious criticism from the 20th century working in the opposite direction. In an epigram by an anonymous woman[51] passion (*hawā*) is described in terms of tastes: it may be sweet (*ḥulw*) or bitter (*murr*); in the course of only three lines the verb 'to taste' (*dhāqa*) and the word 'taste' (*ṭaᶜm*) are each used three times. The metaphor is commonplace and only a Jummayn would conclude that the poem is really about eating.

On the surface level of texts food is not very prominent in erotic imagery. There are some obvious cases, of course: breasts are often compared to pomegranates, and those acquainted with homo-erotic verse will know who are meant by those who love figs.[52] A man and a girl, exchanging lewd gestures combined with appropriate allusions, advertize their 'fresh asparagus' and 'white bread', respectively.[53] 'Kitchen' (*maṭbakh*) may stand for the female pudendum.[54] But there is not much else, in spite of the richness of sex-related imagery in Arabic. Conversely, sex is absent from most descriptions of food, except occasionally a scurrilous comparison that may be found in jesting verse.[55] One surmises that this may be due to the fact that food and sex, the two appetites of belly and genitals (*shahwat al-baṭn* and *shahwat al-farj*) are too close to each another to be interesting to Arab poets or prose writers, who on the whole prefer imagery of a more far-fetched variety.

The most basic link between food and sex has already been briefly discussed in the first chapter, in connection with the display of generosity with food. In bedouin society this was the surest means not only of acquiring posthumous glory but of progeny. That a cultural habit such as this was acquired genetically, by means of a straightforward Darwinian evolution, has been convincingly demonstrated by Matt Ridley in two recent works that contain a synthesis of current research on sex and human evolution.[56] Human language, and by extension literature, plays its part in this process: its purpose is less to inform than to persuade and to deceive. A *qaṣīda* or report referring to a fictive or exaggerated prodigal slaughtering of camels may be more effective than actual generosity which remains unsung.

2. Dreams Sweet and Savoury

In the preceding chapter mention has been made of Ibn Sūdūn's stories of people having excessively sweet dreams, Cockaignian fantasies induced perhaps by a dose of hashish. In ordinary dreams food may play more modest roles. The Arabs assiduously continued the ancient tradition of explaining dreams and several compilations were made, combining Middle Eastern material with Greek classics such as the influential work by Artemidorus. Although these works often present and explain real, or allegedly real, dreams, far more space is given to hypothetical dreams about given objects, persons, concepts, situations or actions. Whether or not the interpretations given have any validity, these works offer some interesting insights into the associations allotted to many elements of mediaeval Arab civilization. Three such compilations will be used here. Two of these, like Artemidorus, are arranged thematically and have chapters on food: the work attributed to the father of Arabic oneirocriticism, Ibn Sīrīn (d. 110/728), but in fact written by a much later author, al-Dārī,[57] and another by Ibn Shāhīn (d. 872/1468).[58] The third work, by ᶜAbd al-Ghanī al-Nābulusī (d. 1143/1731), is primarily arranged alphabetically, although within one letter items are grouped thematically. Because the authors tend to incorporate as much earlier material as they can lay their hands on, it is relatively easy to extract many different and even contradictory interpretations of the same dream, which must have been of considerable help to users searching for favourable signs. Dreaming of *fālūdhaj*, for instance, is mostly deemed positive, as one would expect, yet it may denote hemiplegia (*fālij*) - false etymology being one of the favourite and time-honoured techniques of dream interpretation.[59] Dreaming of eating pork generally has negative associations in our Muslim authors, expectedly; yet we also read: 'Pork in a dream is good for everybody; dreaming of eating roast pork is very favourable and indicates a quick profit.'[60] In this case the reason is obvious: it is taken straight from Artemidorus.[61] Elsewhere, arbitrariness seems to reign. Nevertheless, some general tendencies may be discerned.

Dreaming of edible things is mostly explained as indicating material possessions, wealth and livelihood; meat in particular serves this purpose. Eating meat in a dream is generally something positive; surprisingly, a dissenting voice is heard in Pseudo-Ibn Sīrīn: 'meat stands for pains and illnesses; buying it means a disaster; succulent meat means death, eating it means absence',[62] a rare vegetarian attitude that is swamped by many positive statements about meat in this and the other sources. The logic of the interpreters is at times impeccable but leads to unexpected results: if eating meat means gaining power and dominance, and a snake means an enemy, than eating snake meat stands for subduing an opponent.[63] Few foodstuffs or dishes are in themselves to be interpreted negatively: a bad omen is usually connected with particular characteristics or circumstances occurring in the dream. Yet some food is obviously to some degree despised, especially when associated with the poor and the lower classes in general. Thus the beans called *lūbiyā*[64] stand for 'grief and sorrow',[65] as do cooked chickpeas[66] and *kishk*.[67] The social status of the food reflects upon the meaning of the dream, as can be expected. Al-Nābulusī explains that food of 'kings' stands for prestige and high standing, that of the 'police' (*shurṭa*) for adultery and partaking of forbidden things, that of the poor for repentance and divine guidance, and that of the bedouin for travel.[68]

Obviously, attitudes towards simple food are ambivalent. On the one hand, poor food is merely the negative counterpart of rich food, on the other it is given a morally and religiously positive sense, an interpretation coming from circles of the pious and mystics, to whom al-Nābulusī belonged. A similar ambivalence is shown in al-Nābulusī's comment on dreams about being hungry: it stands for death, fear, unbelief, poverty, loss; but 'according to others, (dreaming of) hunger is better than (dreaming of) satiety. . . He who dreams of being hungry for a long time will attain blessing after need and he will get wealth in proportion to his hunger.'[69] Sweets come in for the same ambivalence: according to al-Nābulusī they may stand for good things such as piety, marriage, pleasant words, being freed, being cured from disease and many other good things; yet sweetness may also denote illness. Much depends on the dreamer: thus sweet dreams may refer to the 'sweetness of religion' for true believers and to the 'sweetness of this world' for the sinner.[70] Similarly, dreaming of 'counterfeit fare' (*muzawwar*), dishes without meat intended for ailing people, is positive for a dreamer who is ill but negative for a healthy person.[71] Dreamers should not overstep the boundaries of their social class: the poor ought to dream of coarse bread (*khushkār*), the rich of white bread (*ḥuwwārā*). For dreaming of the former means poverty to the rich, dreaming of the latter bodes illness to the poor.[72]

Our authors are blissfully unaware of Freud. Sexual dreams, discussed with considerable frankness in some detail, are given down-to-earth interpretations often wholly unrelated to sexual matters; conversely, it cannot be said that sex was much on the mind of the oneirocritics, since they are more restrained in their interpretations than their twentieth-century colleagues. Sexualia are not frequently mentioned as *secundum interpretationis*; one will look in vain for obviously obscene explanations of suggestive foodstuffs like banana, carrots, asparagus, cucumbers[73] or figs. Marriage and other links between the sexes are by no means absent, however. The association of honey with sex and love-play (among other things) is found in the dream books too.[74] A loaf may mean a wife for a bachelor;[75] eating from a table could mean the same.[76] Dreaming of cheese (*jubn*) is marriage to a bachelor, a boy to a pregnant women, cowardice (also *jubn*) to a fighter.[77] He who dreams that he is performing ritual prayer while eating *ʿaṣīda*, *khabīṣ* or *fālūdhaj* will kiss a woman while fasting (a legally dubious act).[78] Plucking a ripe date means a rich and blessed marriage.[79] A table is sometimes said to stand for a woman;[80] to a bachelor it means marriage.[81] Consequently, eating from an overturned table may be explained as anal intercourse;[82] the image is known from other sources.[83] Poultry is more than once associated with women: one the one hand, consuming poultry could mean that one is deceived by one's wife; on the other hand chicken meat generally denotes benefit coming from women.[84]

Another recurrent oneirocritic equation is that of food and speech. Swallowing someone's sour food stands for hearing unpleasant words from him,[85] sweets may denote pleasant words,[86] whoever dreams of eating *ʿaṣīda* may hear joyful tidings,[87] and chewing stands for talking much.[88] Thus the various metaphorical and associative roles of food that were found in the literary sources discussed in this study are confirmed in the dream books, although it must be stressed, again, that the dizzying quantity of different interpretations ensures that the oneirocritic texts could be used to prove almost anything one wants. Both in literary criticism and oneirocriticism it is taken for granted that things may stand for other things. The difference is that in the latter this principle is compulsory and rigorously applied: everything means something else; whereas in literature not everything is metaphorical and figurative, except to those extremist searchers for deeper layers found amongst mystics, esoterici and some modern literary critics.

3. Texts and Tastes

One of the levels where food and texts come together is the perhaps universal occurrence of gustatory and culinary metaphors in literary criticism. There are many metaphors to be found in the metalanguage of the critics. Abd El-Fattah Kilito has studied some of these in a brief article, in which he mentions, among other things, the poem as a concrete product (clothes, jewellery) or as a body;[89] alimentary imagery is not discussed, in spite of the very common concept of 'taste' in literary criticism. In Europe, the term 'taste' became prominent in criticism in the late 17th century,[90] but long before that time gustatory terms such as *mel*, *fel*, *acetum* and *sal* ('honey', 'gall', 'vinegar' and 'salt') had been applied to various kinds of styles and modes; comparing words to honey is as old as literature itself (cf. Homer, *Iliad* i.49). The literal and figurative combine in a startling image in Ezekiel (2:8–9, 3:1–3), who is commanded to eat a book-roll and finds it 'as honey for sweetness', even though 'there was written therein lamentations, and mourning, and woe'.

In Arabic, gustatory metalanguage takes several forms. It was already pointed out that texts (the Koran, or Ibn Qutayba's anthology *ᶜUyūn al-akhbār*) are compared to a banquet; or that the terms for 'short poem' (*qiṭᶜa*) and 'formal ode' (*qaṣīda*) have some remote alimentary associations: 'piece (e.g. of meat)' and 'marrow-bone' (or 'dried meat'), respectively, although to my knowledge these meanings have not been exploited by literary critics. There is an interesting juxtaposition of food and text in a saying attributed to the Prophet: 'Use the two cures: honey and the Koran!';[91] it is in line with this saying that Ibn Qayyim al-Jawziyya, in his work on 'medicine of the Prophet', lists the Koran in an alphabetical list of foodstuffs.[92] The saying intends to convey the idea that the holy text is a potent cure, but at the same time it is suggested that the Koran is as sweet as honey.

Rabīᶜa Ibn Ḥudhār, appointed arbiter between four seventh-century poets, says to one of them, al-Zibriqān: 'Your poetry is like undercooked meat that is fit neither to be eaten nor to be left raw, to be used later.'[93] It is a pity that this impressionistic image is not explained: perhaps it means that the judge discerned a lack of polish; obviously, he found the poetry not quite digestible, hastily concocted, just as al-Shammākh described the hasty and furtive talk with his beloved as 'undercooked roast meat'.[94] In another version of this story it is one of the four poets, ᶜAbda Ibn al-Ṭabīb, who says to al-Zibriqān, describing his poetry: 'You found a slaughtered camel and have taken some nice bits and some bad bits.'[95]

Most often, the various tastes are applied to different kinds of discourse. ᶜĀ'isha is reported to have said, 'Make your children recite poetry so that their tongues will be sweet (*ta*ᶜ*dhub*)'.[96] There are countless instances of particular poems, passages or lines called 'sweet', either ᶜ*adhb* or, more often, *ḥulw*; jesting (*hazl*) or joking (*fukāha*, related to *fākiha* 'fruit') is frequently called 'sweet' and contrasted with 'bitter' seriousness (*jidd*). Even sad poems may be sweet: al-Mubarrad speaks of 'sweet elegies'.[97] 'Saltiness' (*malāḥa*), in Arabic, has associations that differ from those in Europe, for it does refer not so much to piquancy and raciness as to elegance, grace, beauty and wit; the same root produces *mulḥa*, 'pleasantry, anecdote, witticism'. The metaphorical difference between 'sweet/beautiful' and 'savoury/salty/pretty' is difficult to define. When applied to a beautiful human face, the former, it is said, is suitably attributed to the eyes, the former to the smile;[98] but in matters of style and eloquence no such distinctions are offered. A speech may juxtapose the sweet and the bitter: 'A tale tasting like honey, its beginning sweet, its end like bitter *khuṭbān* [a plant]'.[99] Sweetness and saltiness may be combined; an eleventh-century anthologist speaks of verses by Mihyār al-Daylamī (d. 428/1037) possessing 'an elegant (*malīḥ*) and sweet (ᶜ*adhb*) composition, and salt with sweetness is something wonderful'.[100] 'Piquancy' is sometimes rendered by *iḥmāḍ*, which is not very different from *hazl*; literally it means 'making sour or acid'.[101] The various tastes – often nine different tastes are discerned – were listed and categorized by scientists,[102] cooks[103] and lexicographers[104]; but even though their classifications are not rarely found in literary sources,[105] nobody tried to apply them systematically to literary criticism. Yet the word *dhawq* ('taste') received some attention from the critics.

'Tasting' in the sense of 'experiencing' is an old and common metaphor, found many times in the Koran. Al-Jāḥiẓ may have been the first to deal with the metaphorical uses of *dhawq* and its near-synonym *ṭa*ᶜ*m*.[106] Literary theorists use the term *dhawq* to express an undefinable quality, a *je ne sais quoi*, necessary for judging and, above all, making good poetry, for it seems that in Arabic the word 'taste' is more often used when speaking of the production of good style than of its reception by a listener or reader. The poet and theorist Ibn Ṭabāṭabā (d. 322/934) remarks at the beginning of his work on poetics that 'whoever has a sound nature and taste does not need to apply (the science of) prosody in order to compose poetry'.[107] Good poems are enjoyed by the mind just as subtly composed and delicious tastes are enjoyed by the palate;[108] bad products are rejected and the verb *majja*, literally 'to spit out', is very often used in this sense. Synaesthetically, the ears may be said to 'spit out' a bad poem.[109] 'Taste' is a quality as much of the critic as of the text that he tastes. This was memorably expressed by al-Mutanabbī in his famous line in which he criticizes his critics: 'He who has a bitter and sick mouth will find pure water bitter';[110] like Malvolio, they 'taste with distempered appetite'.[111]

Much later, Ibn Khaldūn (d. 808/1406) devotes a chapter to the concept of 'taste' in literary criticism;[112] he argues that it is strongly linked with language: those whose mother tongue is not Arabic cannot hope to acquire *dhawq*. His linguistic outlook is understandable since literary criticism, to him and most writers on poetics, is above all rooted in stylistics (*bayān* or *balāgha*). Throughout the centuries, 'sweetness' (*ḥalāwa* or *ᶜudhūba*) is usually attributed to diction and wording (*lafẓ*) rather than content and meaning (*maᶜnā*).

Apart from taste and tastes, gustatory metaphors are scarce in critical metalanguage, where sartorial terms (related to clothes, texts as textiles) are more prominent especially in the terminology of figures of speech (*badīᶜ*). One culinary term is sometimes found: a felicitous short interpolation in a sentence or line of verse may be called *ḥashw al-lawzīnaj*, 'almond-stuffed lozenge', as in the often-quoted line by ᶜAwf Ibn Muḥallim (d. c. 220/835):

> Eighty years - may [God] make you reach them! - have put my hearing in need of an interpreter.

Here, says al-Thaᶜālibī (who tells us that he has written a little book on the subject, entitled *ḥashw al-lawzīnaj*), the parenthesis is better than what surrounds it, just as the stuffing of *lawzīnaj* is tastier than its shell.[113] The term, it seems, was coined by al-Ṣāḥib Ibn ᶜAbbād.[114] Ibn Aflaḥ (d. 535/1141) informs us that he heard someone describe a similar happy parenthesis by al-Mutanabbī as *ḥashw al-qaṭā'if*.[115] There are no other terms for tropes or figures of speech derived from gastronomy. The terminology for literary genres and modes has no equivalents of, for instance, 'satire' and 'farrago', both derived from Latin and originally meaning 'hotch-potch, medley' (*satura*) or 'mishmash';[116] only *fukāha*, 'joking', has edible connotations, being related to *fākiha* 'fruit', as pointed out above.

This relatively meagre harvest will not, I trust, take away the overall impression that this study has aimed at making. The connections between dishes and discourse in Arabic are close and varied. The metalanguage of literary critics may not be food-centred; another kind of metalanguage, that of metaphors in book-titles, has more to offer. Books are called *Zād al-maᶜād*, 'The Provision for the Hereafter', *Zubdat al-ḥalab* 'Butter from the Milk', *Qūt al-qulūb*, 'Food for the Hearts',[117] *Nishwār al-muḥāḍara*, 'The Cud of Conversation', *Mawā'id al-afrāḥ fī fawā'id al-nikāḥ*, 'The Tables of the Wedding Feast: On the Benefits of Marriage' or *al-Kashkūl* 'The Begging Bowl'. If the present book had been written in Arabic some centuries earlier, it might have been entitled something like *Ṭaᶜām al-kalām wa-kalām al-ṭaᶜām*, 'The Food of Speech and the Speech of Food'.

Notes

Chapter I – Introduction

1 Translated by Arberry, see his 'A Baghdad Cookery-Book', p. 32.

2 Ibn Abī Uṣaybiʿa, *ʿUyūn al-anbā'*, p. 50.

3 See Norman Kiell, 'Food in Literature: A Selective Bibliography'. A recent addition is, for instance, the sometimes appetizing, at times distinctly unsavoury but in any case richly loaded monograph entitled *The Loaded Table: Representations of Food in Roman Literature*, by Emily Gowers.

4 Translated as *A Feast of Words: Banquets and Table Talk in the Renaissance.*

5 Ibn al-ʿAdīm, *al-Wuṣla ilā l-ḥabīb fī waṣf al-ṭayyibāt wa-l-ṭīb*, ed. Sulaymā Maḥjūb and Durriyya al-Khaṭīb (Vol. I is an introduction of more than 400 pp. by Sulaymā Maḥjūb on Arab culinary history).

6 Ibn Sayyār al-Warrāq, *Kitāb al-ṭabīkh*, ed. Kaj Öhrnberg and Sahban Mroueh. The editors hope to publish a translation and copious annotations (Introduction, p. iv). See also Kaj Öhrnberg, 'Ibn Sattār al-Warrāq's *Kitāb al-wuṣla ilà al-ḥabīb/Kitāb al-ṭabbākh*', in Manuela Marín & David Waines (eds.), *La alimentación en las culturas islámicas.*

7 Ed. by Manuela Marín and David Waines, Beirut - Wiesbaden, 1993. For a promised edition of another work, see Garbutt, 'Ibn Jazlah'.

8 For recent surveys of the literature on the history of Arab and Middle Eastern food, see the editors' Introduction (pp. 11-21) of Marín & Waines (eds.), *La alimentación*, and Peter Heine, 'Cultuur en culinaria'.

9 The same may be said of María Jesús Rubiera Mata, 'La dieta de Ibn Quzmān'.

10 Maxime Rodinson, 'Recherches', pp. 112-16.

11 Sabry Hafez, 'Food as a Semiotic Code in Arabic Literature'.

12 On classical Arabic literature, see also Geert Jan van Gelder, 'Eten, etiquette en ethiek: voedsel in de klassiek-Arabische literatuur', in Van Gelder & Buitelaar (eds.), *Eet van de goede dingen*, pp. 59-78.

13 Bürgel, 'Die ekphrastischen Epigramme', pp. 273-74.

14 Table manners are often described or prescribed in anthologies,

works on religious ethics and behaviour (such as al-Ghazālī's *Iḥyā' ᶜulūm al-dīn*), in at least one cookery book (Ibn Sayyār al-Warrāq, *al-Ṭabīkh*) and in a treatise by Jamāl al-Dīn Yaḥyā Ibn ᶜAbd al-ᶜAẓīm al-Jazzār, butcher and poet, in his *Fawā'id al-mawā'id*; see Renato Traini, 'Un trattatello di galateo ed etica conviviale'. See also my 'Arabic Banqueters: Literature, Lexicography and Reality'.

15 Cf. Manuela Marín and David Waines, 'The Balanced Way: Food for Pleasure and Health in Medieval Islam'.

16 Originally they may have come from different roots. Vollers suggested that *adab* might be a back-formation of from *ādāb*, plural of *da'b* 'custom'; see e.g. S.A. Bonebakker, 'Early Arabic Literature and the term *adab*'.

17 Ibn Rashīq, *ᶜUmda*, i, 211. Conversely, bad food may hinder the making of poetry, as Ibn Qutayba says (*al-Shiᶜr wa-l-shuᶜarā'* p. 81). Al-Jāḥiẓ, however, denies this (*Ḥayawān*, iv, 380-81). See Bettini, 'Alimentation et poésie', pp. 74 ff.

18 Ibn Rashīq, *ᶜUmda*, i, 214.

19 See e.g. David Waines and Manuela Marín, 'Foodways and the socialization of the individual'.

20 Jeanneret, *A Feast of Words*, p. 247.

21 Michel de Montaigne, *The Complete Essays*, tr. by M.A. Screech, Harmondsworth, 1993, p. 1071 (*Essays*, III,9); cf. Jeanneret, *A Feast of Words*, p. 139.

22 John Wilmot, Earl of Rochester, *The Complete Poems*, ed. David M. Vieth, New Haven and London, 1977, p. 144.

23 al-Shirbīnī, *Hazz al-quḥūf*, p. 223.

24 al-Wahrānī, *Manāmāt*, pp. 72-74.

25 Ibn al-Nadīm, *Fihrist*, p. 152, Yāqūt, *Muᶜjam al-udabā'*, xviii, 11.

26 See e.g. Joan Smith, *Hungry for you*, Eira Patnaik, 'The Succulent Gender'.

27 For a plethora of examples on this theme, see the chapter 'Of the Bibliophagi or Book-Eaters' in Holbrook Jackson, *The Anatomy of Bibliomania*, New York, 1950, pp. 154-73, Jeanneret, *A Feast of Words*, pp. 127-39, Curtius, *European Literature*, pp. 134-36.

28 See Sabry Hafez, 'Food as a Semiotic Code in Arabic Literature', whose introduction ably employs all the required state-of-the-art buzz-words that I intend to avoid as best I can in the present study.

29 See on Greek literature e.g. Andrew Dalby, *Siren Feasts: A History of Food and Gastronomy in Greece*, London, 1996; John Wilkins, David Harvey & Mike Dolson (eds.), *Food in Antiquity*, Exeter, 1995; Jeanneret, *A Feast of Words*, ch. 6 ('Classical Banquets', pp. 140-71).

Chapter II – Early Poetry: Feeding as Good Breeding

1 Much though I should like to use gender-neutral language, only the masculine pronoun is appropriate, since in the great majority of cases it is the man who feeds and acquires the concomitant honour, even though his female relations may do all the work; see Willy Jansen, '"Eet! en ik zal zeggen wie je bent"'. An example of a woman receiving a male

guest is Khulayda Bint Badr, sister of al-Zibriqān (1st/7th century), who in spite of a lampoon on her by al-Mukhabbal was subsequently a kind hostess to the aged and invalid poet ('she put him up, showed him favours, honoured him and gave him a servant girl', al-Iṣfahāni, *al-Aghānī*, xiii, 196). There is no explicit mention of food or husband, but the former is of course implied.

2 al-Tha[c]ālibī, *Ādāb al-mulūk*, p. 99, followed by examples: the caliph al-Amīn and the famous general Abū Dulaf al-Qāsim Ibn [c]Īsā, who would gladly part with gifts of gold and silver, but begrudged their table companions a bite of bread.

3 al-Iṣfahānī, *Aghānī*, xxiv, 148–50.

4 e.g. *al-Aghānī*, xvii, 367; cf. R.A. Nicholson, *A Literary History of the Arabs*, pp. 85–6. In a sequel to this story, Ḥātim is accepted by Māwiyya Bint [c]Afzar as her husband and preferred to other suitors because he had fed her, when she had disguised herself as a slave girl, with the hump and rump of a camel, whereas the others – including the famous poet al-Nābigha al-Dhubyānī – had offered her its penis and its tail (*al-Aghānī*, xvii, 380–86).

5 *al-Aghānī*, xxii, 279–80.

6 al-Marzūqī, *Sharḥ Dīwān al-ḥamāsa*, pp. 1653–4, *al-Aghānī*, iii, 74.

7 al-Maydānī, *Majma[c] al-amthāl*, ii, 422, and often expressed in similar terms, see Van Gelder, 'Persons as Texts / Texts as Persons in Classical Arabic Literature' (forthcoming).

8 See the two recent stimulating books by Matt Ridley, *The Red Queen: Sex and the Evolution of Human Nature*; idem, *The Origins of Virtue*, pp. 85–124 (ch. 5: 'Duty and the Feast: In which human generosity with food is explained', ch. 6: 'Public Goods and Private Gifts: In which no man can eat a whole mammoth').

9 Muḥammad Ibn Ḥabīb, *al-Munammaq*, pp. 103–4; cf. Ibn Hishām, *Sīra*, i, 136, transl. Guillaume, p. 58.

10 al-Ya[c]qūbī, *Tārīkh*, i, 250.

11 Johan Huizinga, *Homo ludens*, p. 87. The derivation from *[c]aqara*, 'to hock (a beast)' seems obvious; but see J. Sadan's entry 'Nadīm' in *The Encyclopaedia of Islam*, New Edition (p. 850a), for a different etymology.

12 *al-Aghānī*, xvi, 284–89.

13 *al-Aghānī*, xxi, 282–3, cf. Abū [c]Ubayda, *Naqā'iḍ Jarīr wa-l-Farazdaq*, pp. 413–18, 1070.

14 A series of such contests is described in Muḥammad Ibn Ḥabīb, *Munammaq*, pp. 104–16.

15 Muḥammad Ibn Ḥabīb, *Munammaq*, p. 104–5.

16 *al-Aghānī*, xxii, 321–2.

17 *al-Aghānī*, xxii, 341–2.

18 The following lines are taken from the section 'the best lines of *hijā'* by the [c]Arab [i.e. the early poets]' in al-Ḥātimī, *Ḥilyat al-muḥāḍara*, i, 345–49.

19 See on this and the preceding line Van Gelder, *The Bad and the Ugly*, p. 37, with more references.

20 See e.g. Jacobi, *Studien*, p. 1.

21 e.g. Ibn Sīda, *Mukhaṣṣaṣ*, iv, 126.

22 There are innumerable studies and surveys of the early *qaṣīda*; mention may be made of Ewald Wagner, *Grundzüge der klassischen arabischen Dichtung. Band I: Die altarabische Dichtung*, and Renate Jacobi, *Studien zur Poetik der altarabischen Qaside*.

23 See below, p. 18.

24 al-Ma^{c}arrī, *Risālat al-ṣāhil wa-l-shāḥij*, pp. 123–28. Another complaining camel is heard in the *Epistles* of the 10th-century 'Sincere Brethren'; the hardships of travelling and carrying burdens are mentioned, but being eaten is apparently not resented (*Rasā'il Ikhwān al-Ṣafā'*, ii, 216).

25 Ibn Qutayba, *Kitāb al-Ma^{c}ānī*, pp. 365–601 (from p. 437 onwards eating is no longer central and the author drifts off into associated topics such as wine, music and court scenes).

26 e.g. Abū Dhu'ayb, in al-Sukkarī, *Ash^{c}ār al-Hudhaliyyīn*, p. 79, Ibn Qutayba, *Ma^{c}ānī*, pp. 365–66.

27 Labīd, *Dīwān*, p. 216.

28 Ibn Qutayba, *Ma^{c}ānī*, p. 372.

29 *al-Mufaḍḍaliyyāt*, pp. 126–27, as translated by Lyall, *The Mufaḍḍalīyāt: an anthology of ancient Arabian odes (. . .), Vol. II: Translation and notes*, pp. 84–85; also al-Khālidiyyān, al-*Ashbāh wa-l-naẓā'ir*, ii, 100–101.

30 Food, conversation and a non-metaphorical blanket are offered to a guest in a short anonymous poem in Abū Tammām's *Ḥamāsa* (al-Marzūqī, *Sharḥ Dīwān al-ḥamāsa*, p. 1750).

31 Recent translations and commentaries are found in Jones, *Early Arabic Poetry*, II, 52–86 and Stetkevych, 'Regicide and Retribution'.

32 Stetkevych, 'Regicide and retribution', pp. 262–64 and 277–78.

33 'Regicide and Retribution', p. 264.

34 Ridley, *The Origins of Virtue*, p. 90.

35 Translation by A.F.L. Beeston, in his 'An Experiment with Labīd', p. 6; see also Jones, *Early Arabic Poetry*, II, 164–202 and Stetkevych, 'Voicing the Mute Immortals: The *Mu^{c}allaqa* of Labīd and the Rite of Passage' of her *The Mute Immortals Speak*.

36 See the standard work by Arnold van Gennep, *The Rites of Passage*, p. 29: 'The rite of eating and drinking . . . is clearly a rite of incorporation, of physical union, and has been called a sacrament of communion.'

37 For lists of these and other terms, see e.g. al-Jāḥiẓ, *Bukhalā'*, pp. 213–15, Ibn Qutayba, *K. al-ma^{c}ānī*, pp. 377–78, Ibn Durayd, *Jamhara*, pp. 1270–71, Ibn ^{c}Abd Rabbih, *^{c}Iqd*, vi, 292, al-Marzubānī, *Nūr al-qabas*, p. 289, al-Tawḥīdī, *al-Baṣā'ir wa-l-dhakhā'ir*, viii, 50–51, al-Tha^{c}ālibī, *Fiqh al-lugha*, pp. 169–70, Ibn Sīda, *Mukhaṣṣaṣ*, iv, 120–21, al-Rāghib al-Iṣfahānī, *Muḥāḍarāt al-udabā'*, i, 395, al-Sharīf al-Murtaḍā, *Amālī (Ghurar al-fawā'id)*, i, 354–56, al-Ghuzūlī, *Maṭāli^{c} al-budūr*, ii, 43–44, Ibn Ḥijja, *Thamarāt al-awrāq*, p. 479, Nāṣīf al-Yāzijī, *Majma^{c} al-baḥrayn*, pp. 24–25, Sulaymā Maḥjūb, introd. to Ibn al-^{c}Adīm, *al-Wuṣla ilā l-ḥabīb*, i, 93–95.

38 See T. Fahd, entry 'Maysir' in *The Encyclopaedia of Islam*, New Edition.

39 *al-Mufaḍḍaliyyāt* no. 17 vss. 71-74 (pp. 101-2); cf. Lyall's translation in *The Mufaḍḍalīyāt*, pp. 61-2 and the study with translation by Thomas Bauer, 'Muzarrids Qaṣīde vom reichen Ritter und dem armen Jäger'.

40 Translation by Lyall, *The Mufaḍḍalīyāt*, p. 96; *al-Mufaḍḍaliyyāt*, p. 141, al-Akhfash al-Aṣghar, *al-Ikhtiyārayn*, pp. 94-5, Ibn Maymūn, *Muntahā l-ṭalab*, i, 185. The caliph ^{c}Abd al-Malik apparently liked the idea of cleaning one's hands in the way described by the poet (al-Mubarrad, *Kāmil*, i, 327, *al-Aghānī*, xxi, 26-7).

41 Dhū l-Rumma, *Dīwān*, pp. 177, 180, Ibn Qutayba, *Ma^{c}ānī*, pp. 379-80. Some commentators explain the 'black one' as a pair of bellows.

42 *al-Mufaḍḍaliyyāt*, p. 403.

43 Ibn Qutayba, *Ma^{c}ānī*, pp. 381-82.

44 See Ibn Manẓūr, *Lisān al-^{c}arab*, s.v. *n-sh-m*.

45 R.T. Wilson, *The Camel*, London, 1984, p. 73; see also al-Jāḥiẓ, *Bukhalā'*, p. 216, transl. Pellat, 'Ǧāḥiẓiana, II: Le dernier chapître des *Avares* de Ǧāḥiẓ', p. 327.

46 *al-Aghānī*, xxi, 213-14; the complete poem in al-Sukkarī, *Sharḥ ash^{c}ār al-Hudhaliyyīn*, (iii) 1198-1204.

47 Ḥassān Ibn Thābit, *Dīwān*, p. 396, al-Jāḥiẓ, *Bukhalā'*, p. 231, al-Jāḥīẓ, *Ḥayawān*, v, 329, al-Rāghib al-Iṣbahānī, *Muḥāḍarāt*, i, 377; more references in Paul Kunitzsch & Manfred Ullmann, *Die Plejaden in den Vergleichen der arabischen Dichtung*, München, 1992, p. 90.

48 al-Marzubānī, *Muqtabas*, p. 277. I am not certain of the meaning of *(tharīd) al-ḥawāqin*; perhaps '*tharīd* (fit) for bellies'.

49 A *ṣā^{c}* is a dry measure equal to some 4.2 litres, equivalent to 3.24 kg of wheat.

50 Ibn Qutayba, *^{c}Uyūn al-akhbār*, iii, 204, Ibn ^{c}Abd Rabbih, *al-^{c}Iqd al-farīd*, vi, 301-2, al-^{c}Askarī, *Dīwān al-ma^{c}ānī*, i, 304-5, al-Marzubānī, *Nūr al-qabas*, 137-8, al-Mu^{c}āfā al-Jarīrī, *al-Jalīs al-ṣāliḥ al-kāfī*, ii, 261-62, al-Tawḥīdī, *al-Baṣā'ir wa-l-dhakhā'ir*, iv, 204, al-Sharīshī, *Sharḥ Maqāmāt al-Ḥarīrī*, iv, 156.

51 On these and similar expressions connected with laughter, see Kathrin Müller, *'Und der Kalif lachte, bis er auf den Rücken fiel'*.

52 e.g. al-Tha^{c}ālibī, *Fiqh al-lugha*, p. 170, in a list of Bedouin dishes; for similar lists, see e.g. Ibn ^{c}Abd Rabbih, *al-^{c}Iqd al-farīd*, vi, 290-92, Ibn Durayd, *Jamharah*, p. 1270-1, Sulaymā Maḥjūb, introd. to Ibn al-^{c}Adīm, *al-Wuṣla ilā l-ḥabīb*, i, 41-48. Ibn Sīda lists and discusses many terms connected with food in his great thesaurus, *al-Mukhaṣṣaṣ*, iv, 118-49, v, 2-58; see e.g. iv, 143-49 for the pattern *fa^{c}īla*.

53 See al-Maydānī, *Majma^{c} al-amthāl*, i, 98, Ibn Durayd, *Jamhara*, pp. 536, 1049, 1270 and other dictionairies (*Lisān al-^{c}Arab, Tāj al-^{c}arūs*) s.v. *ḤYS*, and the entry 'Ḥays' in *The Encyclopaedia of Islam*, New Edition, Supplement.

Chapter III – Eating and the New Ethos

1 See Metlitzki, *The Matter of Araby*, pp. 210-19 ('The Muslim Paradise as the Land of Cokaygne'); Pleij, *Dromen van Cocagne*, pp. 235-39.

2 This is a usual interpretation of *ṭalḥ*. In the versification of this passage ascribed to Umayya Ibn Abī l-Ṣalt, a contemporary of the Prophet, we find *mawz* 'bananas', see al-Maqdisī, *al-Bad' wa-l-ta'rīkh*, i, 202.
3 al-Ghazālī, *Iḥyā' ʿulūm al-dīn*, iv, 539–40.
4 al-Ghazālī, *Iḥyā'*, iv, 539, cf. al-Bukhārī, *Ṣaḥīḥ*, 'Manāqib al-anṣār' (63) no. 51, 'Tafsīr' (65) on sura 2:56, 'Riqāq' (81) nos. 44 and 51, Muslim, *Ṣaḥīḥ*, 'Munāfiqīn' (50) no. 30.
5 al-Ghazālī, *Iḥyā'*, iv, 540, cf. Muslim, *Ṣaḥīḥ*, 'Janna' (51) no. 18, al-Dārimī, *Sunan*, 'Riqāq' (20) no. 104.
6 Arberry, 'A Baghdad Cookery-Book', p. 32, Ibn al-ʿAdīm, *al-Wuṣla ilā l-ḥabīb*, p. 479, al-Tujībī, *Fuḍālat al-khiwān*, p. 29. Ibn Sayyār and the anonymous author of *Kanz al-fawā'id* do not fully exploit the Koranic possibilities in their prefaces.
7 al-Bukhārī, *al-Ṣaḥiḥ*, 'Aṭʿima' (70) no. 6, cf. no. 48, 'Aymān' (83) no. 22 and 'Manāqib' (61) no. 25.
8 al-Muṭahhar Ibn Ṭāhir al-Maqdisī, *al-Bad' wa-l-ta'rīḳh*, v, 37.
9 al-Bukhārī, *Ṣaḥīḥ*, 'Aṭʿima' (70) no. 23.
10 al-Bukhārī, *Ṣaḥīḥ*, 'Aṭʿima' (70) nos. 12, 13.
11 al-Bukhārī, *Ṣaḥīḥ*, 'Aṭʿima' (70) no. 32.
12 al-Bukhārī, *Ṣaḥīḥ*, 'Aṭʿima' (70) no. 25; cf. al-Jāḥiẓ, *Bukhalā'*, 74. Later, the saying is found reversed: '*Tharīd* is superior to other food as ʿĀ'isha is superior to all other women', *Alf layla wa-layla*, Cairo: Maktabat Ṣubayḥ, n.d., ii, 316, Enno Littmann (übers.), *Die Erzählungen aus den Tausendundein Nächten*, Wiesbaden, 1953, iii, 668.
13 al-Bukhārī, *Ṣaḥīḥ*, 'Aṭʿima' (70) no. 21.
14 al-Bukhārī, *Ṣaḥīḥ* 'Aṭʿima' (70) nos. 10, 14, cf. 'Dhabā'iḥ' (72) no. 33.
15 al-Bukhārī, *Ṣaḥīḥ*, 'Dhabā'iḥ' (72) no. 13.
16 See *EI2*, art. 'ʿAbd Allāh Ibn Djudʿān' (Ch. Pellat).
17 *Aghānī*, viii, 329–30, al-Jāḥiẓ, *al-Awṭān wa-l-buldān*, 116–17, al-Thaʿālibī, *Thimār al-qulūb*, p. 609, al-Ghuzūlī, *Maṭāliʿ al-budūr*, ii, 79. 'The *fālūdhaj* of Ibn Judʿān' became proverbial, see *Thimār al-qulūb*, p. 123.
18 al-Jāḥiẓ, *al-Bayān*, i, 18, idem, *al-Awṭān*, 117, Ibn Qutayba, *Maʿānī*, p. 380, al-Qālī, *Amālī*, i, 122, *Aghānī*, viii, 329, al-ʿAskarī, *Dīwān al-maʿānī*, i, 301–2, etc.
19 In a poem attributed to a famous parasite it is called *ʿayn al-qaṣīd*, which may be rendered as 'the very thing that is desired' but perhaps also as 'the choice part of the poem', linking food and poetry (al-Baghdādī, *Taṭfīl*, p. 141, Ibn al-Jawzī, *Adhkiyā'*, p. 207).
20 Ibn Māja, *Sunan*, (ii,) 1108–9 (*Kitāb al-aṭʿima, bāb al-fālūdhaj*).
21 al-Wāqidī, *al-Maghāzī*, (ii,) 427, cf. Ibn Hishām, *Sīra*, ii, 297, tr. Guillaume, p. 494, and many other works of *ḥadīth* and history.
22 al-Masʿūdī, *Murūj*, iii, 220–22.
23 al-Muʿāfā al-Jarīrī, *Jalīs*, ii, 271–73 (two versions, interrupted by a report on the frugality of the Prophet's Companions).
24 Ibn al-Ṭiqṭaqā, *al-Fakhrī*, p. 150.
25 Ibn al-Ṭiqṭaqā, *al-Fakhrī*, pp. 102–3.
26 e.g. Maḥjūb in Ibn al-ʿAdīm, *Wuṣla*, Introduction, pp. 183–86.
27 al-Masʿūdī, *Murūj*, iv, 7–8, Ibn al-Ṭiqṭaqā, *Fakhrī*, p. 101.
28 al-Thaʿālibī, *Ādāb al-mulūk*, pp. 155–56.

29 al-Farazdaq, *Dīwān*, i, 389, al-Mubarrad, *Kāmil*, ii, 64.
30 al-Jāḥiẓ, *Bukhalā'*, p. 203. On *shubāriqāt*, apparently a meat dish, see the editor's note pp. 400–401; Ibn Durayd, *Jambara*, pp. 1120, 1208, 1212; cf. Persian *pēshpārcha* or *pēshpāra* or *pēshāra* (Steingass, *Persian-English Dictionary*).
31 cf. the version in al-Ghazālī, *Iḥyā'*, iii, 98.
32 al-Ṭabarī, *Tārīkh*, i, 2253; a garbled version in al-Ābī, *Nathr al-durr*, vii, 362.
33 al-Jāḥiẓ, *Bayān*, i, 286.
34 *Aghānī*, viii, 40–41.
35 al-Jāḥiẓ, *al-Bukhalā'*, pp. 221–22, translated by Ch. Pellat in 'Ǧāḥiẓiana, II: Le dernier chapitre des *Avares* de Ǧāḥiẓ', pp. 330–31.
36 Ibn Qutayba, *ᶜUyūn al-akhbār*, iii, 199.
37 al-Masᶜūdī, *Murūj*, iv, 167–68, al-Jahshiyārī, *al-Wuzarā'*, pp. 146–47, Ibn al-Ṭiqṭaqā, *al-Fakhrī*, pp. 243–44.
38 On this topic, see e.g. Bettini, 'Alimentation et poésie: un exemple du *tağhīl al-Ğiāhiliyya*', pp. 78ff.
39 Bashshār Ibn Burd, as translated by A.F.L. Beeston in his *Selections from the poetry of Baššār*, p. 50, Arabic text p. 12; cf. Bashshār Ibn Burd, *Dīwān*, i, 390.
40 Bashshār, *Dīwān*, iii, 140–41.
41 *al-darmak al-manfūṭ*: *darmak* is 'white, refined, flour'; the editor glosses *manfūṭ* as *maṭbūkh*. I wonder if the correct reading is perhaps *manqūṭ* (cf. the verb *tanaqqaṭa* 'to eat bits of bread one after the other').
42 The edition has *al-juᶜal al-muṣallā* and explains the second word as 'roasted' (root *ṢLY*). But see al-Jāḥiẓ, *al-Ḥayawān*, vi, 393–94 on the scarab that seems to be praying (*muṣallī*); cf below, p. 32.
43 Bashshār, *Dīwān*, iii, 208–10; said when provoked by the remark of a Bedouin, on hearing that Bashshār was a non-Arab client (*mawlā*): 'What do *mawālī* know of poetry!'; cf. *Aghānī*, iii, 166–67.
44 Abū Nuwās, *Dīwān*, ii, p. 13. The line became a standard example of the figure of speech called *hazl yurād bihi l-jidd* ('jesting with a serious purport'), see Van Gelder, 'Mixtures of Jest and Earnest in Classical Arabic Literature', Part II, p. 179.
45 See al-Jāḥiẓ, *Ḥayawān*, v, 565–66 on eating locusts' eggs.
46 al-Jāḥiẓ, *Ḥayawān*, vi, 88–89, Ibn Qutayba, *ᶜUyūn al-akhbār*, iii, 210–11, al-Damīrī, *Ḥayāt al-ḥayawān*, ii, 79–80, Ibn ᶜAbd al-Barr, *Bahjat al-majālis*, ii, 81, al-Zamakhsharī, *Rabīᶜ al-abrār*, iv, 466.
47 al-Jāḥiẓ, *Ḥayawān*, vi, 398. On eating, to our tastes, unusual species, see Marvin Harris, *Good to Eat: Riddles of Food and Culture*, ch. 8.
48 According to Wehr's dictionary, its present meaning is 'truffle'; here it is apparently an animal, cf. *al-Ḥayawān*, iv, 144, vi, 20, 360, al-Thaᶜālibī, *Thimār al-qulūb*, pp. 509–10, al-Damīrī, *Ḥayāt al-ḥayawān al-kubrā*, ii, 51.
49 According to al-Jāḥiẓ (ibid., vi, 384, 388) this is the same animal as the *umm ḥubayn*, somewhat like a chameleon, but smaller; cf. al-Damīrī, *Ḥayāt al-ḥayawān al-kubrā*, i, 288.

50 On this animal, see M.V. McDonald, 'Two mysterious animals in the *Kitāb al-Ḥayawān* of al-Jāḥiẓ: the *sim*^{c} and the ^{c}*isbār*', (where some suggestions are reviewed but no final identification is given).
51 al-Jāḥiẓ, *Ḥayawān*, vi, 392–93. On the 'praying' scarab, see above, note 42.
52 *Ḥayawān*, vi, 393.
53 al-Ma^{c}arrī, *Risālat al-ṣāhil wa-l-shāḥij*, p. 148 (in a longer passage on eating lizards and snakes, pp. 147–52).
54 al-Ṭabarī, *Tārīkh*, i, 2241.
55 al-Tawḥīdī, *al-Imtā*^{c} *wa-l-mu'ānasa*, i, 79–80.
56 al-Jāḥiẓ, *Ḥayawān*, ii, 317, Ibn Qutayba, *Ma*^{c}*ānī*, p. 267, al-Baghdādī, *Khizāna*, iv, 383. Al-Barīṣ is, according to the commentators, a river, or a place, in Damascus.
57 al-Tanūkhī, *Nishwār al-muḥāḍara*, i, 204.
58 al-Jāḥiẓ, *Ḥayawān*, vi, 90–92, cf. Ibn Qutayba, ^{c}*Uyūn*, iii, 210, Ibn ^{c}Abd al-Barr, *Bahjat al-majālis*, ii, 82–83, al-Zamakhsharī, *Rabī*^{c} *al-abrār*, iv, 476, (wrongly reading *dhi'āb* instead of *dhibāb*; second line bowdlerized). On the dish called *bazmāward* (*Rabī*^{c} *al-abrār* has *zumāward*) which here includes wasps' grubs, popular in Khurāsān (where al-Faḍl had been governor), see also al-Jāḥiẓ, *Ḥayawān*, iii, 323, iv, 44, Ahsan, *Social Life*, pp. 81–82 (who has 'hornets' instead of 'hornet's grubs'!).
59 al-Sharīf al-Raḍī, *Nahj al-balāgha*, ii, 70–75.
60 al-Ābī, *Nathr al-durr*, i, 231.
61 al-Ābī, *Nathr al-durr*, ii, 30.
62 Ibn al-Ṭiqṭaqā, *Fakhrī*, p. 336; on his frugality cf. al-Mas^{c}ūdī, *Murūj*, v, 98.
63 al-Tha^{c}ālibī, *Ādāb al-mulūk*, p. 199, quoting Abū Isḥāq al-Ṣābi'.
64 al-Ghazālī, *Iḥyā'* ^{c}*ulūm al-dīn*, iii, 80–99.
65 *Iḥyā'*, ii, 2–20, translated and richly annotated by Hans Kindermann, *Über die guten Sitten beim Essen und Trinken*.
66 al-Tawḥīdī, *Imtā*^{c}, iii, 1–85.
67 *Imtā*^{c}, iii, 2.
68 *Imtā*^{c}, iii, 20–23 and cf. iii, 83; partly quoted in al-Ghuzūlī, *Maṭāli*^{c} *al-budūr*, ii, 62–63. On the genre, see Joseph Sadan, 'Kings and Craftsmen - A Pattern of Contrasts. On the History of a Mediaeval Arabic Humoristic Form', see Part I, p. 25.
69 *Imtā*^{c}, iii, 83.
70 *Imtā*^{c}, iii, 22.
71 *Imtā*^{c}, iii, 22.
72 *Imtā*^{c}, iii, 20.
73 *Rasā'il Ikhwān al-Ṣafā'*, i, 358–61.
74 *Rasā'il Ikhwān al-Ṣafā'*, ii, 315–17.
75 *Rasā'il Ikhwān al-Ṣafā'*, ii, 317–18.
76 al-Tha^{c}labī, *Qiṣas al-anbiyā'*, pp. 32–33.
77 al-Ghazālī, *Iḥyā'* ^{c}*ulūm al-dīn*, iv, 109–20.
78 *Rasā'il Ikhwān al-Ṣafā'*, ii, 319–23.
79 *Rasā'il Ikhwān al-Ṣafā'*, iii, 13.
80 For *d.bk.dān* read something like *daykadān* (Persian *dēgdān*).
81 *Rasā'il Ikhwān al-Ṣafā'*, iii, 25–28 (story and explanation).

82 *Rasā'il Ikhwān al-Ṣafā'*, ii, 392.
83 *Rasā'il Ikhwān al-Ṣafā'*, iii, 156–60.
84 al-Tha^{c}labī, *Qiṣaṣ al-anbiyā'*, p. 24.
85 See the commentaries and the several works on the histories of the prophets, such as al-Tha^{c}labī, *Qiṣaṣ al-anbiyā'*, pp. 26–27 (also mentions camphor), al-Muṭahhar al-Maqdisī, *al-Bad' wa-l-ta'rīkh*, ii, 93 (mentions the bitter colocynth).
86 al-Baghdādī, *Tārīkh Baghdād*, xiii, 270, cf. al-Tanūkhī, *Nishwār*, vii, 29.
87 e.g. Qatāda, in al-Tha^{c}labī, *Qiṣaṣ al-anbiyā'*, p. 26.

Chapter IV – *Adab*, or the Text as a Banquet

1 above, p. 3.
2 Ibn Qutayba, *^{c}Uyūn al-akhbār*, i, *lām*.
3 al-Jāḥiẓ, *Bukhalā'*, p. 213, al-Mubarrad, *Kāmil*, ii, 51, al-Mu^{c}āfā al-Jarīrī, *Jalīs*, iii, 329–30, al-Sharīf al-Murtaḍā, *Amālī*, i, 354, 358 (see marginal gloss in note 3), al-Dārimī, *Sunan*, ii, 429, 431, 433 (chapter *Faḍā'il al-Qur'ān*); more references in Bonebakker, 'Early Arabic Literature', pp. 410–11.
4 Jean Thenaud, quoted in Jeanneret, *A Feast of Words*, p. 133, in a rich section entitled 'Metaphors of bibliophagy'.
5 Ibn Qutayba, *^{c}Uyūn*, iii, 197–301.
6 *^{c}Uyūn al-akhbār*, iii, 197.
7 *^{c}Uyūn al-akhbār*, iii, 201. I do not know why Ibn al-Jawzī included this pleasant hyperbole in his collection of sayings by stupid people (*Akhbār al-ḥamqā wa-l-mughaffalīn*, p. 116).
8 *^{c}Uyūn al-akhbār*, iii, 198. For the idiom 'eating the property of orphans', see e.g. sura 4:10.
9 *^{c}Uyūn al-akhbār*, iii, 214.
10 *^{c}Uyūn al-akhbār*, iii, 216–19, cf. al-Jāḥiẓ, *al-Bukhalā'*, 108–11.
11 *^{c}Uyūn al-akhbār*, iii, 224. The text has 'a *ṣā^{c}*', i.e. a dry measure corresponding to c. 4 litres.
12 Both anecdotes *^{c}Uyūn al-akhbār*, iii, 226; for the latter cf. Ibn Abī Ṭāhir Ṭayfūr, *Balāghāt al-nisā'*, pp. 254–55.
13 *^{c}Uyūn al-akhbār*, iii, 233–64. Some anecdotes on misers are taken from al-Jāḥiẓ's *Bukhalā'*.
14 *^{c}Uyūn al-akhbār*, iii, 265–69.
15 *^{c}Uyūn al-akhbār*, iii, 276; cf. the version in al-Shirbīnī, *Hazz al-quḥūf*, Cairo: al-Maktaba al-Maḥmūdiyya, n.d., p. 173. Again, I cannot agree with Ibn al-Jawzī, who gives this as another illustration of the sayings of stupid Bedouins (*Akhbār al-ḥamqā wa-l-mughaffalīn*, p. 118).
16 Ibn ^{c}Abd Rabbih, *al-^{c}Iqd al-farīd*, vi, 290–378.
17 *al-^{c}Iqd*, vi, 290.
18 See Van Gelder, 'Musāwir al-Warrāq and the beginnings of Arabic gastronomic poetry'.
19 *al-^{c}Iqd*, vi, 307–32.
20 *al-^{c}Iqd*, vi, 332–34. On Isḥāq Ibn ^{c}Imrān, see C. Brockelmann, *Geschichte der arabischen Litteratur*, I, 232, Suppl. I, 417.

21 *al-^{c}Iqd*, vi, 174–204 (on misers), 204–15 (parasites). Fedwa Malti-Douglas has studied the literary aspects of the stories about misers and parasites in *Structures of Avarice* and 'Structure and Organization in a Monographic *Adab* Work', respectively.

22 *^{c}Iqd*, ii, 456–59: *bāb al-adab fī l-mu'ākala*.

23 al-Rāghib al-Iṣbahānī, *Muḥāḍarāt al-udabā' wa-muḥāwarāt wa-l-shu^{c}arā' wa-l-bulaghā'*, i, 376–411 (*al-aṭ^{c}ima*).

24 e.g. Ibn Sayyār's *Kitāb al-ṭabīkh*, Ibn al-^{c}Adīm's *al-Wuṣla ilā l-ḥabīb* and the anonymous *Kanz al-fawā'id*.

25 or *ṣifa*, as in Ibn ^{c}Abd Rabbih, *^{c}Iqd*, vi, 293.

26 *Muḥāḍarāt*, i, 382.

27 A proverb attributed to Aktham Ibn Ṣayfī, cf. Abū ^{c}Ubayd al-Bakrī, *Faṣl al-maqāl fī sharḥ al-amthāl*, p. 73, al-Maydānī, *Majma^{c} al-amthāl*, i, 388, etc.

28 This saying is found in many sources, al-Jāḥiẓ, *Bayān*, i, 18 being among the earliest. The expression 'bees' saliva' is meant to have positive connotations, cf. Ibn al-Rūmī's line (*Dīwān*, p. 1144), 'You may say [of honey]: bees' saliva, praising it; / and if you blame it, you say: wasps' vomit.'

29 For an extended version, see al-Zamakhsharī, *Rabī^{c}*, ii, 689, al-Ibshīhī, *Mustaṭraf*, i, 177. The idea is that the angel of Death would be distracted or placated by a tasty dish.

30 A famous 'fool'; see e.g. Ulrich Marzolph, *Arabia ridens*, indexes of vols. 1 and 2.

31 Other versions (e.g. al-Zamakhsharī, *Rabī^{c}*, ii, 691, al-Ibshīhī, *Musta-ṭraf*, i, 178) have 'rancid'.

32 Sura 16:68.

33 Instead of the traditional dates?

34 A man notorious for his stupidity, see e.g. Ibn Qutayba, *^{c}Uyūn*, ii, 52, Ibn ^{c}Abd Rabbih, *^{c}Iqd*, vi, 151–52.

35 The Umayyad singer Aḥmad al-Naṣbī, nevertheless, is said to have died of eating a hot *fālūdhaja* too eagerly, al-Iṣfahānī, *al-Aghānī*, vi, 63–4 (al-Iṣfahānī does not believe it).

36 The earliest occurrence seems to be al-Jāḥiẓ, *Bukhalā'*, pp. 178–79; see Marzolph, *Arabia ridens*, ii, 19 for more sources.

37 Ibn ^{c}Abd al-Barr, *Bahjat al-majālis*, ii, 72–86 (*al-ṭa^{c}ām wa-l-akl*).

38 al-Zamakhsharī, *Rabī^{c} al-abrār*, ii, 671–760: *al-ṭa^{c}am wa-alwānuhu wa-dhikr al-iṭ^{c}ām wa-l-ḍiyāfa wa-l-akl wa-l-akala wa-l-jū^{c} wa-l-shiba^{c} wa-mā yata^{c}allaqu bi-dhālika*.

39 A town in Iraq. Among its specialities, al-Qazwīnī lists young chicken (*Āthār al-bilād*, p. 446).

40 Unclear; 'a certain medicine' according to the dictionaries.

41 al-Zamakhsharī, *Maqāmāt*, pp. 112–23.

42 Ibid., p. 125.

43 A sweet dish made of dates, flour and butter according to the dictionaries, but many other ingredients are given for the numerous recipes found e.g. in Ibn Sayyār, *al-Ṭabīkh*, pp. 246–59.

44 *Rabī^{c} al-abrār*, ii, 673.

45 *Rabī^{c} al-abrār*, ii, 759.

46 I limit myself here to published editions. The large anthology by Ibn Ḥamdūn (d. 562/1166), *al-Tadhkira al-Ḥamdūniyya*, contains a chapter on eating behaviour and food, as yet unpublished; see Iḥsān ^{c}Abbās's edition of vol. 1 (Beirut, 1983), p. 29. Mention should be made of *al-Imtā^{c} wa-l-mu'ānasa* by al-Tawḥīdī (d. after 400/1010), which, though not an *adab* encylopaedia, ranges widely over *adab* themes and includes a long chapter on food and eating (iii, 1–85).

47 *al-Mustaṭraf fī kull fann mustaẓraf*, i, 176–87 (*al-ṭa^{c}ām wa-ādābuhu wa-l-ḍiyāfa wa-l-ḍayf wa-akhbār al-akala wa-mā jā'a ^{c}anhum*).

48 *Mustaṭraf*, i, 178.

49 The tree providing the horrible food of those in Hell, see suras 44:43–46 and 56:52–52.

50 Also in al-Azdī, *Ḥikāyat Abī l-Qāsim*, p. 100. Aubergine (*bādhinjān*) had a bad reputation. Ibn Qur^{c}a's image is found already in Ibn Qutayba *^{c}Uyūn al-akhbār*, iii, 288 (Abū l-Ḥārith Jummayz: 'I will not eat it: the colour of a scorpion, like a cupping-glass') and cf. the partly obscene epigram of eight lines against the aubergine by Abū Hilāl al-^{c}Askarī in his *Dīwān al-ma^{c}ānī*, i, 303, ending: 'their skins resemble bellies of scorpions, their heads are like the noses of cupping-glasses'. Very negative is also the author of the 17th-century didactic poem on dietetics, *Natā'ij al-fikar*, see Armin Schopen & Oliver Kahl, *Die Natā'iǧ al-fikar des Ša^{c}bān ibn Sālim aṣ-Ṣan^{c}ānī*, p. 41 (transl. pp. 129–30, commentary pp. 230–31). Positive epigrams: Kushājim, in Ibn Sayyār, *al-Ṭabīkh*, p. 116, Anon., *Mustaṭraf*, ii, 226–27, in a section of poetical descriptions of fruit. Cf. also al-Ghuzūlī, *Maṭāli^{c} al-budūr*, ii, 31–32, al-^{c}Āmilī, *al-Mikhlāt*, p. 119.

51 al-Ghuzūlī, *Maṭāli^{c} al-budūr*, ii, 18–89. Drinking wine is extensively discussed in a separate section, see i, 128–75.

52 *Maṭāli^{c} al-budūr*, ii, 2–18 and 89–93, respectively.

53 *Maṭāli^{c} al-budūr*, ii, 34.

54 al-Tha^{c}ālibī, *Khāṣṣ al-khāṣṣ*, p. 153.

55 For a structuralist literary study of these two works, see Malti-Douglas, *Structures of Avarice*.

56 On which see Malti-Douglas, 'Structure and Organization'.

57 Badī^{c} al-Zamān al-Hamadhānī, *Maqāmāt*, pp. 73–77, tr. W.J. Prendergast, *The Maqámát of Badí^{c} al-Zamán al-Hamadhání*, pp. 70–73. On the relationship between banquets and the *maqāma* or related forms, see Kilito, *Les séances*, pp. 143–54, Omri, '"There is a Jāḥiẓ for Every Age"', pp. 32–35.

58 Translation by Prendergast, p. 71.

59 *Maqāmāt*, pp. 104–17, tr. Prendergast, pp. 88–97. On this *maqāma* see J.T. Monroe, *The art of Badī^{c} az-Zamān al-Hamadhānī as picaresque narrative*, pp. 145–60, F. Malti-Douglas, '*Maqāmāt* and *adab*: 'al-Maqāma al-Maḍīriyya' of al-Hamadhānī', D. Beaumont, 'A mighty and never ending affair: Comic anecdote and story in medieval Arabic literature'.

60 I thank Mr Christian Peltz (Tübingen) for bringing this passage to my attention.

61 al-Ma^{c}arrī, *Risālat al-ṣāhil wal-shāḥij*, p. 228. On the riddles in this

work, see Pieter Smoor, 'Enigmatic Allusion and Double Meaning in Ma[c]arrī's newly-discovered *Letter of a Horse and a Mule*'.

62 A proverb, see al-Maydānī, *Majma[c] al-amthāl*, i, 75.

63 Sura 13:38.

64 On *sikbāj* see e.g. the lemma by Shawkat M. Toorawa in *The Encyclopaedia of Islam*, New Edition; Ahsan, *Social Life*, p. 83.

65 al-Ma[c]arrī, *Risālat al-ṣāhil wa-l-shāḥij*, pp. 287–89. The solution appears on p. 364.

66 See also ch. V, p. 88.

67 *Maqāmāt*, pp. 176–80, tr. Prendergast, pp. 135–38.

68 al-Baghdādī, *Tatfīl*, p. 119.

69 *Alf layla wa-layla* ed. Ṣubayḥ i, 122–23, ed. Mahdī pp. 373–76; see e.g. the translation of Husain Haddawy, *The Arabian Nights*, pp. 289–92. The story is also found in *al-Ḥikāyāt al-[c]ajība*, pp. 64–68.

70 Leonee Ormond, 'Cayenne and Cream Tarts: W.M. Thackeray and R.L. Stevenson', in Peter L. Caracciolo (ed.), *The* Arabian Nights *in English Literature*, pp. 178–96 (see 182–84).

71 Ibn Buṭlān, *Da[c]wat al-aṭibbā'/The Physicians' Dinner Party*, pp. 14–25, Ibn Buṭlān, *Das Ärztebankett*, pp. 61–74. Beaumont ('A Mighty and Never Ending Affair', pp. 152–59) has already linked Ibn Buṭlān's banquet with al-Hamadhānī's *maḍīra* story.

72 al-Tanūkhī, *al-Faraj ba[c]d al-shidda*, ii, 387–88, idem, *Nishwār al-muḥāḍara*, i, 251.

73 See the review by Elaine Showalter in *The Times Literary Supplement*, 25 February 1994, p. 10, of Maud Ellmann, *The Hunger Artists: Starving, Writing and Imprisonment*, London, 1993.

74 al-Baghdādī, *Tatfīl*, p. 125.

75 See below, p. 58.

76 al-Mutanabbī, *Dīwān*, pp. 35–36.

77 *Wa-laysa li-llāhi bi-mustankarin an yajma[c]a l-[c]ālama fī wāḥidī* (Abū Nuwās, *Dīwān*, i, 185).

78 al-Mutanabbī, *Dīwān*, pp. 36–37. See Van Gelder, 'Al-Mutanabbī's Encumbering Trifles' *Arabic and Middle Eastern Literatures* 2 (1999).

79 Ibn Rashīq, *[c]Umda*, i, 80.

80 Ibn Rashīq, *[c]Umda*, i, 82.

81 Ibn Bassām, *Dhakhīra*, I, 235–36.

82 Ibn Ḥijja, *Thamarāt al-awrāq*, pp. 94–95, al-Anṭākī, *Tazyīn al-aswāq*, i, 297, cf. Arazi, *Amour divin*, p. 113.

83 Ibn al-Mu[c]tazz, *Ṭabaqāt al-shu[c]arā'*, p. 377, attr. to Sa[c]īd Ibn Ṣ.mṣ.m (read probably Ḍamḍam) in al-Bayhaqī, *Maḥāsin*, p. 310.

84 Ghars al-Ni[c]ma, *al-Hafawāt al-nādira*, pp. 224–27, also in al-Tanūkhī, *Nishwār*, vii, 174–77.

85 al-Ḥarīrī, *Maqāmāt*, p. 572, al-Sharīshī, *Sharḥ*, iv, 140.

86 Shortened from al-Ḥarīrī, *Maqāmāt*, p. 574, al-Sharīshī, *Sharḥ*, iv, 141–42. Exceptionally, food may be paid for with verse, see pp. 55, on Ibn Shuhayd and Khālid al-kātib.

87 al-Wahrānī, *Manāmāt*, pp. 92–93, also in al-Ghuzūlī, *Maṭāli[c] al-budūr*, ii, 189.

88 al-Wahrānī, *Manāmāt*, p. 115.

89 *Rasā'il Badī^c al-Zamān al-Hamadhānī*, in the margin of Ibn Ḥijja al-Ḥamawī, *Khizānat al-adab*, pp. 225–26; cf. al-Tha^cālibī, *Yatīma*, iv, 262, and his *Khāṣṣ al-khāṣṣ*, pp. 13–14.
90 al-Maydānī, *Majma^c al-amthāl*, i, 492.
91 al-Mubarrad, *Kāmil*, ii, 319–20, as translated by Jaakko Hämeen-Anttila, 'Khālid Ibn Ṣafwān – The man and the legend' (see translation, p. 103, and Arabic text, pp. 150–51).
92 The words are from a poem attributed to ^cUtba Ibn Bujayr or Miskīn al-Dārimī, see al-Marzūqī, *Sharḥ Dīwān al-Ḥamāsa*, p. 1719 and cf. pp. 1098, 1577. A variant, *inna l-ḥadītha jānibun mina l-qirā*, is a *rajaz* line by an anonymous poet, *ibid.*, p. 1750, attributed to al-Shammākh (with *ṭarafun* instead of *jānibun*) in *al-Aghānī*, ix, 168.
93 *Iḥyā' ^culūm al-dīn*, ii, 7, 8, German translation in Hans Kindermann, *Über die guten Sitten beim Essen und Trinken*, pp. 13, 16 (cf. notes pp. 121–24).
94 [Ps.-]Jāḥiẓ, *al-Tāj fī akhlāq al-mulūk*, pp. 18–19.
95 Mas^cūdī, *Murūj*, i, 262 (= ii, 108–110).
96 e.g. al-Washshā', *al-Muwashshā*, p. 130, Ibn Sayyār, *Ṭabīkh*, p. 336.
97 Jamāl al-Dīn Yaḥyā Ibn ^cAbd al-^cAẓīm al-Jazzār, *Fawā'id al-mawā'id*, fol. 5^v–6^r; see on this work Renato Traini, 'Un trattatello di galateo ed etica conviviale: le *Fawā'id al-mawā'id* di Ibn al-Ǧazzār'.
98 Ibn Sayyār, *Ṭabīkh*, pp. 338–39.
99 Ibn Sayyār, *Ṭabīkh*, p. 339; not in the *Dīwān*.
100 al-Qifṭī, *Inbāh al-ruwāt*, iv, 125, also (without the pun on *adab*) in al-Tha^cālibī, *Yatīmat al-dahr*, ii, 351.
101 al-Mas^cūdī, *Murūj al-dhahab*, v, 250–58 (= old ed. viii, 391–409), translated by A.J. Arberry in his 'A Baghdad Cookery-Book', pp. 21–30.
102 The correct rendering would be 'Pale as a lover's complexion'.
103 'A Baghdad Cookery-Book', 28–29; the Arabic text in *Murūj al-dhahab*, v, 256 (= viii, 404–5), Kushājim, *Dīwān*, pp. 366–67, and (with some variants) Ibn Sayyār al-Warrāq, *Kitāb al-ṭabīkh*, p. 241.
104 For other 'banquet poems', see my article 'Musāwir al-Warrāq and the beginnings of Arabic gastronomic poetry'.
105 *Murūj al-dhahab*, v, 188–90 (= viii, 239–42), translated by Paul Lunde and Caroline Stone in al-Masudi, *The Meadows of Gold: the Abbasids*, pp. 372–77.
106 *Murūj*: *thawat*, *Dīwān*: *nawat* (chosen for this translation), *Zahr al-ādāb*: *ghalat*, *Jam^c al-jawāhir*: *hawat*!
107 Reading, with the *Dīwān*, *qānā* instead of *fa-atā* or *fa-idhā*, found in the other sources.
108 Reading *bintuhā* with the *Dīwān* instead of *duhnuhā* in *Murūj*, since it seems to fit better with *ṣahīr*, 'molten fat', implying a pun with *ṣihr* 'son/brother-in-law'.
109 Reading, with the *Dīwān* and *Dīwān al-ma^cānī*, *mudaqqaqāt* instead of *muraqqaqāt* found in the other soures. On *mudaqqaqa* see e.g. Ibn Sayyār, *Ṭabīkh*, pp. 194–95, Arberry, 'A Baghdad Cookery-Book', pp. 190–91, 195, Ibn al-^cAdīm, *Wuṣla*, pp. 524, 537–38, 541–42, 880, *Kanz al-fawā'id*, index.

110 *Dīwān*: *mulassanun* [read *mulsanun*, *metri causa*] *wa-mudannarū*; most of the other texts have *mulbasun wa-mudaththarū*.

111 al-Mas^{c}ūdī, *Murūj*, v, 188–89 (= viii, 239–40); see also Ibn al-Rūmī, *Dīwān*, p. 954, Ibn Abī ^{c}Awn, *al-Tashbīhāt*, p. 286, Abū Hilāl al-^{c}Askarī, *Dīwān al-ma^{c}ānī*, i, 294, al-Ḥuṣrī, *Zahr al-ādāb*, p. 342, idem, *Jam^c al-jawāhir*, p. 287, al-Rāghib al-Iṣbahānī, *Muḥāḍarāt*, i, 377. My translation is more literal and less poetical than that of Lunde and Stone (*op. cit.*, pp. 375–76).

112 Rhuvon Guest, *Life and Works of Ibn er Rûmî*, p. 49; cf. al-Ḥuṣrī, *Zahr al-ādāb*, p. 347, al-Ḥuṣrī, *Jam^c al-jawāhir*, p. 290.

113 Ibn al-Rūmī, *Dīwān*, pp. 232–38, see vss. 70–85, quoted by al-Ḥuṣrī in his *Zahr*, pp. 345–46 and *Jam^c al-jawāhir*, p. 288.

114 Bürgel, 'Die ekphrastischen Epigramme'; on fruit, food and drinks, see pp. 273–98, Arabic text pp. 315–305 (retrogr.); cf. al-Tha^{c}ālibī, *al-Yatīma*, iv, 175–87.

115 Bürgel, 'Die ekphrastischen Epigramme', p. 295; on this sweet, not identified by Bürgel, see e.g. the recipes in Ibn al-^{c}Adīm, *Wuṣla*, p. 642, *Kanz al-fawā'id*, pp. 109, 117.

116 Bürgel, 'Die ekphrastischen Epigramme', p. 293.

117 Bürgel, 'Die ekphrastischen Epigramme', pp. 287–88.

118 al-Mas^{c}ūdī, *Murūj* v, 133 (= viii, 104).

119 al-Mas^{c}ūdī, *Murūj*, v, 15–16 (= vii, 215–18).

120 al-Mas^{c}ūdī, *Murūj*, iv, 312–13 (= vii, 32–35). Peter Heine (*Kulinarische Studien*, p. 25) casts an undeserved slur upon al-Ma'mūn's name as a cook: he interprets, wrongly it seems, the judgement on his concoction as negative, being over-spiced. On the contrary, it is praised highly by being compared to musk.

121 al-Shābushtī, *Diyārāt*, pp. 186–87.

122 Ibn al-Nadīm, *Fihrist*, pp. 116, 317.

123 Ibn al-Nadīm, *Fihrist*, pp. 122, 317, Yāqūt, *Mu^{c}jam al-udabā'*, i, 198.

124 Ibn al-Nadīm, *Fihrist*, pp. 143, 317, Yāqūt, *Mu^{c}jam al-udabā'*, xv, 144, Ibn Khallikān, *Wafayāt*, iii, 374.

125 Ibn al-Nadīm, *Fihrist*, pp. 145, 317, Yāqūt, *Mu^{c}jam al-udabā'*, ii, 242.

126 Ibn al-Nadīm, *Fihrist*, Anmerkungen, p. 56 (*ad* p. 139), Ḥājjī Khalīfa, *Kashf al-ẓunūn*, (ii,) 1432. For more early authors of cookery books, see e.g. the editors' introduction to Ibn Sayyār's *Kitāb al-ṭabīkh*, pp. v–viii, Kaj Öhrnberg, 'Ibn Sattār al-Warrāq's *Kitāb al-wuṣla ilà al-ḥabīb/Kitāb al-ṭabbākh*: Another Ms of Ibn Sayyār al-Warrāq's *Kitāb al-ṭabīkh*', pp. 30–31.

127 See e.g. *al-Zahra* by Ibn Dāwūd al-Iṣbahānī (d. 297/909).

128 Often called Maḥmūd Ibn al-Ḥusayn (or al-Ḥasan!) or Abū l-Fatḥ in the source. Several of the poems are not found in the printed edition of Kushājim's *Dīwān* (cf. pp. 96, 102, 108, 113–14, 116, 117, 129).

129 *murrī*, see e.g. Muhammad Manazir Ahsan, *Social Life Under the Abbasids*, p. 105.

130 I do not understand *w-'ḍ^{c}f*; read perhaps *wa-ṣfuf*.

131 I prefer the reading *al-narjis*, given as a variant in the critical apparatus to *al-rukhbīn* ('sour milk' or 'butter-milk') in the text.

132 Ibn Sayyār, *al-ṭabīkh*, p. 180. On *narjisiyya* see also Ibn Sayyār, pp. 178–79, 181–83, Ibn al-ᶜAdīm, *al-Wuṣla ilā l-ḥabīb*, pp. 575–76, Arberry, 'A Baghdad Cookery-Book', p. 192, al-Tujībī, *Faḍalat* [or rather *Fuḍālat*] *al-khiwān*, pp. 114, 165, *Kanz al-fawā'id*, p. 43. Ibrāhīm's recipe, turned into prose, transformed into a modern recipe and provided with an appetizing photograph of the result, may be found in David Waines, *In a Caliph's Kitchen*, pp. 84–85.

133 e.g. seventeen lines on a *rībāsiyya* (poultry with gooseberry) by al-Ḥāfiẓ Muḥammad Ibn al-Wazīr, pp. 157–58.

134 See above, note 39.

135 Ibn Sayyār, *Ṭabīkh*, pp. 76–77; the translation is tentative in some places, the text being metrically corrupt in a few lines.

136 *Dīwān*, pp. 2648–49, 17 couplets; also al-Masᶜūdī, *Murūj*, v, 252 (= viii, 396–98).

137 *Wāhan thanāyāka wa-kadman kadman*; al-Masᶜūdī has *Imla' thanāyāka wa-kdim kadman*, which does not scan.

138 On this last expression, see A. Mez in *Abulḳāsim*, xxix (ad p. 11 of the text). Abū Riyāsh, the messy eater described above (pp. 58–59), is also described as *rajīm shayṭān al-maᶜida* (al-Thaᶜālibī, *Yatīma*, ii, 351, al-Qifṭī, *Inbāh*, iv, 125).

139 Ibn Sayyār, *Ṭabīkh*, p. 186.

140 See Wolfhart Heinrichs, 'Scherzhafter badīᶜ bei Abū Nuwās'.

141 Abū l-Qāsim al-Ḥasan Ibn Ḥabīb al-Nīsābūrī, *ᶜUqalā' al-majānīn*, pp. 166–67.

142 *ᶜUqalā' al-majānīn*, pp. 168–69; cf. p. 170 (spiritual *ᶜaṣīda*) and 205–6 ('the *fālūdh* of those who possess spiritual knowledge'). These metaphorical recipes differ from the more concrete versified recipes in medieval Europe described by Melitta Weiss Adamson, 'The Games Cooks Play: Non-Sense Recipes and Practical Jokes in Medieval Literature', pp. 177–95.

143 See above, note 96.

144 *al-Ṭabīkh*, p. 338.

145 *al-Aghānī*, xviii, 317–18. The last line is a variation on a well-known proverb.

146 *fa-duqqa daqqa l-kawdaniyyi l-dayrajī*: the editor explains *kawdaniyy* as 'elephant'. Ullmann, *Untersuchungen*, p. 111 (reading *fa-daqqa*) translates 'da stampfte er, wie das langsam einherschreitende Maultier stampft'. I suspect *dayraj* might be a mistake for *dayzaj* (Persian *dēza*) 'ash-coloured, striped' (said of horses).

147 *al-Aghānī*, xviii, 319.

148 For an example of drinking, exceptionally, between courses, see al-Iṣfahānī, *Aghānī*, xvi, 10.

149 al-Ṣafadī, *Wāfī*, xxi, 45–50.

150 Ahsan, *Social Life under the Abbasids*, p. 111; elsewhere (p. 164) he quotes A. Mez, *The Renaissance of Islam*, p. 396: 'Even in the most dissolute period, wine was never taken with meals'. Ahsan does not mention that wine was often drunk afterwards; for, as Mez says (p. 397), 'Inspite *[sic]* of the Quranic prohibition drinking became widely-diffused.'

151 Ibn al-Khaṭīb, *Nufāḍat al-jirāb*, as quoted in Aḥmad Mukhtār al-ᶜAbbādī (ed.), *Mushāhadāt Lisān al-Dīn al-Khaṭīb fī bilād al-Maghrib wa-l-Andalus*, pp. 122-23.
152 al-Rashīd Ibn al-Zubayr, *al-Dhakhā'ir wa-l-tuḥaf*, pp. 107-8.
153 al-Thaᶜālibī, *Thimār al-qulūb*, pp. 165-67, idem, *Laṭā'if al-maᶜārif*, pp. 72-75, transl. Bosworth, *The Book of Curious and Entertaining Information*, pp. 99-101 (with more references). See also Manuela Marín, 'Sobre Būrān y *būrāniyya*'.
154 Ibn Bassām, *al-Dhakhīra*, ed. Cairo, IV, i, 99 (in the section on ᶜAbd al-ᶜAzīz b. Muḥammad al-Sūsī).
155 al-Ḥanafī, *Maqāmāt*, pp. 62-71.
156 al-Musabbiḥī, *Akhbār Miṣr fī sanatayn (414-415 H)*, pp. 134-36; several critical replies by various other writers (pp. 137-45) also abound with culinary references.
157 Koran, sura 3:134.
158 A hemistich by Muslim Ibn al-Walīd, cf. his *Dīwān*, p. 164.
159 al-Musabbiḥī, *Akhbār*, p. 135. The line by ᶜAbd Banī l-Ḥasḥās in his *Dīwān*, p. 55.
160 Following the text of Mahdī's edition (p. 374); in *al-Ḥikāyāt al-ᶜajība* (pp. 65-66) one finds white bread, *harīsa*, *sikbāj* with duck, kid, *maḍīra* with chicken fattened with pistachio nuts, *ṭabāhajāt*, *būrāniyya*, *lawzīnaj*, *qaṭā'if*, *khabīṣa* with almonds, followed by wine and fruit.
161 *Aghānī*, xix, 141-42, Rosenthal, *Humor in Early Islam*, pp. 49-50, al-Muᶜāfā al-Jarīrī, *Jalīs*, ii, 265; cf. the versions *Aghānī*, xix, 151 (Rosenthal, *Humor*, p. 63), al-Jāḥiẓ, *Bukhalā'*, p. 149, Ibn Qutayba, *ᶜUyūn*, iii, 260-61, Ibn ᶜAbd Rabbih, *ᶜIqd*, vi, 182, al-Rāghib al-Iṣfahānī, *Muḥāḍarāt*, i, 410.
162 al-Ḥarīrī, *Maqāmāt*, pp. 199-214, al-Sharīshī, *Sharḥ*, ii, 104-39.
163 *min gharab*: made of a kind of wood, or of silver, according to the commentators.
164 al-Tanūkhī, *Faraj*, iv, 358-69, idem, *Nishwār*, iv, 177-90 (taken from Ibn al-Jawzī, *Muntaẓam*), al-Anṭākī, *Tazyīn al-aswāq*, i, 351-53, *Alf layla wa-layla* (Mahdī), pp. 304-15 (transl. Haddawy pp. 228-38). See also Ashtiany, 'al-Tanūkhī's *al-Faraj baᶜd al-shidda* as a literary source', pp. 111-13.
165 See on these two dishes e.g. Arberry, 'A Baghdad Cookery-Book', pp. 35-36, Ibn Sayyār, *Ṭabīkh*, pp. 150-54, Ahsan, *Social Life*, p. 84.
166 al-Tanūkhī, *Faraj*, iv, 129-32, idem, *Nishwār*, iii, 195-97, al-Damīrī, *Ḥayāt*, ii, 228, al-ᶜĀmilī, *Mikhlāt*, pp. 49-50, Ibn Baṭṭūṭa, *Riḥla*, pp. 213-14. The Persian mystical poet Rūmī has used the story in his *Mathnawī*, see the illustration in B. Lewis (ed.), *The World of Islam*, London, 1976, p. 136.
167 al-Iṣfahānī, *Aghānī*, xxiii, 98.
168 *Alf layla wa-layla* (Ṣubayḥ) ii, 200-202.
169 *Alf layla wa-layla* (Ṣubayḥ) iii, 184.
170 Gerhardt, *The Art of Story-Telling*, p. 331.
171 Abū l-Muṭahhar al-Azdī, *Ḥikāyat Abī l-Qāsim al-Baghdādī / Abulḳāsim: ein bagdâder Sittenbild*.

172 *Ḥikāyat Abī l-Qāsim*, p. 2, al-Jāḥiẓ, *Bayān*, i, 70.

173 *Ḥikāya*, p. 3. Shmuel Moreh, in his stimulating discussion of the *risāla*, leaves out all the positive elements from Abū l-Qāsim's description, thus distorting the picture (*Live Theatre and Dramatic Literature in the Medieval Arabic World*, p. 99).

174 *Ḥikāya*, p. 146.

175 *Ḥikāya*, p. 6.

176 *Ḥikāya*, p. 10. The last word, *qudūr*, puns on *qidr* 'pot' and *qadar*, 'lot, fate'. The poem is found anonymously in al-Khaṭīb al-Baghdādī, *al-Taṭfīl*, p. 86, al-Aqfahsī, *al-Qawl al-nabīl bi-dhikr al-taṭfīl*, p. 169.

177 *Ḥikāya*, p. 10; cf. the advice of parasites in al-Baghdādī, *Taṭfīl*, 141–45 (partly in al-Tanūkhī, *Nishwār*, vii, 147–49) and 162; e.g. 'Eat the *fālūdh* when it is there; leave the vegetables, they are no good. / But attack the kid . . .'

178 The epithets are unclear; Hawīd is 'the territory of Samarqand' (Steingass, *Persian-English Dictionary*).

179 Daqūq or Daqūqā: a place in al-Jazīra (cf. *EI2* s.v.).

180 *Ḥikāya*, p. 38.

181 *ḥabbat al-khaḍrā'*: an early reference to hashish, it seems; cf. the following word (*shahdānaj*) and see Rosenthal, *The Herb*, index s.v. *ḥabba*, *khaḍrā'* and *shahdānaj*.

182 *Ḥikāya*, p. 40. Mez gives some explanations in his notes and glossary, other terms may be found in cookery books edited since Mez made his edition.

183 *Ḥikāya*, p. 42.

184 *Ḥikāya*, pp. 91–92; cf. Hamadhānī, *Maqāmāt*, p. 93, transl. Prendergast, p. 82.

185 *Ḥikāya*, p. 99.

186 *Ḥikāya*, pp. 99–102.

187 *Ḥikāya*, p. 19.

188 Ismail El Outmani, *Anatomies of Subversion in Arabic and Spanish Literatures: Towards a Redefinition of the Picaresque*, pp. 100–106.

189 *Ḥikāya*, p. 4.

190 *Ḥikāya*, p. 16; *maraqtu* 'I pierced' could also be interpreted as 'I filled with broth'. The translation of *ʿaṣīb* is based on the context; literally it may mean 'tripe'; cf. also p. 137: *wa-ʿaṣībin shawāhu tannūru mifsā-/ka fa-alqayta taḥtahū jūdhābah*.

191 *Ḥikāya*, p. 62.

192 *Ḥikāya*, p. 63.

193 *Ḥikāya*, p. 97.

194 Ibn al-Jarrāḥ, *al-Waraqa*, pp. 128–31, al-Marzubānī, *Muʿjam al-shuʿarā'*, p. 184.

195 Ibn al-Jarrāḥ, *Waraqa*, p. 129.

196 Ibn al-Jarrāḥ, *Waraqa*, pp. 130–31.

Chapter V – Food for Satire and Parody

1 al-Jāḥiẓ, *Ḥayawān*, i, 267 (with more examples), ii, 124, *al-Bukhalā'*, p. 235, Ibn Qutayba, *Ma^{c}ānī*, p. 254, *^{c}Uyūn*, iii, 212, al-Tawḥīdī, *Mathālib*, p. 302, al-Rāghib al-Iṣbahānī, *Muḥāḍarāt al-udabā'*, i, 386. Not found in the *Dīwān*, ed. Beirut, Dār Ṣādir.

2 al-Jāḥiẓ, *Ḥayawān*, i, 267, ii, 159–60, iv, 41, al-Jāḥiẓ, *Bukhalā'*, p. 234.

3 al-Jāḥiẓ, *Ḥayawān*, i, 268, 319, *al-Bukhalā'*, p. 235.

4 The poet is al-Kumayt Ibn Ta^{c}laba.

5 The poet is Sālim Ibn Dāra. For the story and the poetry, see e.g. al-Jāḥiẓ, *al-Bayān wa-l-tabyīn*, iv, 38–39, ps.-Jāḥiẓ, *al-Maḥāsin wa-l-aḍdād*, p. 87–88, al-Maydānī, *Majma^c al-amthāl*, i, 156–57, al-Baghdādī, *Khizānat al-adab*, iii, 266–67, vii, 521–23.

6 Abū Nuwās, *Dīwān*, ii, 8–9.

7 By Ḍabīs Ibn Rāfi^c al-^{c}Aḍalī, al-Sukkarī, *Sharḥ ash^{c}ār al-Hudhaliyyīn*, pp. 729–31, al-Jāḥiẓ, *al-Bukhalā'*, p. 235; cf. *Sharḥ ash^{c}ār al-Hudhaliyyīn*, pp. 731–32 and 737 for lines by different poems on the same event.

8 *Sharḥ ash^{c}ār al-Hudhaliyyīn*, p. 781, Ḥassān Ibn Thābit, *Dīwān*, p. 251. The virgins mentioned in connection with meat somehow echo Imra' al-Qays's *Mu^{c}allaqa* in which virgins throw pieces of meat with fat at each other; cf. also, from a short poem by al-Farazdaq: '. . . while the pot was boiling with white pieces of camel hump fat; the bobbing up of the humps in it was like virgins looking at other virgins' (*Dīwān*, i, 203, reading *tir^{c}īb* instead of *targhīb*; cf. al-Jāḥiẓ, *Bukhalā'*, p. 225, transl. Ch. Pellat in *Arabica* 2 [1955] 332–33).

9 Abū ^{c}Ubayda, *Naqā'iḍ Jarīr wa-l-Farazdaq*, pp. 1085–86, cf. al-Mubarrad, *Kāmil*, i, 99–100, al-Jāḥiẓ, *al-Bayān*, i, 190, al-Marzubānī, *Mu^{c}jam al-shu^{c}arā'*, p. 480, al-Baghdādī, *Khizānat al-adab*, vi, 523, 527. The poet is Abū l-Muhawwish al-Faq^{c}asī or Abū l-Hawas al-Asadī or Yazīd Ibn al-Ṣa^{c}iq.

10 Ibn ^{c}Abd Rabbih, *^{c}Iqd*, ii, 462, al-Baghdādī, *Khizānat al-adab*, vi, 527; cf. Ibn Qutayba, *Adab al-kātib*, pp. 13–14.

11 al-Jāḥiẓ, *Ḥayawān*, iii, 66–67, cf. al-Baghdādī, *Khizānat al-adab*, vi, 527.

12 Ḥassān Ibn Thābit, *Dīwān*, p. 153.

13 al-Jāḥiẓ, *Bukhalā'*, p. 235.

14 al-Akhfash, *Ikhtiyārayn*, pp. 214–15, al-^{c}Askarī, *Maṣūn*, p. 86; the whole poem in Ibn Maymūn, *Muntahā l-ṭalab*, iii, 237–38.

15 The *qāḍī* Ismā^{c}īl Ibn Ḥammād, in al-Jāḥiẓ, *Ḥayawān*, v, 27.

16 Ibn Qutayba, *al-Ma^{c}ārif*, p. 621, al-Muṭahhar Ibn Ṭāhir al-Maqdisī, *al-Bad' wa-l-ta'rīkh*, iv, 31–32.

17 For a different garbled account of the Eucharist, see above, p. 42.

18 J.G. Frazer, *The Golden Bough: A Study in Magic and Religion*, pp. 629–48; see e.g. pp. 641–44, on Aztec idols made of dough and eaten sacramentally.

19 *Alf layla wa-layla*, transl. Littmann, iv, 502.

20 al-Jāḥiẓ, *Ḥayawān*, i, 234, iv, 41, 61, 94.
21 See the commentaries on Koran 5:60; cf. Jarīr, *Dīwān*, p. 601: 'You say the snort-nose pig was a Jewish tribe? I say it was your father.' – On pigs in Islam, see F. Viré, art. 'Khinzīr' in *EI2*, Richard A. Lobban Jr., 'Pigs and their prohibition'; on eating pork in general, Marvin Harris, *Good to Eat*, ch. 4: 'The Abominable Pig' (pp. 67–87).
22 Jarīr, *Dīwān*, p. 858.
23 Referring to the Bedouin game of *maysir* to divide portions of a slaughtered camel.
24 Jarīr, *Dīwān*, pp. 156–59, *Naqā'iḍ Jarīr wa-l-Akhṭal*, pp. 175–76.
25 *Naqā'iḍ Jarīr wa-l-Akhṭal*, p. 208, Jarīr, *Dīwān*, p. 750. The verb used in the *Naqā'iḍ* (*nazat*) suggests that she is after sexual rather than alimentary delights.
26 *addat li-* in both editions; read *adat li-*? The same expression also in al-Akhṭal's poem to which Jarịr responds (*Naqā'iḍ Jarīr wa-l-Akhṭal*, p. 139).
27 *Naqā'iḍ Jarīr wa-l-Akhṭal*, pp. 147–48, Jarīr, *Dīwān*, p. 239.
28 *bi-l-Kunāsati*, referring to a famous location in al-Kufa, favoured by poets for their performances. It could be literally translated, in this context, as 'amongst the offal'.
29 Jarīr, *Dīwān*, p. 232, *Naqā'iḍ Jarīr wa-l-Akhṭal*, p. 126.
30 Jarīr, *Dīwān*, p. 675.
31 For the story see e.g. Geert Jan van Gelder, *The Bad and the Ugly*, pp. 24–25.
32 See Ignaz Goldziher, 'Ṣâliḥ b. ᶜAbd al-Ḳuddûs und das Zindîḳthum während der Regierung des Chalifen al-Mahdî', p. 125, Geert Jan van Gelder, 'Musāwir al-Warrāq', p. 327.
33 See, besides illustrations in this study, the poem discussed and translated in my 'The Joking Doctor: Abū l-Ḥakam ᶜUbayd Allāh Ibn al-Muẓaffar (d. 549/1155)', pp. 217–28; or the long poem by al-Wāsānī (d. 1004) in al-Thaᶜālibī, *Yatīmat al-dahr*, i, 339–48: examples of the Painful Dinner, 'one of the chief themes for satiric description' (Highet, *The Anatomy of Satire*, p. 221).
34 pp. 59–60.
35 Ibn Shuhayd, *Risālat al-tawābiᶜ wa-l-zawābiᶜ*, pp. 162–66, translated in James T. Monroe, *Risālat at-tawābiᶜ wa z-zawābiᶜ / The Treatise of Familiar Spirits and Demons by Abū ᶜĀmir ibn Shuhaid al-Ashjaᶜī, al-Andalusī*, pp. 74–76.
36 Monroe, *op. cit.*, p. 76, changing his 'unique wind' into 'withering wind' (cf. Sura 51:41).
37 Abū l-ᶜAtāhiya, *Dīwān*, p. 351.
38 al-Khaṭīb al-Baghdādī, *Taṭfīl*, p. 166, al-Aqfahsī, *al-Qawl al-nabīl bi-dhikr al-taṭfīl*, p. 158.
39 al-Khaṭīb al-Baghdādī, *Taṭfīl*, pp. 166–68, al-Aqfahsī, *al-Qawl al-nabīl*, pp. 158–59.
40 Reading *rikhla*; the editions have *d.khla*.
41 See Ibn Sayyār al-Warrāq, *ṭabīkh*, pp. 165–66, Anon., *Kanz al-fawā'id*, pp. 30–31, 45–46, 52, 193.
42 *zallat* (al-Baghdādī); or 'are humbled' (*dhallat*, al-Aqfahsī).

43 Reading *inqāl* or *anqāl* instead of *anfāl*, which I do not understand.
44 *Alf layla wa-layla* (Mahdī), p. 172; the translation by Haddawy (pp. 107–8) obscures the reference to the convention of asking one's companions to turn aside with the camels to reminisce at an abandoned camp-site. See the German versions in Littmann's translation, i, 152, iii, 268, v, 571. The meaning of *khubz al-maᶜārīj* is not known.
45 al-Maᶜarrī, *Risālat al-ghufrān*, pp. 268 ff.
46 *Risālat al-ghufrān*, pp. 281–84.
47 Muᶜāfā al-Jarīrī, *al-Jalīs al-ṣāliḥ al-kāfī*, iii, 280, and cf. above, p. 23.
48 *Risālat al-Ghufrān*, p. 271.
49 See R. A. Nicholson, *Studies in Islamic Poetry*, pp. 134–36.
50 The extensive discussion, in the form of letters, is preserved in Yāqūt, *Muᶜjam al-udabā'*, iii, 175–213.
51 e.g. al-Ṭabarī, *Tārīkh*, i, 1934, 1975, Ibn Ḥubaysh, *al-Ghazawāt*, i, 54, 57, al-Jāḥiẓ, *Ḥayawān*, v, 530, al-Bāqillānī, *Iᶜjāz al-Qur'ān*, p. 157, al-Khaṭṭābī, *Bayān iᶜjāz al-Qur'ān*, p. 55, Ibn ᶜAbd Rabbihi, *ᶜIqd*, ii, 66.
52 See W.M. Watt, *Muḥammad at Medina*, pp. 134–35.
53 al-Ṭabarī, *Tārīkh*, i, 1934, al-Bāqillānī, *Iᶜjāz*, p. 157.
54 Translation of the three passages by Arberry. The translation obscures the morphological similarity: *Wa-l-mubadhdhirāti zarᶜā / wa-l-ḥāṣidāti ḥaṣdā / wa-l-dhāriyāti qamḥā / wa-l-ṭāḥināti ṭāḥnā / wa-l-khābizāti khabzā* . . . (Musaylima); *Wa-l-dhāriyāti dharwā / fa-l-ḥāmilāti wiqrā* . . . (sura 51), *Wa-l-nāziᶜāti gharqā / wa-l-nāshiṭāti nashṭā* . . . (sura 79), *Wa-l-ᶜādiyāti ḍabḥā / fa-l-mūriyāti qadḥā / fa-l-mughīrāti ṣubḥā* . . . (sura 100). See also the openings of suras 37 and 77.
55 See on these Koranic introductory passages Angelika Neuwirth, 'Der Horizont der Offenbarung. Zur Relevanz der einleitenden Schwurserien für die Suren der frühmekkanischen Zeit', in Udo Tworuschka (ed.), *Gottes ist der Orient, Gottes ist der Okzident: Festschrift für Abdoldjavad Falaturi* . . ., Köln - Wien, 1991, pp. 3–39, esp. 5–13.
56 The same applies to another, obscene piece of rhymed prose attributed to Musaylima, with sexual intercourse and human reproduction as its theme; see e.g. Ṭabarī, *Tārīkh*, i, 1917–18, *Aghānī*, xxi, 34, al-Bāqillānī, *Iᶜjāz*, p. 157.
57 See D.B. MacDonald & S.A. Bonebakker, art. 'Iḳtibās' in *EI2*.
58 al-Ābī, *Nathr al-durr*, ii, 251–52, al-Khaṭīb al-Baghdādī, *Taṭfīl*, pp. 120–21, al-Aqfahsī, *al-Qawl al-nabīl*, pp. 81–82, more references in Ulrich Marzolph, *Arabia Ridens*, ii, 180 (no. 766).
59 *kharaqtu* (as in al-Baghdādī), cf. the following; al-Aqfahsī has *jaraftu* 'I scooped', Ibn al-Jawzī has *jarra* 'he drew'.
60 al-Khaṭīb al-Baghdādī, *Taṭfīl*, pp. 172–74, al-Aqfahsī, *al-Qawl al-nabīl*, pp. 162–63, Ibn al-Jawzī, *al-Adhkiyā'*, pp. 207–8; more references in Marzolph, *Arabia Ridens*, ii, 229 (no. 1035). All Koranic translations are Arberry's.
61 See e.g. Ṣafī al-Dīn al-Ḥillī, *Sharḥ al-Kāfiya al-badīᶜiyya*, pp. 326–27, Ibn Ḥijja al-Ḥamawī, *Khizānat al-adab*, pp. 539–54, al-Tanasī, *Naẓm*

al-durr wa-l-ᶜiqyān / Westarabische Tropik, pp. 309–32, German introd. pp. 58–64, *Shurūḥ al-Talkhīṣ*, iv, 509–14, al-ᶜAbbāsī, *Maᶜāhid al-tanṣīṣ*, ii, 166–67, al-Zarkashī, *al-Burhān fī ᶜulūm al-Qur'ān*, i, 481–85, al-Suyūṭī, *al-Itqān*, i, 386–91.

62 See *EI2* s.v. 'Busḥāḳ' with more references; A.J. Arberry, *Classical Persian Literature*, pp. 410–12, Daniela Meneghini Correale, 'Tra il serio e il faceto. Parte seconda: Ḥāfiẓ e Busḥāq', Heshmat Moayyad, art. 'Busḥāq', in *Encyclopaedia Iranica*, iv (London, 1990).

63 Lithograph edition, Cairo, AH 1280. I am grateful to Dr Arnoud Vrolijk, Leiden, who has recently made an edition of this text, for providing me with a copy and for several useful suggestions concerning the text. On Ibn Sūdūn (not found worthy of a lemma in *EI2*) see *GAL* II, 18–19, *S* II, 11, F. Kern, 'Neuere ägyptische Humoristen und Satiriker', pp. 31–36, 49–58, Manuela Marín, 'Literatura y gastronomía', pp. 138–49, 152.

64 Ibn Sūdūn, *Nuzha*, p. 3, Kern, 'Neue ägyptische Humoristen und Satiriker', pp. 32, 51.

65 On this topic, see G.J.H. van Gelder, 'Mixtures of Jest and Earnest in Classical Arabic Literature'.

66 'geistlosen Reimereien': Kern, 'Neuere ägyptischen Humoristen und Satiriker', p. 33.

67 *Nuzha*, p. 2.

68 *Nuzha*, pp. 53–54.

69 Recipes in *Kanz al-fawā'id*, pp. 35, 37, 121–22, 271; cf. Ibn Sayyār, *Ṭabīkh*, pp. 247, 249, 256 etc.

70 Dozy, *Supplément*, s.v., *Kanz al-fawā'id*, p. 127 and cf. index s.v. *qaṭr*.

71 *Nuzha*, p. 47, cf. p. 54: 'O bananas, o syrup, visit my dwelling, visit!'

72 Or 'sea'; but *baḥr* usually means the Nile to Egyptians, cf. *Nuzha*, p. 67: 'The *baḥr* is a *baḥr* even though they call it the Nile'.

73 *Nuzha*, p. 48, cf. Kern, 'Neuere ägyptische Humoristen', pp. 33, 52. An older example attributed to Ibn Hāni' ('Night is night and day is day / A mule is a mule, an ass is an ass' etc.) in Ibn al-Dawādārī, *Kanz al-durar*, vi, 246, attrib. to Abū Nuwās in al-Qazwīnī, *Āthār al-bilād*, p. 327, or to Ibn Ḥazm, cf. *Rasā'il Ibn Ḥazm*, iv, 354.

74 *ᶜuslūl*: perhaps a mock-formation of *ᶜasal*.

75 On 'killing' hashish see F. Rosenthal, *The Herb: Hashish versus Medieval Muslim Society*, pp. 59–60.

76 See e.g. al-Bukhārī, *Ṣaḥīḥ*, 'Ṭalāq' (68) nos. 7, 37, 'Libās' (77) nos. 6, 23; cf. below, ch. VI note 42.

77 al-Ābī, *Nathr al-durr*, iv, 260, al-Rāghib al-Iṣbahānī, *Muḥāḍarāt al-udabā'*, ii, 163, al-Ghuzūlī, *Maṭāliᶜ al-budūr*, i, 272.

78 Marín, 'Literatura y gastronomía', pp. 146–48, F. Rosenthal, *The Herb*, pp. 14, 57, 65, 79–80, 94, 144, 158.

79 *Kanz al-fawā'id*, p. 122, *al-Wuṣla ilā l-ḥabīb*, pp. 644, 651.

80 Without doubt derived from Persian or Ottoman-Turkish *mushk* (Arabic *misk*), 'musk' (information from Dr Arnoud Vrolijk).

81 *Kanz al-fawā'id*, pp. 106–7, *al-Wuṣla*, p. 644.

82 *Nuzha*, pp. 68–69. A similar edible building appears p. 75.

83 *Nuzha*, pp. 74–75.

84 Rosenthal, *The Herb*, pp. 23–24; for the red eyes pp. 77–78.

85 *Kanz al-fawā'id*, p. 115, *al-Wuṣla ilā l-ḥabīb*, pp. 640–41, 835, Marín, 'Literatura y gastronomía', p. 157.
86 *Nuzha*, pp. 71–72.
87 *Nuzha*, p. 120.
88 al-Wahrānī, *Manāmāt*, p. 112.
89 See Dozy, *Supplément,* s.v., Marín, 'Literatura y gastronomía', p. 156 with more references.
90 *Nuzha*, pp. 69–70.
91 *khushkanānak*, cf. Dozy, *Supplément* s.v. *khushkunānij*.
92 *Nuzha*, p. 78.
93 'Neuere ägyptische Humoristen und Satiriker', p. 34.
94 *Nuzha*, pp. 96–97; the poem transliterated and translated by Kern, 'Neuere ägyptische Humoristen und Satiriker', pp. 34–35.
95 al-Baghdādī, *Taṭfīl*, pp. 175–80, al-Tanūkhī, *Nishwār*, vii, 155–61, al-Qalqashandī, *Ṣubḥ al-aʿshā*, xiv, 360–65.
96 Marín, 'Literatura y gastronomía', p. 152.
97 See e.g. *EI*², art. 'Ibn al-Ḥadjdjādj' (D.S. Margoliouth & Ch. Pellat).
98 *Nuzha*, pp. 129–33, cf. Kern, 'Neuere ägyptische Humoristen und Satiriker', pp. 36 and 55–58 (Arabic text); see also 42–43 for a later elaboration. The reading Qurdān with *u* is explicitly given by Ibn Sūdūn.
99 The word *maṭlūz* or more likely *muṭalwaz* (*muṭawlaz* in Kern's text) is unclear. My translation adopts Kern's suggestion that it may mean 'elongated' and assumes that it may be a Sūdūnian coinage. The reading *muṭawliz* in the Oxford autograph is equally enigmatic (information from Dr Arnold Vrolijk).
100 *Nuzha*, pp. 143–45.
101 See J. Heyworth-Dunne, 'Arabic Literature in Egypt in the Eighteenth century with some Reference to Poetry and Poets', pp. 686–87; Muḥammad Sayyid Kīlānī, *al-Adab al-miṣrī fī ẓill al-ḥukm al-ʿuthmānī*, pp. 204–6; Shawqī Ḍayf, *ʿAṣr al-duwal wa-l-imārāt: Miṣr wa-l-Shām (Tārīkh al-adab al-ʿarabī, VI)*, pp. 384–86; al-Jabartī, *ʿAjā'ib al-āthār fī l-tarājim wa-l-akhbār*, ii, 189–92, transl. Philipp & Perlmann, I, 411–14.
102 On this and similar poems, see Geert Jan van Gelder, 'Arabic Didactic Verse'.
103 al-Jabartī, *ʿAjā'ib*, ii, 190.
104 See E. Wagner, 'Die arabische Rangstreitdichtung und ihre Einordnung in die allgemeine Literaturgeschichte' and his article 'Munāẓara' in *EI2*.
105 *Munāẓarat al-tīn wa-l-ʿinab*, by Muḥammad Ibn Muḥammad Ibn Muḥammad Ibn al-Muḥibb, see W. Ahlwardt, *Verzeichnis der arabischen Handschriften*, vii, 554 (no. 8592).
106 There are many references to this debate; e.g. al-Sijistānī, *al-Nakhl*, p. 46 (*al-ḥabala khayr am al-nakhla?*), Ibn al-Faqīh, *al-Buldān*, pp. 118–27, al-Qālī, *Amālī*, ii, 58, al-Ābī, *Nathr al-durr*, vi, 44, 48, Ahlwardt, *Verzeichnis*, vii, 554 (*Munāẓarat al-ʿinab wa-l-ruṭab*), M. Steinschneider, 'Rangstreit-Literatur', p. 29 (*Munāẓarah bayn al-ruṭab wa-l-ʿinab*). In the debate on 'palm-tree (*nakhl*) vs. crops (*zarʿ*)',

often mentioned, the latter is sometimes said to stand for the vine. When this topic is discussed in the circle of the famous philologian Abū ^{c}Amr Ibn al-^{c}Alā', the poet al-Sayyid al-Ḥimyarī takes his leave after a while, finding it too frivolous (al-Iṣfahānī, *Aghānī*, vii, 267).

107 ^{c}Alī Ibn Muḥammad Ibn al-Shāh al-Ṭāhirī (4th/10th century), a member of the Mīkālī family, wrote a *Kitāb ḥarb al-jubn ma^{c}a l-zaytūn* ('The War of Cheese and Olives'), and a *Kitāb al-laḥm wa-l-samak* ('Meat and Fish'), Yāqūt, *Mu^{c}jam al-udabā'*, xiv, 156, Ṣafadī, *Wāfī*, xxii, 160-61. An anonymous poem of 28 lines with a debate between oil (*zayt*) and meat in Aḥmad al-Hāshimī, *Jawāhir al-adab fī ṣinā^{c}at inshā' al-^{c}arab*, pp. 182 f.

108 J. Finkel, 'King Mutton, A curious Egyptian tale of the Mamluk period'.

109 'Sobre alimentación y sociedad (el texto árabe de la «La guerra deleitosa»)'. An important tool for the identification of the numerous dishes mentioned in the text is the probably contemporary anonymous cookbook *Kanz al-fawā'id fī tanwī^{c} al-mawā'id*, edited by Manuela Marín and David Waines. See also Manuela Marín, 'Literatura y gastronomía'. I cannot explain why the word *ḥarb* in the title is construed as a masculine, contrary to normal usage.

110 'King Mutton', p. 15.

111 See pp. 98, 99, 106, 114, 119, 120. Finkel translates *'Place des Tables'* (pp. 11, 13, 16, 17).

112 Ibn Shāhīn, *Ishārāt*, ii, 332, al-Nābulusī, *Ta^{c}ṭīr*, ii, 250.

113 Finkel, 'King Mutton', p. 142.

114 'leg was entangled with leg': Koran 75:29, *al-Ḥarb*, p. 115 (not identified by the translator, Finkel, 'King Mutton', p. 14); or 'bowls like basins and firm-standing cooking-pots': Koran 34:13, *al-Ḥarb al-ma^{c}shūq* p. 108 (not identified by the editor). Interestingly, it has been suggested that this Koranic phrase is itself a quotation from a line attributed to the pre-Islamic poet Imra' al-Qays, see Ibn Abī l-Iṣba^{c} (d. 654/1256), *Taḥrīr al-taḥbīr*, p. 380 (not found in the *Dīwān* of Imra' al-Qays or elsewhere).

115 Finkel, *op. cit.*, 125.

116 Finkel, *op. cit.*, 143.

117 See also Rodinson, 'Recherches', pp. 113-15.

118 Jack Goody, *Cooking, Cuisine and Class: A Study in Comparative Sociology*, (ch. 4: 'The high and the low: culinary culture in Asia and Europe', pp. 97-153, see pp. 127-33 on Arab food).

119 p. 88, Finkel's translation, p. 2.

120 A variant recorded in the critical apparatus, *mishmishiyya*, is found in *Kanz*, pp. 37, 56.

121 Dozy, *Supplément*, mentions *qishmish* or *kishmish* (a kind of grape).

122 All these dishes are taken from p. 92 of the Arabic text.

123 al-Ghuzūlī, *Maṭāli^{c} al-budūr*, ii, 55.

124 al-Tīfāshī, *Nuzhat al-albāb*, pp. 104-5.

125 al-Ghuzūlī, *Maṭāli^{c} al-budūr*, ii, 41; cf. Ch. Pellat, art. 'Khubz' in *EI2*.

126 al-Zamakhsharī, *Rabī^{c} al-abrār*, ii, 67.

127 Unidentified, quoted in al-Tawḥīdī, *Imtā^{c}*, iii, 75.

128 Tr. Collins, in Al-Muqaddasi, *The Best Divisions for Knowledge of the Regions: A Translation of* Aḥsan al-Taqasim fi Ma^{c}rifat al-Aqalim, p. 46; al-Muqaddasī, *Aḥsan al-taqāsīm*, p. 44.

129 Arberry, 'A Baghdad Cookery-Book', pp. 198–99; cf. Ibn Sayyār al-Warrāq, *Ṭabīkh*, pp. 138–41 (various recipes for *harīsa*), Ibn al-^{c}Adīm, *Wuṣla*, pp. 621–23, 647 (*harīsat fustuq*), al-Tujībī, *Fuḍālat al-khiwān*, pp. 94, 148–49; Kindermann, *Über die guten Sitten*, pp. 89, 241–42, Ahsan, *Social Life*, pp. 131–32.

130 *Die Nahrung der Herzen: Abū Ṭālib al-Makkīs Qūt al-qulūb*, eingeleitet, übersetzt und kommentiert von Richard Gramlich, III, see pp. 266–390 (Parts 39 and 40) on food and eating habits.

131 Ibn al-Jawzī, *Talbīs Iblīs*, pp. 184–95.

132 al-Tha^{c}ālibī, *Thimār al-qulūb*, pp. 174–75, al-Zamakhsharī, *Rabī^c al-abrār*, iii, 592.

133 See e.g. Mhammed Ferid Ghazi, 'Un groupe social: «les Raffinés»'.

134 al-Washshā, *al-Muwashshā*, pp. 129–31, Ibn al-Waššā', *Das Buch des buntbestickten Kleides*, aus dem Arab. übers. von Dieter Bellman, ii, 80–83.

135 Quoted by permission from a draft of: Michael Cooperson, 'Ibn Ḥanbal and Bishr al-Ḥāfī: A Case Study in Biographical Tradition', *Studia Islamica* 86 (1997) 71–101 (where the quoted passage is no longer found).

136 Ibn Khallikān, *Wafayāt*, i, 65.

137 Ibn Ḥijja al-Ḥamawī, *Thamarāt al-awrāq*, pp. 445–46.

138 Yāqūt, *Mu^{c}jam al-udabā'*, xviii, 89–93.

139 See e.g. Ibn Sayyār al-Warrāq, *al-Ṭabīkh*, pp. 159–60, Arberry, 'A Baghdad Cookery-Book', p. 46.

140 e.g. Ibn Sayyār al-Warrāq, *al-Ṭabīkh*, pp. 152–54, Arberry, 'A Baghdad Cookery-Book', p. 36.

141 *fī l-khaysh*; the editor's explanation ('jute clothes') is incorrect.

142 Yāqūt, *Mu^{c}jam al-udabā'*, xviii, 92.

143 See e.g. M. Bakhtin, *L'œuvre de François Rabelais et la culture populaire au Moyen Age et sous la Renaissance*, pp. 285–30 on the literary tradition of the grotesque banquet.

144 Tawḥīdī, *Imtā^c*, iii, 77.

145 Yūsuf Ibn Muḥammad al-Shirbīnī, *Hazz al-quḥūf fī sharḥ qaṣīd Abī Shādūf*, Cairo: al-Maktaba al-Maḥmūdiyya, n.d. The bowdlerized 'edition' by Muḥammad Qandīl al-Baqlī, significantly entitled *Qaryatunā l-Miṣriyya qabla l-Thawra*, Cairo, 1963 (date of preface) is unreliable. The best introduction to the work is Gabriel Baer, 'Shirbīnī's Hazz al-Quḥūf and its Significance'; see also M. Peled, 'Nodding the Necks: A Literary Study of Shirbīnī's *Hazz al-Quḥūf* and Ch. Vial, '*Le Hazz al-Quhūf* de al-Širbīnī est-il un échantillon d'*adab* populaire?'. The word *qiḥf* has several meanings, including 'brainpan', 'skull-cap' and 'yokel, bumpkin'.

146 *Hazz*, p. 2.

147 See e.g. Abd Al Raheim A. Abd Al Raheim, '*Hazz al-Quḥūf:* A new source for the study of the *fallāḥīn* of Egypt in the xviith and xviiith centuries'.

148 *Hazz*, p. 3. For references to and quotations from Ibn Sūdūn, see also pp. 40, 58, 71, 100, 102, 155.
149 *Hazz*, pp. 146-209.
150 Thus instead of the more usual *khushkanānak* or *khushknānaj*; e.g. Arberry, 'A Baghdad Cookery-Book', p. 212, Ibn Sayyār al-Warrāq, *Ṭabīkh*, pp. 271-73, Ibn al-^{c}Adīm, *Wuṣla*, pp. 656, 805; Dozy (*Supplement* i, 372b, cf. 373b) thinks the form with *t* may be a mistake, but it is attested elsewhere (see Yūsuf al-Maghribī, *Daf^c al-iṣr ^{c}an kalām ahl Miṣr*, p. 58), Marín, 'Literatura y gastronomía', p. 142 n. 18.
151 See Dozy, *Supplément*, s.v. *bayṣār* (with *ṣād*); Ibn Razīn al-Tujībī, *Fuḍālat al-khiwān fī ṭayyibāt al-ṭa^{c}ām wa-l-alwān*, pp. 56-57.
152 See Françoise Aubaile-Sallenave, '*Al-Kishk*: The past and present of a complex culinary practice'.
153 *Hazz*, p. 15.
154 *Hazz*, p. 26.
155 *Hazz*, p. 115, see Abd El Raheim, '*Hazz*', p. 261, Baer, *Fellah and Townsman*, pp. 14-15.
156 Neither *The New Grove Dictionary of Music and Musicians* nor *The New Oxford Companion to Music* (Oxford, 1994) have an entry on it, while *Collins Encyclopedia of Music* (London, 1984) does have one but misspells it ('cacophany').
157 Kern, 'Neuere ägyptische Humoristen und Satiriker', pp. 40-41.
158 *julubbān* in Standard Arabic, *gulbān* in M. Hinds & El-Said Badawi, *A Dictionary of Egyptian Arabic*, *gilbān* according to al-Shirbīnī, *Hazz*, p. 168.
159 Most of the poem is translated by Abd Al Raheim, '*Hazz al-Quḥūf*: A New Source', pp. 260, 266-68 (vss. 24-5 and 46 are omitted for no apparent reason).
160 *Hazz*, p. 149.
161 On the Feast of Sacrifice, see *Hazz*, p. 198.
162 This word I have not been able to find elsewhere (the entry in Dozy, *Supplement*, goes back to *Hazz al-quḥūf* through Mehren, *Et Par Bidrag*). Al-Shirbīnī's etymologies of the word (149-50) are spurious. Perhaps it is a corruption of *bīrāf*, a dish described in *Kanz al-fawā'id*, pp. 187-88.
163 *Hazz*, pp. 148-49.
164 *Fellah and Townsman*, p. 22.
165 *Hazz*, pp. 131-39.
166 *Hazz*, pp. 172-74, translated by Finkel, 'King Mutton', pp. 132-36. In the following fragments Finkel's translation is used.
167 *Hazz*, p. 174, Finkel, 'King Mutton', p. 136.
168 See e.g. Pleij, *Dromen van Cocagne*, pp. 175-76, 398-400.
169 If feasts are involved, they are not necessarily always Islamic. Mez (*The Renaissance of Islam*, pp. 418-27) gives examples of Christian, old Persian and other festivals being eagerly celebrated by Muslims.
170 *Hazz*, pp. 223-24.
171 Baer, *Fellah and Townsman*, index s.v. Sandūbī.

Chapter VI – Alimentary Metaphors

1 Attributed to the early Islamic poet Nahshal Ibn Ḥarrī in al-Zamakhsharī, *Kashshāf*, s.v. *ṬYB*.
2 al-Ghazālī, *Iḥyā' ᶜulūm al-dīn*, iii, 79-107.
3 Ibn ᶜAbd Rabbihi, *ᶜIqd*, vi, 300, al-Tijānī, *Tuḥfat al-ᶜarūs wa-mutᶜat al-nufūs*, p. 353; the last of the three is often replaced with 'inserting flesh into flesh', e.g. al-Thaᶜālibī, *Laṭā'if al-luṭf*, p. 93 (attrib. to Aḥmad Ibn al-Ṭayyib al-Sarakhsī), id., *Khāṣṣ al-khāṣṣ*, p. 56 (al-Sarakhsī), al-Qazwīnī, *Āthār al-bilād*, p. 390 (al-Sarakhsī), al-Shirbīnī, *Hazz al-quḥūf*, p. 173 (anon., but attrib. to 'the Imām ᶜAlī' in Finkel's translation, 'King Mutton', p. 133).
4 al-Ghuzūlī, *Maṭāliᶜ al-budūr*, ii, 39. *Mā'ida* is usually translated as 'table', but unlike *khiwān* it implies food being laid on it, as the lexicographers and exegetes say.
5 For the story of Umm Zarᶜ, see e.g al-Bukhārī, *Ṣaḥīḥ (kitāb al-Nikāḥ, bāb Ḥusn al-muᶜāshara)*, Muslim, *Ṣaḥīḥ (kitāb Faḍā'il al-ṣaḥāba, bāb dhikr ḥadīth Umm Zarᶜ)*, al-Ābī, *Nathr al-durr*, iv, 70-73, al-Suyūṭī, *Muzhir*, ii, 532-36; F. Rosenthal, 'Muslim Social Values and Literary Criticism: Reflections on the Ḥadīth of Umm Zarᶜ', *Oriens* 34 (1994) 31-56; for the commentary quoted, see Ibn Abī Ṭāhir Ṭayfūr, *Balāghāt al-nisā'*, p. 114 (I suspect the inserted comment to be much later than the author's time), Muḥammad Fu'ād ᶜAbd al-Bāqī, *al-Lu'lu' wa-l-marjān fīmā ttafaqa ᶜalayh al-Shaykhān*, Cairo, n.d., iii, 146.
6 al-Iṣfahānī, *Aghānī*, xi, 185.
7 *Harīsa*, according to tradition, was recommended to the Prophet by the angel Gabriel, see e.g. J.C. Bürgel, 'Love, Lust and Longing: Eroticism in Early Islam', p. 90, Kindermann, *Über die guten Sitten*, p. 241. For aphrodisiacs, see the books on erotology such as *Rujūᶜ al-shaykh ilā ṣibāh fī l-quwwa ᶜalā l-bāh* ('The Old Man's Rejuvenation in his Power of Copulation') by al-Tīfāshī (attrib. to Ibn Kamāl Bāshā), Cairo, 1309; see also C. Pellat, art. 'Djins' in *EI2*, Malek Chebel, *Encyclopédie de l'amour en Islam*, s.v. 'aphrodisiaques'.
8 *Alf layla wa-layla*, ed. Muhsin Mahdi, pp. 126-38, *The Arabian Nights*, transl. by Husain Haddawy, pp. 66-77.
9 Both taken from Ibn al-Muqaffaᶜ, *al-Adab al-kabīr*, pp. 42 and 90.
10 al-Tanūkhī, *Nishwār*, ii, 172-83, also Ibn Ḥijja al-Ḥamawī, *Thamarāt al-awrāq*, in the margin of al-Ibshīhī, *Mustaṭraf*, ii, 166-74.
11 al-Tanūkhī, *Nishwār*, ii, 174.
12 *Alf layla wa-layla*, ii, 188-91, tr. Littmann, iii, 124-30.
13 Ibn Qayyim al-Jawziyya, *Rawḍat al-muḥibbīn*, p. 328. He supports the quotation with a well-known *ḥadīth* (included in the compilations of al-Bukhārī and Muslim, chapter *al-Nikāḥ*) in which the Prophet recommends marriage to those that are able to have sexual intercourse, while others are enjoined to fast. In fact, there is a difference, because here, it would seem, fasting is not meant to suppress sexual urges. See on the parallels between eating or fasting and sex or chastity also Ibn al-Qayyim, *Rawḍat al-muḥibbīn*, pp. 132-33 and 219.

14 al-Marzūqī, *Sharḥ Dīwān al-ḥamāsa*, pp. 1853. The commentator adds a similar anonymous epigram: 'If you are in love, eat all the fat you can find: / Drive passion and (her) aloofness away from your heart with indigestion. / He who eats has no sickness to fear in matters of love.'
15 al-Marzūqī, *Sharḥ*, p. 1854.
16 al-Tawḥīdī, *Imtā*ᶜ, iii, 8-9.
17 *The Arabian Nights*, translated by Husain Haddawy, p. 6.
18 Francesco Gabrieli, 'Ǧamīl al-ᶜUdrī: Studio critico e raccolta dei frammenti', p. 159; al-Anṭākī, *Tazyīn al-aswāq*, i, 106; attributed to 'a Bedouin' in al-Mubarrad, *Kāmil*, ii, 12 and see Ibn ᶜAbd Rabbih, *ᶜIqd*, iii, 484, vi, 213, 299.
19 Ibn al-Jarrāḥ, *al-Waraqa*, p. 123, al-Zamakhsharī, *Rabīᶜ al-abrār*, ii, 726; cf. al-Aqfahsī, *al-Qawl al-nabīl*, p. 32, and see the encomiastic passage on bread in the *Maqāma zarᶜiyya* by a certain Naṣr al-Dīn al-Ḥusaynī, in al-Ḥanafī (*et al.*), *Maqāmāt*, pp. 322-26.
20 Ibn al-Jarrāḥ, *Waraqa*, pp. 123-24.
21 See Sezgin, *Geschichte*, ii, 593, 696.
22 A dish like *isfīdbāj*, see Dozy, *Supplément*, al-Tujībī, *Fuḍālat al-khiwān*, pp. 103-4, 154.
23 See al-Tujībī, *Fuḍālat al-khiwān*, pp. 95-96, 204 (with beef or fish, not camel meat!).
24 Read probably *wa-jarīshu l-samīdh* instead of *wa-jayshu l-samīdh*.
25 Ibn Bassām, *Dhakhīra*, i, 557.
26 See Marzolph, *Arabia ridens*, indexes s.v. Abū l-Ḥārit ummayn.
27 al-Ḥuṣrī, *Jamᶜ al-jawāhir*, p. 336 (where Ḥusayn should be read Jummayn or Jummayz), al-Mubarrad, *Kāmil*, ii, 11-12.
28 al-Zamakhsharī, *Rabīᶜ al-abrār*, iv, 281.
29 al-Marzūqī, *Sharḥ*, p. 1851.
30 Diᶜbil, *Dīwān*, p. 170.
31 al-Rāghib al-Iṣbahānī, *Muḥāḍarāt*, ii, 186.
32 See e.g. Ridley, *The Origins of Virtue*, pp. 87-89.
33 al-Jāḥiẓ, *Rasā'il*, I, 386-87 and 391-92, al-Ḥuṣrī, *Zahr al-ādāb*, pp. 145, 147; on this form, see Sadan, 'Kings and Craftsmen'.
34 al-Thaᶜālibī, *Khāṣṣ al-khāṣṣ*, p. 53.
35 In both words a change of punctuation could yield forms of the verb *nāka*. In another version of this story, the first speaker calls the boy a *kashkiyya*, while the second replies, 'Yes, once!', apparently since *kashkiyya* can be converted, or perverted, into *kunta niktahu*, 'Have you ever buggered him?' (Ibn al-Jawzī, *Dhamm al-hawā*, p. 98).
36 Ibn al-Muqaffaᶜ, *al-Adab al-kabīr* p. 90.
37 *Alf layla wa-layla*, iii, 140, transl. Littmann, iv, 263-64.
38 ᶜAlī Ibn al-Ḥusayn al-ᶜAqīlī in a poem 'in praise of drinking in the morning' which begins with a description of a meal (al-Ṣafadī, *Wāfī*, xxi, 46).
39 al-Thaᶜālibī, *Siḥr al-balāgha*, pp. 37-38; cf. also his *Khāṣṣ al-khāṣṣ*, pp. 56-60.
40 A line by al-Ḥāfiẓ (Muḥammad Ibn al-Wazīr), in Ibn Sayyār al-Warrāq, *Ṭabīkh*, p. 143.
41 Ibn al-Rūmī, *Dīwān*, pp. 61-62. The point of the 'slumber' (*ighfā'*) escapes me.

42 al-Thaᶜālibī, *Tatimma*, p. 213. On the 'sweet little honey', see above, p. 92; cf. also Ibn Qayyim al-Jawziyya, *Rawḍat al-muḥibbīn*, p. 80, where it is said that a woman, once she has tasted 'the sweet little honey of a man', cannot bear to be without it. For a plump woman compared to a water-melon, see al-Farazdaq, *Dīwān*, ii, 55.
43 al-Tīfāshī, *Nuzhat al-albāb*, p. 108. The woman answers, 'Ask my husband, he'll tell you, for he has tasted both myself and your wife.'
44 *Alf layla wa-layla*, transl. Littmann, iv, 455.
45 Gowers, *The Loaded Table*.
46 For a pre-Islamic example of self-starvation and force-feeding, see the story of Maᶜbad Ibn Zurāra (Ibn ᶜAbd Rabbih, *ᶜIqd*, v, 140, Abū ᶜUbayda, *Ayyām al-ᶜArab qabla l-Islām*, ii, 139).
47 Maud Ellmann, *The Hunger Artists: Starving, Writing and Imprisonment*, London, 1993. See Elaine Showalter's review in *The Times Literary Supplement*, 25 February 1994, p. 10. Ellmann has a predecessor in Audrey Richards, *Hunger and Work in a Savage Tribe* (London, 1932, see Goody, *Cooking, Cuisine and Class*, p. 15).
48 See, for instance, Eira Patnaik, 'The Succulent Gender: Eat Her Softly'.
49 al-ᶜAbbās Ibn al-Aḥnaf, *Dīwān*, p. 202.
50 *Aghānī*, viii, 364.
51 al-Muᶜāfā al-Jarīrī, *Jalīs*, ii, 87, Ibn al-Sarrāj, *Maṣāriᶜ al-ᶜushshāq*, i, 164, Ibn Qayyim al-Jawziyya, *Rawḍat al-muḥibbīn*, p. 186, al-Anṭākī, *Tazyīn al-aswāq*, i, 44.
52 One or two examples must suffice: 'He plants his neighbour's cucumber in his own fig' (Diᶜbil, *Dīwān*, p. 302, Ibn al-Muᶜtazz, *Ṭabaqāt al-shuᶜarā'*, p. 267). A man who likes boys as well as girls is said to 'eat figs and pomegranates' (*Alf layla wa-layla*, iii, 215, transl. Littmann, iv, 694). See also al-Jurjānī, *Muntakhab*, pp. 100-101.
53 al-Tanūkhī, *Nishwār al-muḥāḍara*, ii, 279-80.
54 Diᶜbil, *Dīwān*, p. 165; an anonymous epigram in Ibn Qayyim al-Jawziyya, *Rawḍat al-muḥibbīn*, p. 83.
55 e.g. an apricot likened to a *glans penis* daubed with yellow *khalūq* perfume (Abū l-Makārim al-Muṭahhar Ibn Muḥammad al-Baṣrī, in al-Thaᶜālibī, *Tatimma*, p. 27), turnips likened to penises without *glans* (Manṣūr Ibn al-Ḥusayn al-Ābī, ibid., p. 121).
56 Matt Ridley, *The Red Queen*; idem, *The Origins of Virtue*.
57 See [Ps.-]Ibn Sīrīn, *Muntakhab*, i, 92-100, 'On kinds of food, sweets, and meat and related things (. . .)', cf. i, 223-33 on fruits, i, 234-40 on cereals and vegetables.
58 Ibn Shāhīn, ii, 329-33: 'On dreaming about kinds of food and edibles and their being served onto foodcloths and tables'; cf. ii, 333-36 on meat, fat, and dairy products, ii, 188-96 on fruits, ii, 20-204 on vegetables, ii, 204-208 on cereals.
59 al-Nābulusī, *Taᶜṭīr*, i, 162, ii, 125.
60 al-Nābulusī, *Taᶜṭīr*, i, 198-99.
61 Artemidorus, *Taᶜbīr al-ru'yā*, p. 140.
62 [Ps.-]Ibn Sīrīn, *Muntakhab*, i, 94, Ibn Shāhīn, *Ishārāt*, ii, 333 (attr. to a certain Abū Saᶜīd al-Wāᶜiẓ).
63 reference mislaid; cf. Ibn Shāhīn, *Ishārāt*, ii, 334, al-Nābulusī, *Taᶜṭīr*, i, 171.

64 The dictionaries give 'green beans', 'string beans', 'cowpea', 'hyacinth bean', 'lablab' (Wehr); 'French beans', 'kidney beans' (Hava); 'cowpea(s)', 'black-eyed pea(s) or bean(s)' (Hinds/Badawi). See also Bolens, 'Le haricot vert en andalousie'.
65 Ibn Shāhīn, *Ishārāt*, ii, 331.
66 Ibn Shāhīn, *Ishārāt*, ii, 331.
67 Ibn Shāhīn, *Ishārāt*, ii, 330; cf. ii, 332 and [Ps.-]Ibn Sīrīn, *Muntakhab*, i, 97, al-Nābulusī, *Taᶜṭīr*, ii, 193.
68 al-Nābulusī, *Taᶜṭīr*, ii, 61.
69 al-Nābulusī, *Taᶜṭīr*, i, 117.
70 al-Nābulusī, *Taᶜṭīr*, i, 162.
71 Ibn Shāhīn, *Ishārāt*, ii, 331. On *muzawwar*, see Waines and Marín, '*Muzawwar*: Counterfeit fare for fasts and fevers'.
72 Artemidorus, *Taᶜbīr al-ru'yā*, p. 139, al-Nābulusī, *Taᶜṭīr*, i, 185.
73 But cucumbers (*qiththā'*) may denote pregnancy, [Ps.-]Ibn Sīrīn, *Muntakhab*, i, 240, al-Nābulusī, *Taᶜṭīr*, ii, 162.
74 al-Nābulusī, *Taᶜṭīr*, ii, 94–95.
75 [Ps.-]Ibn Sīrīn, *Muntakhab*, i, 93.
76 Ibn Shāhīn, *Ishārāt*, ii, 332.
77 al-Nābulusī, *Taᶜṭīr*, i, 119.
78 [Ps-]Ibn Sīrīn, *Muntakhab*, i, 97, 99, al-Nābulusī, *Taᶜṭīr*, ii, 94.
79 [Ps-]Ibn Sīrīn, *Muntakhab*, i, 99.
80 e.g. [Ps-]Ibn Sīrīn, *Muntakhab*, i, 94, Ibn Shāhīn, *Ishārāt*, ii, 332–33.
81 Ibn Shāhīn, *Ishārāt*, ii, 332.
82 Ibn Shāhīn, *Ishārāt*, ii, 332.
83 See al-Ḥanafī (late 6th/12th century?), *Maqāmāt*, pp. 80–81, al-Jurjānī, *Muntakhab kināyāt al-udabā'*, p. 86.
84 [Ps.-]Ibn Sīrīn, *Muntakhab*, i, 96, cf. Ibn Shāhīn, *Ishārāt*, ii, 329, al-Nābulusī, *Taᶜṭīr*, i, 26–27 (*iwazz* 'geese'), 58 (*baṭṭ* 'duck') and 220 (*dajāja* 'chicken'); it goes back to Artemidorus, *Taᶜbīr*, p. 142.
85 al-Nābulusī, *Taᶜṭīr*, ii, 61.
86 e.g. al-Nābulusī, *Taᶜṭīr*, i, 162 (*ḥalwā*), ii, 125 (*fālūdhaj*).
87 Ibn Shāhīn, *Ishārāt*, ii, 330.
88 Ibn Shāhīn, *Ishārāt*, ii, 332.
89 Kilito, 'Sur le métalangage métaphorique des poéticiens arabes', *Poétique* 38 (1979) 162–74.
90 Fabian Gudas, art. 'Taste' in Alex Preminger & T.V.F. Brogan (eds.), *The New Princeton Encyclopedia of Poetry and Poetics*, Princeton, 1993, p. 1266.
91 Ibn Māja, *Sunan*, (ii,) 1142 (*Kitāb al-ṭibb, bāb al-ᶜasal*). The saying combines Koran 16:69 (honey as a cure) and 17:82 (the Koran as a cure).
92 Ibn Qayyim al-Jawziyya, *al-Ṭibb al-nabawī*, p. 352.
93 al-Iṣfahānī, *Aghānī*, xiii, 198, xxi, 203, al-Marzubānī, *Muwashshaḥ*, p. 107.
94 al-Jāḥiẓ, *al-Bayān wa-l-tabyīn*, i, 281.
95 al-Marzubānī, *Muwashshaḥ*, p. 108.
96 Ibn ᶜAbd Rabbih, *ᶜIqd*, v, 274.
97 al-Mubarrad, *Kāmil*, ii, 288.

98 Further, *jamīl* ('beautiful') to the human stature, *ḥasan* ('fine, handsome') to the nose, etc.; see al-Anṭākī, *Tazyīn al-aswāq*, ii, 129, al-ᶜĀmilī, *Mikhlāt*, p. 596.
99 An anonymous line quoted in al-Jāḥiẓ, *al-Bayān wa-l-tabyīn*, i, 276.
100 al-Bākharzī, *Dumyat al-qaṣr*, i, 289.
101 See Abu-Haidar, 'The *Kharja* of the *Muwashshaḥ* in a New Light', p. 7.
102 See e.g. Avicenna (Ibn Sīnā), *De anima [Kitāb al-nafs], being the psychological part of Kitāb al-shifā'*, ed. F. Rahman, London, 1959, pp. 75-76, *Rasā'il Ikhwān al-Ṣafā'*, ii, 402, 405, al-Tahānawī, *Kashshāf*, pp. 926-27. On tastes, see also Lucie Bolens, 'L'art culinaire médiéval andalou est baroque', pp. 142-43, idem, 'L'eau dans l'alimentation et la cuisine andalouses', pp. 104-5, T. Fahd, 'Genèse des saveurs d'après l'agriculture nabatéenne', *Rev. de l'Occident musulman* 13-14 (1973) 319-29.
103 Ibn Sayyār, *Ṭabīkh*, p. 16.
104 e.g. al-Thaᶜālibī, *Fiqh al-lugha*, pp. 173-74.
105 e.g. al-Masᶜūdī, *Murūj*, ii, 137 (on the tastes of water), al-Tawḥīdī, *Muqābasāt*, pp. 320-22, al-Ṣafadī, *Ghayth*, i, 268-69, al-ᶜĀmilī, *Kashkūl*, p. 304, Ibn Aydamir, *Durr*, iv, 48 *in margine*, al-Tīfāshī, *Surūr*, p. 175, al-Jabartī, *ᶜAjā'ib al-āthār*, iii, 91-2. (in verse, in the necrology of the author's father, AH 1188; cf. translation by Philipp & Perlmann, i, 670-71). See also Fazlur Rahman, art. 'Dhawḳ' in *EI2*.
106 al-Jāḥiẓ, *Ḥayawān*, v, 28-33. For the difference between the two terms, see al-ᶜAskarī, *Furūq*, p. 254.
107 Ibn Ṭabāṭabā, *ᶜIyār al-shiᶜr*, pp. 5-6.
108 Ibn Ṭabāṭābā, *ᶜIyār al-shiᶜr*, p. 22.
109 Ibn Ṭabāṭabā, *ᶜIyār al-shiᶜr*, p. 5 (*majjat'hu l-asmāᶜ*).
110 al-Mutanabbī, *Dīwān*, p. 220.
111 *Twelfth Night*, I, v.
112 Ibn Khaldūn, *Muqaddima*, (iv,) 1279-82, tr. Rosenthal, iii, 358-62.
113 al-Thaᶜālibī, *Thimār al-qulūb*, pp. 610-12, with more examples; cf. al-Bākharzī, *Dumyat al-qaṣr*, i, 41, the Persian work on stylistics by Rashīd al-Dīn Waṭwāṭ (d. 573/1182), *Ḥadā'iq al-siḥr*, ed. ᶜAbbās Iqbāl, Tehran, n.d., p. 53.
114 al-Thaᶜālibī, *Khāṣṣ al-khāṣṣ*, p. 128.
115 Ibn Aflaḥ, *Muqaddima*, in Van Gelder, *Two Arabic Treatises on Stylistics*, p. 19 (Arabic), Introd. p. 31.
116 Highet, *Anatomy*, pp. 231-33, Jeanneret, *A Feast of Words*, passim.
117 Many more titles beginning with *zād*, *zubda* or *qūt* may be found in bibliographies such as by Ḥājjī Khalīfa, *Kashf al-ẓunūn*, its sequel by Bağdatli İsmail Paşa, *Īḍāḥ al-maknūn*, Carl Brockelmann, *Geschichte der arabischen Litteratur*, etc.

Bibliography

The Arabic article *al-* does not affect the alphabetical order. Names of publishers are given only in the case of some undated editions for the sake of easier identification.

1. Primary Sources: Works in or translated from Arabic

al-ᶜAbbās Ibn al-Aḥnaf, *Dīwān*, Beirut, 1965.

al-ᶜAbbāsī, ᶜAbd al-Raḥīm Ibn ᶜAbd al-Raḥmān, *Maᶜāhid al-tanṣīṣ, sharḥ shawāhid al-Talkhīṣ*, Cairo, AH 1316.

ᶜAbd Banī l-Ḥasḥās, Suḥaym, *Dīwān*, ed. ᶜAbd al-ᶜAzīz al-Maymanī, Cairo, 1950.

al-Ābī, *Nathr al-durr*, Cairo, 1980-1990.

Abū l-ᶜAtāhiya, *Dīwān*, ed. Shukrī Fayṣal, Beirut, 1964 [date of preface].

Abū Nuwās, *Dīwān*, ed. Ewald Wagner & Gregor Schoeler, Wiesbaden, 1958- .

Abū ᶜUbayd al-Bakrī, *Faṣl al-maqāl fī sharḥ al-amthāl*, ed. Iḥsān ᶜAbbās & ᶜAbd al-Majīd ᶜĀbidīn, Beirut, 1983.

Abū ᶜUbayda, *Ayyām al-ᶜArab qabla l-Islām*, ed. ᶜĀdil Jāsim al-Bayātī, Beirut, 1987.

Abū ᶜUbayda, *Naqā'iḍ Jarīr wa-l-Farazdaq*, ed. Anthony Ashley Bevan, Leiden, 1905-1912.

Aghānī, *see* Iṣfahānī, Abū l-Faraj al-.

al-Akhfash al-Aṣghar, *al-Ikhtiyārayn*, ed. Fakhr al-Dīn Qabāwa, Damascus, 1974.

Alf layla wa-layla, Cairo: Maktabat Ṣubayḥ, n.d.

[Alf layla wa-layla] - Enno Littmann (übers.), *Die Erzählungen aus den Tausendundein Nächten*, Wiesbaden, 1953.

[Alf layla wa-layla]: Kitāb Alf layla wa-layla min uṣūlihi al-ᶜarabiyya al-ūlā, ed. Muhsin Mahdi, Leiden, 1984.

[Alf layla wa-layla] - *The Arabian Nights*, Transl. by Husain Haddawy, based on the text ed. by Muhsin Mahdi, New York & London, 1990.

al-ᶜĀmilī, *al-Kashkūl*, Beirut, 1983.

al-ᶜĀmilī, *al-Mikhlāt*, ed. Muḥammad Khalīl al-Bāshā, Beirut, 1985.

al-Anṭākī, *Tazyīn al-aswāq*, ed. Muḥammad Altūnjī, Beirut, 1993.

al-Aqfahsī, Shihāb al-Dīn Aḥmad Ibn al-ᶜImād, *al-Qawl al-nabīl bi-dhikr al-taṭfīl*, ed. Muṣṭafā ᶜĀshūr, Cairo, [1989].

Artemidorus d'Éphèse (Arṭāmīdūrus al-Afsusī), *Kitāb taᶜbīr al-ru'yā / Le livre des songes*, trad. du Grec en Arabe par Ḥunayn b. Isḥāq, éd. crit. avec introd. par Toufic Fahd, Damascus, 1964.

al-Azdī, Muḥammad Ibn Aḥmad Abū l-Muṭahhar, *Ḥikāyat Abī l-Qāsim al-Baghdādī / Abulḳâsim: Ein bagdâder Sittenbild*, mit Anmerkungen hg. von Adam Mez, Heidelberg, 1902.

al-ᶜAskarī, Abū Aḥmad, *al-Maṣūn fī l-adab*, ed. ᶜAbd al-Salām Muḥammad Hārūn, Cairo, 1982.

al-ᶜAskarī, Abū Hilāl, *Dīwān al-maᶜānī*, Cairo, AH 1352.

al-ᶜAskarī, Abū Hilāl, *al-Furūq al-lughawiyya*, ed. Ḥusām al-Dīn al-Qudsī, Cairo, AH 1353.

Badīᶜ al-Zamān al-Hamadhānī, *Maqāmāt*, ed. Muḥammad ᶜAbduh, repr. Beirut, 1973.

[Badīᶜ al-Zamān al-Hamadhānī] - *The Maqámát of Badíᶜ al-Zamán al-Hamadhání*, Translated from the Arabic with an Introd. and Notes historical and grammatical, by W.J. Prendergast, repr. London, 1973.

al-Baghdādī, al-Khaṭīb, *Tārīkh Baghdād*, Cairo, 1931.

al-Baghdādī, al-Khaṭīb, *al-Taṭfīl*, ed. ᶜAbd Allāh ᶜAbd al-Raḥīm ᶜUsaylān, Jeddah, 1986.

al-Baghdādī, Muḥammad Ibn al-Ḥasan, *see under* Secondary Sources, s.v. Arberry.

al-Bākharzī, *Dumyat al-qaṣr*, ed. ᶜAbd al-Fattāḥ al-Ḥulw, vols. 1-2 Cairo, 1968, 1971.

al-Bāqillānī, *Iᶜjāz al-Qur'ān*, ed. al-Sayyid Aḥmad ṭaqr, Cairo, 1963.

Bashshār Ibn Burd, *Dīwān*, ed. Muḥammad al-Ṭāhir Ibn ᶜĀshūr, Tunis, 1976.

[Bashshār Ibn Burd] - A.F.L. Beeston, *Selections from the poetry of Baššār*, Cambridge, 1977.

al-Bayhaqī, Ibrāhīm Ibn Muḥammad, *al-Maḥāsin wa-l-masāwi'*, Beirut, 1970.

al-Bukhārī, *al-Ṣaḥīḥ*, İstanbul, 1979-1981 (chapters and sections numbered as in A.J. Wensinck *et al.*, *Concordance of Indices de la Tradition Musulmane*).

al-Damīrī, *Ḥayāt al-ḥayawān al-kubrā*, Cairo: al-Maktaba al-tijāriyya al-kubrā, n.d.

al-Dārimī, *Sunan*, n.pl.: Dār Iḥyā' al-Sunna al-Nabawiyya, n.d.

Dhū l-Rumma, *Dīwān*, ed. C.H.H. Macartney, Cambridge, 1919.

Diᶜbil, *Dīwān*, ed. ᶜAbd al-Ṣāḥib ᶜImrān al-Dujaylī, Beirut, 1972.

al-Farazdaq, *Dīwān*, Beirut: Dār Ṣādir, n.d.

Ghars al-Niᶜma Muḥammad Ibn Hilāl al-Ṣābi', *al-Hafawāt al-nādira*, ed. Ṣāliḥ al-Ashtar, Damascus, 1967.

al-Ghazālī, *Iḥyā' ᶜulūm al-dīn*, Cairo: Maktabat al-Mashhad al-Ḥusaynī, n.d.

[al-Ghazālī] - Hans Kindermann, *Über die guten Sitten beim Essen und Trinken: Das ist das 11. Buch von al-Ghazzālī's Hauptwerk. Übersetzung und Bearbeitung als ein Beitrag zur Geschichte unserer Tischsitten*, Leiden, 1964.

al-Ghuzūlī, ᶜAlā' al-Dīn ᶜAlī Ibn ᶜAbd Allāh, *Maṭāliᶜ al-budūr fī manāzil al-surūr*, Būlāq, AH 1299-1300.

Ḥājjī Khalīfa, *Kashf al-ẓunūn*, ed. Şerefettin Yaltkaya & Rifat Bilge, İstanbul, 1941-1943.

al-Ḥanafī, Aḥmad Ibn Abī Bakr al-Rāzī, *Maqāmat*, in *Maqāmāt al-Ḥanafī wa-Ibn Nāqiyā*, Istanbul, AH 1330.

al-Ḥarīrī, *Maqāmāt*, ed. Antoine Isaac Silvestre de Sacy, Paris, 1847-1853, repr. Amsterdam, 1968.

Ḥassān Ibn Thābit, *Dīwān*, ed. Sayyid Ḥanafī Ḥasanayn, Cairo, 1983.

al-Ḥikāyāt al-^{c}ajība wa-l-akhbār al-gharība / Das Buch der wunderbahren Erzählungen und seltsamen Geschichten, ed. Hans Wehr, Wiesbaden, 1956.

al-Ḥillī, Ṣafī al-Dīn, *Sharḥ al-Kāfiya al-badī^{c}iyya*, ed. Nasīb Nashāwī, Damascus, 1982.

al-Ḥuṣrī, *Jam^{c} al-jawāhir fī l-mulaḥ wa-l-nawādir*, ed. ^{c}Alī Muḥammad al-Bajāwī, repr. Beirut, 1987.

al-Ḥuṣrī, *Zahr al-ādāb*, ed. Zakī Mubārak, repr. Beirut, 1972.

Ibn ^{c}Abd al-Barr, *Bahjat al-majālis wa-uns al-mujālis*, ed. Muḥammad Mursī al-Khūlī, Beirut, 1981-1982.

Ibn ^{c}Abd Rabbih, *al-^{c}Iqd al-farīd*, ed. Aḥmad Amīn et al., Cairo, 1948-1953.

Ibn Abī ^{c}Awn, *al-Tashbīhāt*, ed. Muḥammad ^{c}Abd al-Mu^{c}īd Khān, London, 1950.

Ibn Abī l-Iṣba^{c} (d. 654/1256), *Taḥrīr al-taḥbīr*, ed. Ḥifnī Muḥammad Sharaf, Cairo, AH 1383.

Ibn Abī Ṭāhir Ṭayfūr, Aḥmad, *Balāghāt al-nisā'*, Beirut, 1987.

Ibn al-^{c}Adīm, *al-Wuṣla ilā l-ḥabīb fī waṣf al-ṭayyibāt wa-l-ṭīb*, ed. Sulaymā Maḥjūb & Durriyya al-Khaṭīb, 2 vols. Aleppo, 1986, 1988.

Ibn Bassām, *al-Dhakhīra fī maḥāsin ahl al-Jazīra*, ed. Iḥsān ^{c}Abbās, Beirut, 1978-1979.

Ibn Bassām, *al-Dhakhīra fī maḥāsin ahl al-Jazīra*, vol. IV, Cairo, 1945.

Ibn Baṭṭūṭa, *al-Riḥla*, Beirut, 1985.

Ibn Buṭlān, *Da^{c}wat al-aṭibbā' / The Physicians' Dinner Party*, ed. with an introd. by Felix Klein-Franke, Wiesbaden, 1985.

Ibn Buṭlān, *Das Ärztebankett*, übers. und mit einer Einl. sowie Anm. versehen von Felix Klein-Franke, Stuttgart, 1984.

Ibn al-Dawādārī, *Kanz al-durar wa-jāmi^{c} al-ghurar*, Wiesbaden, 1960- .

Ibn Durayd, *Jamharat al-lugha*, ed. Ramzī Munīr Ba^{c}labakkī, Beirut, 1987-1988.

Ibn al-Faqīh, *al-Buldān*, ed. M.J. de Goeje, Leiden, 1885.

[Ibn al-Ḥajjār, Aḥmad Ibn Yaḥyā Ibn Ḥasan, *al-Ḥarb al-ma^{c}shūq bayn laḥm al-ḍa'n wa-ḥawāḍir al-sūq*] - Manuela Marín, 'Sobre alimentación y sociedad (el texto árabe de la «La guerra deleitosa»)', *al-Qanṭara* 13:1 (1992) 83-122.

Ibn Ḥamdūn, *al-Tadhkira al-Ḥamdūniyya*, i-ii, ed. Iḥsān ^{c}Abbās, Beirut, 1983-1984.

Ibn Ḥazm, *Rasā'il Ibn Ḥazm*, ed. Iḥsān ^{c}Abbās, vol. IV, Beirut, 1983.

Ibn Ḥijja al-Ḥamawī, *Khizānat al-adab*, Būlāq, AH 1291.

Ibn Ḥijja al-Ḥamawī, *Thamarāt al-awrāq*, ed. Muḥammad Abū l-Faḍl Ibrāhīm, Cairo, 1971.

Ibn Hishām, *al-Sīra al-nabawiyya*, ed. Muṣṭafā al-Saqqā, Ibrāhīm al-Abyārī & ^{c}Abd al-Ḥafīẓ Shalabī, Cairo, 1955.

[Ibn Hishām] - *The Life of Muhammad: A Translation of Isḥāq's* [sic] Sīrat Rasūl Allāh, tr. A. Guillaume, Karachi, 1978.

Ibn Ḥubaysh, *al-Ghazawāt*, ed. Suhayl Zakkār, Beirut, 1992.

Ibn al-Jarrāḥ, *al-Waraqa*, ed. ^{c}Abd al-Wahhāb ^{c}Azzām & ^{c}Abd al-Sattār Aḥmad Farrāj, Cairo, n.d.

Ibn al-Jawzī, *al-Adhkiyā'*, ed. Muḥammad ^{c}Abd al-Raḥmān ^{c}Awaḍ, Beirut, 1986.

Ibn al-Jawzī, *Akhbār al-ḥamqā wa-l-mughaffalīn*, Beirut, 1988.

Ibn al-Jawzī, *Dhamm al-hawā*, ed. Aḥmad ^{c}Abd al-Salām ^{c}Aṭā, Beirut, 1987.

Ibn al-Jawzī, *Talbīs Iblīs*, Beirut, 1994.

Ibn Khaldūn, *al-Muqaddima*, ed. ^{c}Abd al-Wāḥid Wāfī, Cairo, 1960-1962.

Ibn Khaldūn, *The Muqaddimah*, tr. by Franz Rosenthal, Princeton, N.J., 1967.

Ibn Khallikān, *Wafayāt al-a^{c}yān*, ed. Iḥsān ^{c}Abbās, Beirut, 1968-1972.

Ibn al-Khaṭīb, *Mushāhadāt Lisān al-Dīn al-Khaṭīb fī bilād al-Maghrib wa-l-Andalus*, ed. Aḥmad Mukhtār al-^{c}Abbādī, Alexandria, 1958.

Ibn Māja, *al-Sunan*, ed. Muḥammad Fu'ād ^{c}Abd al-Bāqī, Beirut, n.d.

Ibn Manẓūr, *Lisān al-^{c}arab*, ed. ^{c}Alī Shīrī, Beirut, 1988.

Ibn Maymūn, *Muntahā l-ṭalab*, facs. ed. Frankfurt a. M, 1986-1993.

Ibn al-Muqaffa^{c}, *al-Adab al-kabīr*, in Muḥammad Kurd ^{c}Alī (comp.), *Rasā'il al-bulaghā'*, Cairo, 1954, pp. 39-106.

Ibn al-Mu^{c}tazz, *Ṭabaqāt al-shu^{c}arā'*, ed. ^{c}Abd al-Sattār Aḥmad Farrāj, Cairo, 1968.

Ibn al-Nadīm, *al-Fihrist*, ed. Gustav Flügel, Leipzig, 1871-1872.

Ibn Qayyim al-Jawziyya, *Rawḍat al-muḥibbīn*, repr. Beirut, 1992.

Ibn Qayyim al-Jawziyya, *al-Ṭibb al-nabawī*, ed. Shu^{c}ayb al-Arna'ūṭ & ^{c}Abd al-Qādir al-Arna'ūṭ, Beirut, 1985 [part of his *Zād al-ma^{c}ād*, separately edited].

Ibn Qutayba, *Adab al-kātib*, ed. Max Grünert, Leiden, 1901.

Ibn Qutayba, *Kitāb al-ma^{c}ānī l-kabīr fī abyāt al-ma^{c}ānī*, Hyderabad, 1949.

Ibn Qutayba, *al-Ma^{c}ārif*, ed. Tharwat ^{c}Ukāsha, Cairo, 1981.

Ibn Qutayba, *^{c}Uyūn al-akhbār*, Cairo, 1925-1930.

Ibn Rashīq, *al-^{c}Umda fī maḥāsin al-shi^{c}r wa-ādābihi wa-naqdihi*, ed. Muḥammad Muṭyī l-Dīn ^{c}Abd al-Ḥamīd, repr. Beirut, 1972.

Ibn al-Rūmī, *Dīwān*, ed. Ḥusayn Naṣṣār, Cairo, 1973-1981.

Ibn al-Sarrāj, *Maṣāri^{c} al-^{c}ushshāq*, Beirut: Dār Ṣādir, n.d.

Ibn Sayyār al-Warrāq, *Kitāb al-ṭabīkh*, ed. Kaj Öhrnberg and Sahban Mroueh, Helsinki, 1987.

Ibn Shāhīn al-Ẓāhirī, Khalīl, *al-Ishārāt fī ^{c}ilm al-^{c}ibārāt*, printed in vol. ii of al-Nābulusī, *Ta^{c}ṭīr al-anām* (q.v.; *pace* the title-page which mentions Ibn Sīrīn, *Muntakhab al-kalām*).

Ibn Shuhayd, *Risālat al-tawābi^{c} wa-l-zawābi^{c}*, ed. Buṭrus al-Bustānī, Beirut, 1951.

Ibn Shuhayd, *Risālat at-tawābi^{c} wa z-zawābi^{c} / The Treatise of Familiar Spirits and Demons by Abū ^{c}Āmir ibn Shuhaid al-Ashja^{c}ī, al-Andalusī*, Introd., transl. and notes by James T. Monroe, Berkeley etc., 1971.

Ibn Sīda, *al-Mukhaṣṣaṣ*, Cairo, AH 1316-1321.

[Ps.-]Ibn Sīrīn (= al-Ḥusayn Ibn Ḥasan Ibn Ibrāhīm al-Khalīlī al-Dārī), *Muntakhab al-kalām fī tafsīr al-aḥlām*, printed in vol. i of al-Nābulusī, *Ta^cṭīr al-anām* (q.v.).

Ibn Sūdūn, *Nuzhat al-nufūs wa-muḍḥik al-^cabūs*, lithograph ed., Cairo, AH 1280.

Ibn Ṭabāṭabā, *^cIyār al-shi^cr*, ed. ^cAbd al-^cAzīz Ibn Nāṣir al-Māni^c, Riyadh, 1985.

Ibn al-Ṭiqṭaqā, *al-Fakhrī*, ed. H. Derenbourg, Paris, 1894.

al-Ibshīhī, *al-Mustaṭraf fī kull fann mustaẓraf*, Cairo, 1952.

al-Iṣfahānī, Abū l-Faraj, *al-Aghānī*, Cairo, 1927-1974.

al-Jabartī, *^cAjā'ib al-āthār fī l-tarājim wa-l-akhbār*, Cairo, ed. Ḥasan Muḥammad Jawhar *et al.*, 1958-67.

al-Jabartī, *^cAjā'ib al-āthār fī al-tarājim wa-al-akhbār / ^cAbd al-Raṭmān al-Jabartī's History of Egypt*, translated by Thomas Philipp and Moshe Perlmann, Stuttgart, 1994.

al-Jāḥiẓ, *al-Awṭān wa-l-buldān*, in his *Rasā'il*, ed. ^cAbd al-Salām Muḥammad Hārūn, iii-iv (Cairo, 1979), iv, 107-47.

al-Jāḥiẓ, *al-Bayān wa-l-tabyīn*, ed. ^cAbd al-Salām Muḥammad Hārūn, Cairo, 1968.

al-Jāḥiẓ, *al-Bukhalā'*, ed. Ṭāhā al-Ḥājirī, Cairo, n.d.

[al-Jāḥiẓ] - Ch. Pellat, 'Ǧāḥiẓiana, II: Le dernier chapitre des *Avares* de Ǧāḥiẓ', *Arabica*, 2 (1955) 322-52.

al-Jāḥiẓ, *al-Ḥayawān*, ed. ^cAbd al-Salām Muḥammad Hārūn, Cairo, 1965-1969.

[Ps.-]al-Jāḥiẓ, *al-Maḥāsin wa-l-aḍdād*, ed. G. van Vloten, Leiden, 1898.

al-Jāḥiẓ, *Rasā'il*, ed. ^cAbd al-Salām Muḥammad Hārūn, Cairo, [1964]-1979.

[Ps.-]al-Jāḥiẓ, *al-Tāj fī akhlāq al-mulūk*, ed. Aḥmad Zakī, Cairo, 1914.

al-Jahshiyārī, *al-Wuzarā' wa-l-kuttāb*, ed. Muṣṭafā al-Saqqā *et al.*, Cairo, 1980.

[Jamīl Buthayna] - Francesco Gabrieli, 'Ǧamīl al-^cUdrī: Studio critico e raccolta dei frammenti', *RSO* 17 (1938-1939) 41-71, 133-72.

Jarīr, *Dīwān, bi-sharḥ Muḥammad Ibn Ḥabīb*, ed. Nu^cmān Muḥammad Amīn Ṭāhā, Cairo, 1986.

al-Jazzār, Jamāl al-Dīn Yaḥyā Ibn ^cAbd al-^cAẓīm, *Fawā'id al-mawā'id*, MS British Library Or. 6388.

al-Jurjānī, Abū l-^cAbbās Aḥmad Ibn Muḥammad, *al-Muntakhab min kināyāt al-udabā' wa-ishārāt al-bulaghā'*, ed. Muḥammad Shams al-Ḥaqq Shamsī, Hyderabad, 1983.

Kanz al-fawā'id fī tanwī^c al-mawā'id, ed. by Manuela Marín and David Waines, Beirut - Wiesbaden, 1993.

Khālid Ibn Yazīd al-Kātib, *Dīwān* = Albert Arazi, *Amour divin et amour profane dans l'Islam médiéval à travers le Dīwān de Khālid Al-Kātib*, Paris, 1990.

al-Khālidiyyān, *al-Ashbāh wa-l-naẓā'ir*, ed. al-Sayyid Muḥammad Yūsuf, Cairo, 1958-1965.

al-Khaṭṭābī, *Bayān i^cjāz al-Qur'ān*, in *Thalāth rasā'il fī i^cjāz al-Qur'ān*, ed. Muḥammad Khalaf Allāh & Muḥammad Zaghlūl Sallām, Cairo, 1968.

Kushājim, *Dīwān*, ed. Khayriyya Muḥammad Maḥfūẓ, Baghdad, 1970.

Labīd, *Dīwān*, Beirut, 1966.

al-Ma^{c}arrī, Abū l-^{c}Alā', *Risālat al-ghufrān*, ed. ^{c}Ā'isha ^{c}Abd al-Raḥmān, 4th ed, Cairo, n.d.

al-Ma^{c}arrī, Abū l-^{c}Alā', *Risālat al-ṣāhil wa-l-shāḥij*, ed. ^{c}Ā'isha ^{c}Abd al-Raḥmān, Cairo, 1984.

al-Maghribī, Yūsuf, *Daf^c al-iṣr ^{c}an kalām ahl Miṣr*, facs. ed. by ^{c}Abd al-Salām Aḥmad ^{c}Awwād, Moscow, 1968.

al-Makkī, Abū Ṭālib, *Die Nahrung der Herzen: Abū Ṭālib al-Makkīs Qūt al-qulūb*, eingeleitet, übersetzt und kommentiert von Richard Gramlich, III, Stuttgart, 1995.

al-Maqdisī, al-Muṭahhar Ibn Ṭāhir, *al-Bad' wa-l-ta'rīkh*, ed. Clément Huart, Paris, 1899-1919.

al-Marzubānī, Abū ^{c}Ubayd Allāh Muḥammad Ibn ^{c}Imrān, *Mu^{c}jam al-shu^{c}arā'*, ed. ^{c}Abd al-Sattār Aḥmad Farrāj, Cairo, 1960.

al-Marzubānī, *Nūr al-qabas / Die Gelehrtenbiographien des Abū ^{c}Ubaidallāh al-Marzubānī in der Rezension des Ḥāfiẓ al-Yaġmūrī*, ed. Rudolf Sellheim, Wiesbaden, 1964.

al-Marzūqī, *Sharḥ Dīwān al-ḥamāsa*, ed. Aḥmad Amīn & ^{c}Abd al-Salām Hārūn, repr. Beirut, 1991.

al-Mas^{c}ūdī, *Murūj al-dhahab*, éd. Barbier de Meynard & Pavet de Courteille, revue et corrigée par Charles Pellat, Beyrouth, 1966-1979.

[al-Mas^{c}ūdī] - al-Masudi, *The Meadows of Gold: the Abbasids*, translated by Paul Lunde and Caroline Stone, London, 1989.

al-Maydānī, *Majma^c al-amthāl*, ed. Na^{c}īm Ḥusayn Zarzūr, Beirut, 1988.

al-Mu^{c}āfā al-Jarīrī, *al-Jalīs al-ṣāliḥ al-kāfī*, ed. Muḥammad Mursī al-Khūlī & Iḥsān ^{c}Abbās, Beirut, 1993.

al-Mubarrad, *al-Kāmil*, Cairo: al-Maktaba al-tijāriyya al-kubrā, n.d.

al-Mufaḍḍaliyyāt, ed. Aḥmad Muḥammad Shākir and ^{c}Abd al-Salām Muḥammad Hārūn, Cairo, n.d.

The Mufaḍḍalīyāt: an anthology of ancient Arabian odes (. . .), ed. by Charles James Lyall, Vol. II: Translation and notes, Oxford, 1918.

Muḥammad Ibn Ḥabīb, *al-Munammaq fī akhbār Quraysh*, ed. Khūrshīd Aḥmad Fāriq, Hyderabad, 1964.

al-Muqaddasī, *Aḥsan al-taqāsīm fī ma^{c}rifat al-aqālīm*, ed. M.J. de Goeje, ed. secunda, Leiden, 1906.

al-Muqaddasi, *The Best Divisions for Knowledge of the Regions: A Translation of* Aḥsan al-Taqasim fi Ma^{c}rifat al-Aqalim, Transl. by Basil Anthony Collins, rev. by Muhammad Hamid al-Tai, Reading, 1994.

al-Musabbiḥī, *Akhbār Miṣr fī sanatayn (414-415 H)*, ed. William G. Millward, Cairo, 1980.

Muslim, *al-Ṣaḥīḥ*: *Ṣaḥīḥ Muslim bi-sharḥ al-Nawawī*, 18 vols. Beirut, 1972.

Muslim Ibn al-Walīd Ṣarī^c al-Ghawānī, *Dīwān*, ed. Sāmī al-Dahhān, Cairo, 1985.

al-Mutanabbī, *Dīwān*, ed. F. Dieterici, Berlin, 1861.

al-Nābulusī, ^{c}Abd al-Ghanī, *Ta^{c}ṭīr al-anām fī tafsīr al-aḥlām*, 2 vols. Cairo: Dār Iḥyā' al-kutub al-^{c}arabiyya, n.d.

Naqā'iḍ Jarīr wa-l-Akhṭal, ed. Anṭūn Ṣāliḥānī, Beirut, 1922.

al-Nīsābūrī, Abū l-Qāsim al-Ḥasan Ibn Ḥabīb, *^{c}Uqalā' al-majānīn*, ed. ^{c}Umar al-As^{c}ad, Beirut, 1987.

al-Qālī, *Amālī*, Cairo, 1926.

al-Qalqashandī, *Ṣubḥ al-a^{c}shā*, Cairo, 1922.
al-Qazwīnī, Zakariyyā, *Āthār al-bilād*, Beirut, 1979.
al-Qifṭī, *Inbāh al-ruwāt*, ed. Muḥammad Abū l-Faḍl Ibrāhīm, Cairo, 1950–1973.
al-Rāghib al-Iṣbahānī, *Muḥāḍarāt al-udabā' wa-muḥāwarāt al-shu^{c}arā' wa-l-bulaghā'*, Cairo, AH 1287.
Rasā'il Ikhwān al-Ṣafā', Beirut, 1957.
al-Rashīd Ibn al-Zubayr, *al-Dhakhā'ir wa-l-tuḥaf*, ed. Muḥammad Ḥamīd Allāh, Kuwait, 1959.
al-Ṣafadī, *al-Ghayth al-musajjam fī sharḥ Lāmiyyat al-^{c}ajam*, Beirut, 1975.
al-Ṣafadī, *al-Wāfī bi-l-Wafayāt*, Wiesbaden, 1962- .
[Sha^{c}bān Ibn Sālim] – Armin Schopen & Oliver Kahl, *Die Natā'iğ al-fikar des Ša^{c}bān ibn Sālim aṣ-Ṣan^{c}ānī: Eine jemenitische Gesundheitsfibel aus dem frühen 18. Jahrhundert. Text, Übersetzung und Kommentar*, Wiesbaden, 1993.
al-Shābushtī, *al-Diyārāt*, ed. Gūrgīs ^{c}Awwād, repr. Beirut, 1986.
al-Sharīf al-Murtaḍā, *Amālī (Ghurar al-fawā'id)*, ed. Muḥammad Abū l-Faḍl Ibrāhīm, Cairo, 1954.
al-Sharīf al-Raḍī, *Nahj al-balāgha*, ed. Muḥammad ^{c}Abduh, Cairo, n.d.
al-Sharīshī, *Sharḥ Maqāmāt al-Ḥarīrī*, Cairo, 1979.
al-Shirbīnī, Yūsūf Ibn Muḥammad, *Hazz al-quḥūf fī Sharḥ qaṣīd Abī Shādūf*, Cairo: al-Maktaba al-Maḥmūdiyya, n.d.
al-Shirbīnī, Yūsuf Ibn Muḥammad, *Hazz al-quḥūf*, ed. Muḥammad Qandīl al-Baqlī, Cairo, 1963 (date of preface) (= *Qaryatunā l-Miṣriyya qabla l-Thawra*, vol.I).
Shurūḥ al-Talkhīṣ, vol. IV, Cairo, AH 1343.
al-Sijistānī, *al-Nakhl*, ed. Ibrāhīm al-Sāmarrā'ī, Beirut, 1985.
al-Sukkarī, *Ash^{c}ār al-Hudhaliyyīn: Sharḥ ash^{c}ār al-Hudhaliyyīn, ṣan^{c}at Abī Sa^{c}īd . . . al-Sukkarī*, ed. ^{c}Abd al-Sattār Aḥmad Farrāj, Cairo, n.d.
al-Suyūṭī, *al-Itqān*, ed. Muḥammad Abū l-Faḍl Ibrāhīm, Cairo, 1974–75.
al-Ṭabarī, *Tārīkh al-rusul wa-l-mulūk*, ed. M.J. De Goeje et al., Leiden, 1879–1901.
al-Tahānawī, *Kashshāf iṣṭilāḥāt al-funūn / A Dictionary of the Technical Terms used in the Sciences of the Musalmans*, Calcutta, 1862.
al-Tanasī, *Naẓm al-durr wa-l-^{c}iqyān / Westarabische Tropik*, ed. Nuri Soudan, Beirut - Wiesbaden, 1980.
al-Tanūkhī, *al-Faraj ba^{c}d al-shidda*, ed. ^{c}Abbūd al-Shāljī, Beirut, 1978.
al-Tanūkhī, *Nishwār al-muḥāḍara*, ed. ^{c}Abbūd al-Shāljī, Beirut, 1971–1973.
al-Tawḥīdī, *al-Baṣā'ir wa-l-dhakhā'ir*, ed. Wadād al-Qāḍī, Beirut, 1988.
al-Tawḥīdī, *al-Imtā^{c} wa-l-mu'ānasa*, ed. Aḥmad Amīn & Aḥmad al-Zayn, Cairo, 1939–1953.
al-Tawḥīdī, *Mathālib al-wazīrayn*, ed. Ibrāhīm al-Kīlānī, Damascus, 1961 (date of preface).
al-Tawḥīdī, *al-Muqābasāt*, ed. Muḥammad Tawfīq Ḥusayn [incorrectly Ḥasan on the title-page], Beirut, 1989.
al-Tha^{c}ālibī, *Ādāb al-mulūk*, ed. Jalīl al-^{c}Aṭiyya, Beirut, 1990.
al-Tha^{c}ālibī, *Fiqh al-lugha*, Cairo, AH 1318.
al-Tha^{c}ālibī, *Khāṣṣ al-khāṣṣ*, ed. Ḥasan al-Amīn, Beirut, n.d.
al-Tha^{c}ālibī, *Laṭā'if al-luṭf*, ed. ^{c}Umar al-As^{c}ad, Beirut, 1980.

al-Tha^{c}ālibī, *Laṭā'if al-ma^{c}ārif (Latáifo 'l-ma'árif)*, ed. P. de Jong, Leiden, 1867.

al-Tha^{c}ālibī, *The Book of Curious and Entertaining Information (The Laṭā'if al-ma^{c}ārif of Tha^{c}ālibī)*, transl. with introd. and notes by C.E. Bosworth, Edinburgh, 1968.

al-Tha^{c}ālibī, *Siḥr al-balāgha*, ed. ^{c}Abd al-Salām al-Ḥūfī, Beirut, n.d.

al-Tha^{c}ālibī, *Thimār al-qulūb*, ed. Muḥammad Abū l-Faḍl Ibrāhīm, Cairo, 1985.

al-Tha^{c}ālibī, *Tatimmat al-Yatīma*, ed. Mufīd Muḥammad Qumayḥa, Beirut, 1983.

al-Tha^{c}ālibī, *Yatīmat al-dahr*, ed. Muḥammad Muḥyī l-Dīn ^{c}Abd al-Ḥamīd, Cairo, 1947.

al-Tha^{c}labī, *Qiṣaṣ al-anbiyā' al-musammā ^{c}Arā'is al-majālis*, repr. Beirut: Dār al-Ma^{c}rifa, n.d.

al-Tijānī, *Tuḥfat al-^{c}arūs wa-mut^{c}at al-nufūs*, ed. Jalīl al-^{c}Aṭiyya, London, 1992.

al-Tujībī, Ibn Razīn, *Fuḍālat al-khiwān fī ṭayyibāt al-ṭa^{c}ām wa-l-alwān*, ed. Muḥammad Ibn Shaqrūn (Muhammad B.A. Benchekroun), Beirut, 1984 [The first word is often given as *Faḍālat*; I have little doubt that *Fuḍālat* is to be preferred].

al-Wahrānī, Ibn Muḥriz al-, *Manāmāt al-Wahrānī wa-maqāmātuhu wa-rasā'iluhu*, ed. Ibrāhīm Sha^{c}lān & Muḥammad Naghsh, Cairo, 1968.

al-Wāqidī, *al-Maghāzī*, ed. Marsden Jones, London, 1966.

al-Washshā', *al-Muwashshā*, ed. Rudolph E. Brünnow, Leiden, 1886.

[al-Washshā] – Ibn al-Waššā', *Das Buch des buntbestickten Kleides*, aus dem Arab. übers. von Dieter Bellman, Leipzig & Weimar, 1984.

al-Ya^{c}qūbī, *Tārīkh*, Beirut: Dār Bayrūt, n.d.

Yāqūt, *Mu^{c}jam al-udabā'*, ed. Aḥmad Farīd Rifā^{c}ī, Cairo, 1936-1938.

al-Yāzijī, Nāṣīf, *Majma^{c} al-baḥrayn*, Beirut: Maktabat al-ṭullāb, n.d.

al-Zabīdī, Murtaḍā, *Tāj al-^{c}arūs*, ed. ^{c}Abd al-Sattār Farrāj, Kuweit, 1965- .

al-Zamakhsharī, *Asās al-balāgha*, Beirut, 1979.

al-Zamakhsharī, *al-Maqāmāt*, ed. Yūsuf Biqā^{c}ī, Beirut, n.d.

al-Zamakhsharī, *Rabī^{c} al-abrār wa-nuṣūṣ al-akhbār*, ed. Salīm al-Nu^{c}aymī, Baghdād, 1976-1982.

al-Zarkashī, *al-Burhān fī ^{c}ulūm al-Qur'ān*, ed. Muḥammad Abū l-Faḍl Ibrāhīm, Cairo, n.d.

2. Secondary Sources

Abd Al Raheim, Abd Al Raheim A., '*Hazz al-Quḥūf*: A new source for the study of the *fallāḥīn* of Egypt in the xviith and xviiith centuries', *JESHO* 18 (1975) 245-70.

Abu-Haidar, Jareer, 'The *Kharja* of the *Muwashshaḥ* in a New Light', *Journal of Arabic Literature* 9 (1978) 1-13.

Adamson, Melitta Weiss, 'The Games Cooks Play: Non-Sense Recipes and Practical Jokes in Medieval Literature', in Melitta Weiss Adamson (ed.), *Food in the Middle Ages: A Book of Essays*, New York & London, 1995, pp. 177-95.

Ahlwardt, W., *Verzeichnis der arabischen Handschriften*, Berlin, 1887-1899.

Ahsan, Muhammad Manazir, *Social Life Under the Abbasids*, London - New York, 1979.

Arazi, Albert, *see under* Primary Sources, s.v. Khālid Ibn Yazīd al-Kātib.

Arberry, A.J., 'A Baghdad Cookery-Book', *Islamic Culture* 13 (1939) 21-47, 189-214.

Arberry, A.J., *Classical Persian Literature*, London, 1958.

Ashtiany, Julia, 'al-Tanūkhī's *al-Faraj baᶜd al-shidda* as a Literary Source', in Alan Jones (ed.), *Arabicus felix, Luminosus Britannicus: Essays in Honour of A.F.L. Beeston on his Eightieth Birthday*, Reading, 1991, pp. 108-28.

Aubaile-Sallenave, Françoise, '*Al-Kishk*: The past and present of a complex culinary practice', in Zubaida & Tapper (eds.), *Culinary Cultures* (q.v.), pp. 105-39.

Baer, Gabriel, 'Shirbīnī's Hazz al-Quḥūf and its Significance', = ch. 1 in his *Fellah and Townsman in the Middle East: Studies in Social History*, London, 1982.

Bakhtin, Mikhaïl, *L'œuvre de François Rabelais et la culture populaire au Moyen Age et sous la Renaissance*, tr. du Russe par Andrée Robel, Paris, 1970.

Bauer, Thomas, 'Muzarrids Qaṣīde vom reichen Ritter und dem armen Jäger', in Wolfhart Heinrichs & Gregor Schoeler (Hrsgg.), *Festschrift Ewald Wagner zum 65. Geburtstag. Band 2: Studien zur arabischen Dichtung*, Beirut, 1994, pp. 42-71.

Beaumont, Daniel, 'A mighty and never ending affair: Comic anecdote and story in medieval Arabic literature', *JAL* 24:2 (1993) 139-59.

Beeston, A.F.L., 'An Experiment with Labīd', *JAL* 7 (1976) 1-6.

Bolens, Lucie, 'L'art culinaire médiéval andalou est baroque: les ruses de la science au service du goût (XIe-XIIIe siècles)', repr. in her *L'Andalousie du quotidien au sacré, XIe-XIIIe siècles*, Aldershot, 1990 (Variorum, CS 337) (first publ. 1984).

Bolens, Lucie, 'L'eau dans l'alimentation et la cuisine andalouses (XIe-XIIIe siècles)', *Études rurales* 93-94 (1984) 103-21, repr. in her *L'Andalousie du quotidien au sacré, XIe-XIIIe siècles*, Aldershot, 1990.

Bolens, Lucie, 'L'haricot vert en Andalousie et en Méditerranée médiévales (phaseolus, dolichos, lūbiā, judía)', *al-Qanṭara* 8 (1987) 65-86, repr. in her *L'Andalousie du quotidien au sacré, XIe-XIIIe siècles*, Aldershot, 1990.

Bonebakker, S.A., 'Early Arabic Literature and the term *adab*', *Jerusalem Studies in Arabic and Islam* 5 (1984) 389-421.

Brockelmann, C., *Geschichte der arabischen Litteratur*, Leiden, 1937-49.

Bürgel, J. Christoph, 'Die ekphrastischen Epigramme des Abū Ṭālib al-Ma'mūnī. Literaturkundliche Studie über einen arabischen Conceptisten', *Nachrichten der Akad. der Wiss. in Göttingen, I, Philol.-hist. Kl.*, Jhrg. 1865, Nr. 14 (pp. 217-322).

Bürgel, J. C., 'Love, Lust and Longing: Eroticism in Early Islam', in Afaf Lutfi Al-Sayyid-Marsot (ed.), *Society and the Sexes in Medieval Islam*, Malibu, Calif., 1979.

Caracciolo, Peter L. (ed.), *The* Arabian Nights *in English Literature: Studies in the Reception of* The Thousand and One Nights *into British Culture*, New York, 1988.

Chebel, Malek, *Encyclopédie de l'amour en Islam*, Paris, 1995.

Cooperson, Michael, 'Ibn Ḥanbal and Bishr al-Ḥāfī: A Case Study in Biographical Tradition', *Studia Islamica* 86 (1997) 71-101.

Curtius, Ernst Robert, *European Literature and the Latin Middle Ages*, tr. by Willard R. Trask, Princeton, 1973.

Ḍayf, Shawqī, *ʿAṣr al-duwal wa-l-imārāt: Miṣr wa-l-Shām (Tārīkh al-adab al-ʿarabī, VI)*, Cairo, 1984.

Dozy, R. *Supplément aux dictionnaires arabes*, Leiden, 1927.

EI² = *Encyclopaedia of Islam*, New edition, Leiden, 1960- .

Finkel, J., 'King Mutton, A curious Egyptian tale of the Mamluk period', *Zeitschrift für Semitistik und verwandte Gebiete* 8 (1932) 122-48, 9 (1933-34) 1-18.

Frazer, J.G., *The Golden Bough: A Study in Magic and Religion*, abridged ed. London, 1967.

Gabrieli, Francesco, 'Ǧamīl al-ʿUdrī: Studio critico e raccolta dei frammenti', *Rivista degli Studi Orientali* 17 (1938-1939) 41-71, 133-72.

Garbutt, Nina, 'Ibn Jazlah: The Forgotten ʿAbbāsid Gastronome', *Journal of the Economic and Social History of the Orient* 39:1 (1996) 42-44.

Gelder, Geert Jan van, 'Arabic Banqueters: Literature, Lexicography and Reality', in R. Gyselen (ed.), *Banquets d'Orient* (= *Res Orientales*, 4), Bures-sur-Yvette, 1992, 85-93.

Gelder, Geert Jan van, 'Arabic Didactic Verse', in Jan Willem Drijvers and Alasdair MacDonald (eds.), *Centres of Learning: Learning and Location in Pre-Modern Europe and the Near East*, Groningen 1995, pp. 103-117.

Gelder, Geert Jan van, *The Bad and the Ugly: Attitudes towards Invective Poetry* (hijāʾ) *in Classical Arabic Literature*, Leiden, 1988.

Gelder, Geert Jan van, & Marjo Buitelaar (eds.), *Eet van de goede dingen: culinaire culturen in het Midden-Oosten en de Islam*, Bussum, 1995.

Gelder, Geert Jan van, 'The Joking Doctor: Abū l-Ḥakam ʿUbayd Allāh Ibn al-Muẓaffar (d. 549/1155)', in Concepción Vázquez de Benito & Miguel Ángel Manzano Rodríguez (eds.), *Actas XVI Congreso UEAI [Union Européenne des Arabisants et des Islamisants, Salamanca, 1992]*, Salamanca, 1995, pp. 217-28.

Gelder, Geert Jan van, 'Musāwir al-Warrāq and the beginnings of Arabic gastronomic poetry', *J. of Semitic Studies* 36:2 (1991) 309-27.

Gelder, Geert Jan van, 'Mixtures of Jest and Earnest in Classical Arabic Literature', *J. of Arabic Literature* 23:3 (1992) 83-108, 169-90.

Gelder, Geert Jan van, 'Al-Mutanabbī's Encumbering Trifles', *Arabic and Middle Eastern Literatures* 2 (1999) 5-19.

Gelder, Geert Jan van, (ed.), *Two Arabic Treatises on Stylistics: al-Marghīnānī's* al-Maḥāsin fī 'l-naẓm wa-'l-nathr *and Ibn Aflaḥ's* Muqaddima, Istanbul - Leiden, 1987.

Gennep, Arnold van, *The Rites of Passage*, London, 1966 (original French ed. 1908).

Gerhardt, Mia I., *The Art of Story-Telling: A Literary Study of the Thousand and One Nights*, Leiden, 1963.

Ghazi, Mhammed Ferid, 'Un groupe social: «les Raffinés»', *Studia Islamica* 11 (1959) 39-71.

Goldziher, Ignaz, 'Ṣâliḥ b. ᶜAbd al-Ḳuddûs und das Zindîḳthum während der Regierung des Chalifen al-Mahdî', in *Transactions of the Congress of Orientalists, London*, ii (1892), 104-129.

Goody, Jack, *Cooking, Cuisine and Class: A Study in Comparative Sociology*, Cambridge, 1982.

Gowers, Emily, *The Loaded Table: Representations of Food in Roman Literature*, Oxford, 1993.

Guest, Rhuvon, *Life and Works of Ibn er Rûmî (. . .), a Baghdad Poet of the 9th Century of the Christian Era: His Life and Poetry*, London, 1944.

Hafez, Sabry, 'Food as a Semiotic Code in Arabic Literature', in Sami Zubaida and Richard Tapper, (eds.) *Culinary Cultures of the Middle East* (q.v.), pp. 257-80.

Hämeen-Anttila, Jaakko, 'Khālid Ibn Ṣafwān - The man and the legend', *Studia Orientalia* 73 (1994) 69-166.

Harris, Marvin, *Good to Eat: Riddles of Food and Culture*, New York, 1985.

al-Hāshimī, Aḥmad, *Jawāhir al-adab fī ṣināᶜat inshā' al-ᶜarab*, Cairo, AH 1319.

Heine, Peter, 'Cultuur en culinaria: over de studie van de kookkunst in de Arabische cultuurgeschiedenis', in Geert Jan van Gelder & Marjo Buitelaar (eds.), *Eet van de goede dingen* (q.v.), pp. 25-33.

Heine, Peter, *Kulinarische Studien. Untersuchungen zur Kochkunst in arabisch-islamischen Mittelalter*, Wiesbaden, 1988.

Heinrichs, Wolfhart, 'Scherzhafter badīᶜ bei Abū Nuwās', in E. Wagner & K. Röhrborn (Hrsg.), *Kaškūl. Festschrift zum 25. Jahrestag der Wiederbegründung des Instituts für Orientalistik an der Justus-Liebig-Unversität Giessen*, Wiesbaden, 1989, pp. 23-37.

Heyworth-Dunne, J., 'Arabic Literature in Egypt in the Eighteenth century with some Reference to Poetry and Poets', *BSOAS* 9 (1937-1939) 675-89.

Highet, Gilbert, *The Anatomy of Satire*, Princeton, 1962.

Hinds, M. & El-Said Badawi, *A Dictionary of Egyptian Arabic*, Beirut, 1987.

Huizinga, Johan, *Homo ludens: A Study of the Play Element in Culture*, London, 1971.

Jacobi, Renate, *Studien zur Poetik der altarabischen Qaside*, Wiesbaden, 1971.

Jansen, Willy, '"Eet! en ik zal zeggen wie je bent": eetgedrag en persoonlijkheid in de Arabische wereld', in Van Gelder en Buitelaar (eds.), *Eet van de goede dingen* (q.v.), pp. 89-103.

Jeanneret, Michel, *A Feast of Words: Banquet and Table Talk in the Renaissance*, transl. by Jeremy Whiteley and Emma Hughes, Cambridge, 1991 (orig. title *Des mets et des mots: banquets et propos de table à la Renaissance*, 1987).

Jones, Alan (ed., transl. and comm.), *Early Arabic Poetry*, I-II, Reading, 1992, 1996.

Kern, F., 'Neuere ägyptische Humoristen und Satiriker', *Mitteilungen des Seminars für Orientalische Sprachen an der Kön. Friedrich-Wilhelms-Universität zu Berlin* 9 (1906) Zweite Abt., pp. 31-73.

Kiell, Norman, 'Food in Literature: A Selective Bibliography', *Mosaic: A Journal for the Interdisciplinary Study of Literature* 24:3-4 (1991) 211-63.

Kīlānī, Muḥammad Sayyid, *al-Adab al-miṣrī fī ẓill al-ḥukm al-ᶜuthmānī*, Cairo, 1965.

Kilito, Abdelfattah, *Les Séances. Récits et codes culturels chez Hamadhânî et Harîrî*, Paris, 1983.

Kindermann, Hans, *see under* Primary Sources, s.v. al-Ghazālī.

Kraemer, Joel L., *Humanism in the Renaissance of Islam: The Cultural Revival during the Buyid Age*, Leiden, 1986.

Lobban Jr., Richard A., 'Pigs and their prohibition', *IJMES* 26:1 (1994) 57-75.

McDonald, M.V., 'Two mysterious animals in the *Kitāb al-Ḥayawān* of al-Jāḥiẓ: the *simᶜ* and the *ᶜisbār*', *JAL* 22 (1991) 100-107.

Maḥjūb, Sulaymā, 'Tārīkh al-aṭᶜima ᶜinda l-ᶜArab', = Introduction to Ibn al-ᶜAdīm, *Wuṣla* (q.v. under Primary Sources), pp. 21-413.

Malti-Douglas, Fedwa, '*Maqāmāt* and *adab*: 'al-Maqāma al-Maḍīriyya' of al-Hamadhānī', *JAOS* 105 (1985) 247-58.

Malti-Douglas, Fedwa, 'Structure and organization in a monographic *adab* work: *al-Taṭfīl* of al-Khaṭīb al-Baghdādī', *Journal of Near Eastern Studies* 40 (1981) 227-45.

Malti-Douglas, Fedwa, *Structures of avarice: The* Bukhalā' *in medieval Arabic literature*, Leiden, 1985.

Marín, Manuela, & David Waines (eds.), *La alimentación en las culturas islámicas: Una colección de estudios*, Madrid 1994.

Marín, Manuela, & David Waines, 'The Balanced Way: Food for Pleasure and Health in Medieval Islam', *Manuscripts of the Middle East* 4 (1989) 123-32.

Marín, Manuela, 'Literatura y gastronomía: dos textos árabes de época mameluca', in Marín & Waines (eds.), *La alimentación* (q.v.), pp. 137-58.

Marín, Manuela, 'Sobre alimentación y sociedad', *see under* Primary Sources, s.v. Ibn al-Ḥajjār.

Marín, Manuela, 'Sobre Būrān y *būrāniyya*', *al-Qanṭara* 2 (1981) 193-207.

Marzolph, Ulrich, *Arabia ridens*, Frankfurt am Main, 1992.

Mehren, A.F. [von], *Et Par Bidrag til Bedømmelse af den nyere Folkelitteratur i Ægypten*, Copenhagen, 1872.

Meneghini Correale, Daniela, 'Tra il serio e il faceto. Parte seconda: Ḥāfiẓ e Busḥāq', *Annali di Ca' Foscari* (Serie Orientale) 24:3 (1985) 41-89.

Metlitzki, Dorothee, *The Matter of Araby in Medieval England*, New Haven, 1977.

Mez, Adam, *The Renaissance of Islam*, tr. by Salahuddin Khuda Bukhsh and D.S. Margoliouth, London, 1937.

Moayyad, Heshmat, art. 'Busḥāq', in *Encyclopaedia Iranica*, iv, London, 1990.

Monroe, James T., *The art of Badīᶜ az-Zamān al-Hamadhānī as picaresque narrative*, Beirut, 1983.

Moreh, Shmuel, *Live Theatre and Dramatic Literature in the Medieval Arabic World*, Edinburgh, 1992.

Müller, Kathrin, *'Und der Kalif lachte, bis er auf den Rücken fiel': Ein Beitrag zur Phraseologie und Stilkunde des klassischen Arabisch*, München, 1993.

Neuwirth, Angelika, 'Der Horizont der Offenbarung. Zur Relevanz der einleitenden Schwurserien für die Suren der frühmekkanischen Zeit', in Udo Tworuschka (ed.), *Gottes ist der Orient, Gottes ist der Okzident: Festschrift für Abdoldjavad Falaturi (. . .)*, Köln - Wien, 1991, pp. 3-39.

Nicholson, R.A., *A Literary History of the Arabs*, repr. Cambridge, 1966 (1st ed. London, 1907).

Nicholson, R.A., *Studies in Islamic Poetry*, repr. Cambridge, 1969 (1st ed. 1921).

Öhrnberg, Kaj, 'Ibn Sattār al-Warrāq's *Kitāb al-wuṣla ilà al-ḥabīb / Kitāb al-ṭabbākh*, another MS of Ibn Sayyār al-Warrāq's *Kitāb al-ṭabīkh*', in Manuela Marín & David Waines (eds.), *La alimentación en las culturas islámicas*, (q.v.), pp. 23-35.

Omri, Mohammed-Salah, '"There is a Jāḥiẓ for Every Age": narrative construction and intertextuality in al-Hamadhānī's *Maqāmāt*', *Arabic and Middle Eastern Literatures* 1 (1998) 31-46.

Outmani, Ismail El, *Anatomies of Subversion in Arabic and Spanish Literatures: Towards a Redefinition of the Picaresque*, Ph.D. thesis, University of Amsterdam, 1995.

Patnaik, Eira, 'The Succulent Gender: Eat Her Softly', in David Bevan (ed.), *Literary Gastronomy*, Amsterdam, 1988, 59-74.

Peled, M., 'Nodding the Necks: A Literary Study of Shirbīnī's *Hazz al-Quḥūf*', *Die Welt des Islams* 26 (1986) 57-75.

Pellat, C., 'Ǧāḥiẓiana, II' *see under* Primary Sources, s.v. al-Jāḥīẓ.

Pellat, C., art. 'Khubz', in *The Encyclopaedia of Islam*, New Edition, V (Leiden, 1986), 41-43.

Pleij, Herman, *Dromen van Cocagne: Middeleeuwse fantasieën over het volmaakte leven*, Amsterdam, 1997.

Ridley, Matt, *The Origins of Virtue*, London, 1996.

Ridley, Matt, *The Red Queen: Sex and the Evolution of Human Nature*, London, 1993.

Rodinson, Maxime, art. 'Ghidhā'', in *The Encyclopaedia of Islam*, New Edition, II (Leiden, 1965), 1057-72.

Rodinson, Maxime, 'Recherches sur les documents arabes relatifs à la cuisine', *Revue des Études Islamiques*, 1949, 95-165.

Rosenthal, Franz, *The Herb: Hashish versus Medieval Muslim Society*, Leiden, 1971.

Rosenthal, Franz, *Humor in Early Islam*, repr. Westport, Connecticut, 1976.

Rubiera Mata, María Jesús, 'La dieta de Ibn Quzmān: Notas sobre la alimentación andalusí a través de su literatura', in Marín & Waines (eds.), *La alimentación* (q.v.), pp. 126-36.

Sadan, Joseph, 'Kings and Craftsmen - A Pattern of Contrasts. On the History of a Mediaeval Arabic Humoristic Form', *Studia Islamica* 56 (1982) 5-49, 62 (1985) 89-120.

Schopen, Armin, & Oliver Kahl, *see under* Primary Sources, s.v. Shaᶜbān.

Sezgin, Fuat, *Geschichte des arabischen Schrifttums. Band II: Poesie*, Leiden, 1975.

Smith, Joan, *Hungry for You: Essays and Extracts*, London, 1996.

Smoor, Pieter, 'Enigmatic Allusion and Double Meaning in Ma^{c}arrī's newly-discovered *Letter of a Horse and a Mule*', *Journal of Arabic Literature* 12 (1981) 49-73, 13 (1982) 23-52.

Steingass, F., *A Comprehensive Persian-English Dictionary*, repr. Beirut, 1970.

Steinschneider, M., 'Rangstreit-Literatur', *Sitzungsberichte der phil.-hist. Kl. der kaiserl. Akad. der Wiss., Wien*, 155 (1908).

Stetkevych, Suzanne Pinckney, 'Regicide and retribution: The *Mu^{c}allaqa* of Imru' al-Qays', = ch. 7 of her *The Mute Immortals Speak: Pre-Islamic Poetry and the Poetics of Ritual*, Ithaca & London, 1993, pp. 241-85.

Stetkevych, Suzanne Pinckney, 'Voicing the Mute Immortals: The *Mu^{c}allaqa* of Labīd and the Rite of Passage', = ch. 1 of her *The Mute Immortals Speak*, pp. 3-54.

Traini, Renato, 'Un trattatello di galateo ed etica conviviale: le *Fawā'id al-mawā'id* di Ibn al- azzār', in *Studi in onore di F. Gabrieli nel suo ottentesimo compleanno*, Roma, 1984, pp. 783-806.

Ullmann, Manfred, *Untersuchungen zur Rağazpoesie: Ein Beitrag zur arabischen Sprach- und Literaturwissenschaft*, Wiesbaden, 1966.

Vial, Ch., '*Le Hazz al-Quhūf* de al-Širbīnī est-il un échantillon d'*adab* populaire?', in *Rivages et déserts: Hommage à Jacques Berque*, Paris, 1988, pp. 171-81.

Wagner, Ewald, 'Die arabische Rangstreitdichtung und ihre Einordnung in die allgemeine Literaturgeschichte', in *Abh. d. Geistes- u. Sozialwisschensch. Kl. d. Akad. d. Wiss. u. d. Lit. in Mainz*, 1962, no. 8.

Wagner, Ewald, *Grundzüge der klassischen arabischen Dichtung. Band I: Die altarabische Dichtung*, Darmstadt, 1987.

Waines, David, and Manuela Marín, 'Foodways and the socialization of the individual', pre-publication in *Working Papers for volume I: State of the Art. Individual and Society in the Mediterranean Muslim World, Granada (Spain) 24-27 May 1996* (European Science Foundation), pp. 74-87.

Waines, David, and Manuela Marín, '*Muzawwar*: Counterfeit fare for fasts and fevers', *Der Islam* 69:2 (1992) 289-301.

Waines, David, *In a Caliph's Kitchen*, London, 1989.

Watt, W.M., *Muḥammad at Medina*, Oxford, 1956.

Zubaida, Sami, and Richard Tapper, (eds.) *Culinary Cultures of the Middle East*, London, 1994.

Index

The article *al-* does not affect the alphabetical order